THE
NATURAL WORLD
OF THE MAORI

THE NATURAL WORLD OF THE MAORI

Margaret
Orbell

photographs by

Geoff Moon

Sheridan House

© Margaret Orbell
First published in the United States of America in 1985 by Sheridan House Inc.,
145 Palisade Street, Dobbs Ferry, N.Y. 10522

Library of Congress Cataloging in Publication Data

Orbell, Margaret Rose.
    The natural world of the Maori.

    Bibliography: p.
    Includes index.
    1. Maoris.   2. Human ecology — New Zealand.   I. Title.
DU423.A1073   1985   306'.089994   84-23643
ISBN 0-911378-52-9

ISBN 0-911378-52-9

Printed in Hong Kong
Production: David Bateman Ltd, New Zealand

Acknowledgements

My main debt is to the Maori authorities who in the nineteenth and early twentieth centuries recorded their myths, legends, songs and proverbs for later generations. That which is of value in this book belongs to them. The faults are my own. No rātou mā te mātauranga, nōku te hē. Wiremu Maihi Te Rangikaheke, Mohi Ruatapu, Hamiora Pio, Tutakangahau, Matene Te Whiwhi, Te Rangihaeata, Wiremu Te Wheoro, Aperahama Taonui, Te Kahui Kararehe, Piri Kawau, Hoani Wiremu Hipango, Paitini Wi Tapeka, Hoani Patara, Te Paki, Hoani Nahe, Takaanui Tarakawa, Mohi Turei, otirā koutou ko ō hoa maha, kei te mihi atu ra ki a koutou, ki ngā ringa nāna ēnei taonga i whakamau mo ngā uri whakatipu. Tēnā koutou, tēnā koutou, tēnā koutou.

I am also much indebted to the Pakeha students of Maori history and tradition who preserved and published the manuscripts. There are many of these men; their names are in the list of references. In the field of nature lore the most important writer was Elsdon Best, who was given information by Maori authorities in most parts of the country, and especially the Ureweras and the Bay of Plenty. And there are the early Pakeha artists, most notably George French Angas, who provided a faithful visual record.

In this century, Apirana Ngata and Pei Te Hurinui set new standards in the editing and annotation of the songs. At the same time, overseas scholars brought new approaches to the study of Maori tradition. In particular, in the 1950s a Danish historian of religion, J. Prytz Johansen, developed an approach based upon the close, comparative reading of Maori writings. Johansen's methods and his insights have been a major influence upon my work.

For assistance and encouragement in the study of Maori, I am grateful to Wiremu Parker of the Victoria University of Wellington and to Bruce Biggs of the University of Auckland. Two other mentors have passed on. I owe much to Arapeta Awatere and to Beth Ranapia, and I remember them fondly.

For their contribution to this book and and for their patience, Geoff Moon and I are grateful to the editor, Brigid Pike, and the designer, Neysa Moss. For their advice and assistance, I wish to thank Roger Neich of the National Museum, Marian Minson of the Alexander Turnbull Library, my colleagues Lyndsay Head and Bill Nepia, R. M. McDowall, Ray Richards, Hugh Wilson and Gordon Walters.

MARGARET ORBELL

Credits

All photographs not credited hereunder are by Geoff Moon.

I am indebted to the Directors of the following institutions for permission to reproduce photographs of works in their collections:

Alexander Turnbull Library, Wellington: pp. 24 below (by Tamati Ranapiri, 1894), 141 ('Rangitoto Island, extinct volcano no. 2', by Charles Heaphy), 155 (by Charles Heaphy), 192 (Carnell Collection), 195, 213 (by Edward Markham). Auckland Public Library: p. 183. British Library, London: pp. 31 ('New Zealanders fishing', by Sydney Parkinson), 55 ('The inside of a Hippah in New Zealand', by John Webber). British Museum, London: pp. 142 right, 163 below, 181. Dixson Library, Sydney: p. 50 below and bottom left. Gisborne Museum and Arts Centre: p. 189. Hunterian Museum, Glasgow University, Glasgow: p. 67. National Museum, Wellington: pp. 23 below, 24 left, 28 right, 31 below, 32 left (photo W. N. Wilson), 45 above right and below, 47 below right, 57 right, 59 right, 83, 112, 122 (photo Burton Bros), 147 right, 161. Southland Museum and Art Gallery, Invercargill: p. 143 below right.

For permission to take photographs for publication, I am indebted to the Directors of the following institutions:

Auckland Museum: pp. 61 and 159 (photos Theo Schoon); 53 below and 203 (photos Gordon Walters); 51 left, 144-5, 177 right (photos M. Orbell). Canterbury Museum, Christchurch: pp. 75 (lithograph after G. F. Angas), 190 top (photo T. T. Barrow). Hawke's Bay Art Gallery and Museum, Napier: p. 60 (photo G. Walters). National Ethnographic Museum of Sweden, Stockholm: p. 47 above left (photo John Turner). National Museum, Wellington: pp. 9 left, 47 above right, 50 right (photos J. Turner); 35 left and 146 (photos M. Orbell). New Zealand Maori Arts and Crafts Institute, Whakarewarewa: p. 160 (photo Geoff Moon). Otago Museum, Dunedin: p. 214 (detail of carving from house near Lake Taupo, photo Michael de Hamel). Wanganui Regional Museum: p. 35 right (photo M. Orbell).

For permission to take photographs for publication, I am indebted to the owners of the following meeting-houses:

Te Whai a te Motu, Mataatua marae, near Ruatahuna: p. 21 (photo Ans Westra). Hinetapora, Mangahanea, Ruatoria: p. 104 (photo M. Orbell). Whitireia, Whangara: p. 105 (photo M. Orbell). Te Mana o Turanga, Whakato marae, Manutuke: p. 143 (photo M. Orbell). Rongopai (Eriopeta), Repongaere: pp. 169 and 185 (photos G. Walters).

As well, the following provided photographs or artwork:

The late Mrs E. L. Clayton (prints on pp. 78, 101, 106, 116, 126 left); R. Lockley (photo on p. 145 above); M. Lessiter (photos on pp. 36 bottom, 114 middle); R. M. McDowall (photo on p. 147 left); R. Grace (both photos on p. 140); G. Walters (drawings on pp. 7, 8, 156; photo on p. 195 right).

Lithographs and engravings in publications in the Canterbury University Library were photographed by Duncan Shaw-Brown, Merilyn Hooper and Barbara Cottrell of the University's Audio-Visual Aids Department; I am grateful also to the many librarians who helped. The works are as follows:

George French Angas, *The New Zealanders Illustrated*. London 1847, pp. 11, 27 left, 27 right, 30 top right, 45 above left, 46 (all on this page), 47 below left, 48, 49, 56 above, 56 below, 57 left, 59 left, 75, 86 above, 113, 118, 137, 142 right, 171 right, 172 above, 186 left.

W. L. Buller, *A history of the birds of New Zealand*. London 1888, pp. 25 right, 194, 206.

Barnet Burns, *A brief narrative of a New Zealand chief*. London 1844, p. 44.

F. R. Chapman, 'On the working of greenstone'. *Transactions and proceedings of the New Zealand Institute* 1891, vol. 24, p. 52.

James Cook, *A voyage to the Pacific Ocean*. London 1784, p. 55.

Augustus Earle, *Sketches illustrative of the native inhabitants of New Zealand*. London 1838, pp. 12, 38 above (detail).

J. Hawkesworth, *An account of voyages undertaken by the order of his present majesty*. London 1773, pp. 138, 208.

F. R. von Hochstetter, *New Zealand*. Stuttgart 1867, 89, 93.

J. J. H. Labillardière, *Atlas pour servir à la relation du voyage à la recherche de La Pérouse*. Paris 1800, p. 69.

J. L. Nicholas, *Narrative of a voyage to New Zealand*. London 1817, p. 50 below left.

Sydney Parkinson, *A journal of a visit to the South Seas*. London 1784, pp. 94 above, 208.

J. S. Polack, *New Zealand*. London 1838, pp. 86 below, 94 below.

J. S. Polack, *Manners and customs of the New Zealanders*. London 1840, pp. 30 bottom, 52 right, 179.

Richard Taylor, *Te ika a Maui*. London 1855, pp. 30 middle left, 121, 182, 210.

Dumont d'Urville, *Voyage pittoresque autour du monde*. Paris 1839, p. 10.

William Yate, *An account of New Zealand*. London 1835, p. 37 right.

Glossary of Maori words

atua	spirit
kaitaka	fine cloak with taniko border
karakia	spell, ritual chant
kiore	native rat
korowai	cloak decorated with twisted black thrums
kōwhaiwhai	curvilinear patterns, painted or incised
kūmara	sweet potato
mana	power, prestige, status
Māori	person of Maori descent
marae	space in front of house, especially chief's house; courtyard
mauri	life principle, object embodying life principle
mere	short flat striking-weapon of greenstone
ngārara	reptile; in folklore, giant reptile
pā	fortified village, stronghold
Pākehā	person of non-Maori descent (usually European)
patu	short, flat striking-weapon of stone or wood
patupaiarehe	fairy
poi	light ball, attached to string, rhythmically swung by singers and dancers

rāhui	ban on the taking of birds, fish, etc.
rangatira	chief
taiaha	fighting staff with carved head at one end
tāniko	strips of patterned weaving, generally used on borders of cloaks
taniwha	dragon, supernatural being believed to live in water and in the ground
tapu	sacred, under religious restriction
tiki	human image, made generally from greenstone and worn as neck pendant
tohunga	religious expert, priest
tūāhu	shrine, sacred place where many religious rituals were performed
tukutuku	panels of ornamental latticework on the walls of houses
whakapapa	genealogy

MACRONS: In the list above, and elsewhere throughout this book, long vowels in Maori words are shown by macrons, or bars, over the letters concerned.

NOTE ON PLURAL NOUNS

In the Maori language, most nouns do not change their form in the plural. Many Maori words have entered New Zealand English, and in English they are often given a final *s* in the plural, as in *kiwis* and *totaras*. However, speakers of English who are bilingual tend to speak instead of *kiwi* and *totara*. In this book the Maori usage has been followed, except that the words *Maori* and *Pakeha* are sometimes given the English form of the plural, as happens generally in common usage.

Contents

Map of Aotearoa showing places mentioned in the text   1

One
LAND AND PEOPLE   5

Two
WAYS AND MEANS   19

Three
THE WORLD OF LIGHT   65

Four
SHAPING THE LAND   99

Five
THE REALM OF TANGAROA   135

Six
THE CHILDREN OF TANE   167

Epilogue   214
Notes   218
References   223
Some Books on the Natural History of Aotearoa   225
Index   226

AOTEAROA
NEW ZEALAND

Te Rēinga
Cape Reinga

Rangaunu

Ōpoe

Doubtless Bay

Pēwhairangi
Bay of Islands

TE TAI TOKERAU
NORTHLAND

Hokianga

Wairoa

Maunganui

▲ Manaia
Whāngārei

Tokatoka

Kaipara

Repanga Cuvier Island

Rangitoto

▲ Moehau

Tāmaki
Auckland

Coromandel
Peninsula

Manukau

Waikato

WAIKATO

Tūhua Mayor Island

Te Aroha ▲

Whakaari White Island

Tauranga

Whangaparāoa

Whanga
o-kenc
East
Island

Whāingaroa Raglan

Taupiri ▲

Whakatāne

Waiapu

Aotea

Rotoehu

Rotorua

Pūtauaki
▲ Mt
Edgecumbe

Moiū

▲ Hikurangi

Kāwhia

Pirongia ▲

Tarawera

TE TAI RĀWHITI
THE EAST COAST

Waipā

▲ Waioeka

Maungahaumi ▲

Rangitoto ▲

Maungapohatu ▲

Waipaoa

Awakino

UREWERA

Tūranga
Gisborne

Taupō

Tauhara ▲

Waikaremoana

TARANAKI

Pihanga ▲

▲ Tongariro

HERETAUNGA
HAWKE'S BAY

Whakapunake

Taranaki ▲
Mt Egmont

Whanganui
Wanganui

▲ Ngauruhoe
Ruapehu

Te Māhia
Mahia Peninsula

Ahuriri
Napier

Waitōtara

Rangitīkei

Kapiti

TE ŪPOKO
O TE IKA

Mana

Te Ika a Māui
The North Island

Wairarapa

Te Whanga-nui a Tara
Wellington

RAUKAWA
COOK STRAIT

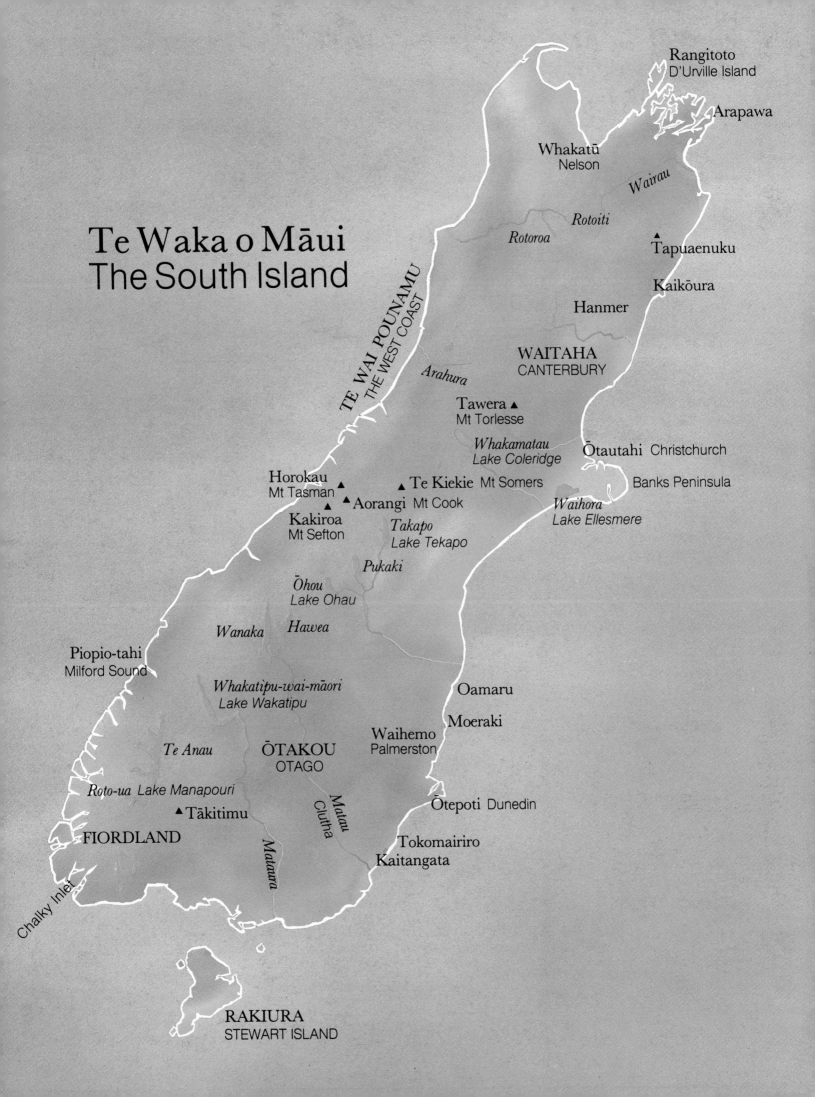

Rangitoto
D'Urville Island

Arapawa

Whakatū
Nelson

Wairau

Rotoiti

Rotoroa

▲ Tapuaenuku

Kaikōura

Hanmer

WAITAHA
CANTERBURY

Te Waka o Māui
The South Island

Arahura

TE WAI POUNAMU
THE WEST COAST

Tawera ▲
Mt Torlesse

Whakamatau
Lake Coleridge

Ōtautahi Christchurch

Banks Peninsula

Horokau
Mt Tasman ▲

▲ Te Kiekie Mt Somers

▲ ▲ Aorangi Mt Cook

Waihora
Lake Ellesmere

Kakiroa
Mt Sefton

Takapo
Lake Tekapo

Pukaki

Ōhou
Lake Ohau

Wanaka   *Hawea*

Piopio-tahi
Milford Sound

Whakatipu-wai-māori
Lake Wakatipu

Oamaru

Moeraki

Te Anau

ŌTAKOU
OTAGO

Waihemo
Palmerston

Roto-ua Lake Manapouri

▲ Tākitimu

Matau
Clutha

Ōtepoti Dunedin

FIORDLAND

Mataura

Tokomairiro
Kaitangata

Chalky Inlet

RAKIURA
STEWART ISLAND

One
LAND
AND
PEOPLE

The ancestors of the Maori came originally from the Asian mainland and lived for thousands of years in the western Pacific. They were farmers who kept pigs and fowls and grew taro, yams, breadfruit, coconuts and bananas, and they were fishermen as well, and skilful shipbuilders. In about 1500 BC, when they were living mostly on the coast of Papua New Guinea and some of its off-shore islands, they began a remarkable series of exploratory voyages, sailing eastwards over great distances to islands where no human beings had lived before. First they crossed the ocean to Fiji, then by 1000 BC some of them were settled in Tonga, Samoa and islands nearby. This area is known now as Western Polynesia. They remained there for about 1000 years, with their languages and cultures becoming more distinctively Polynesian. Then about 2000 years ago, a Samoan expedition sailed out into the vast area of ocean that lies further to the east. Over a period of time, the descendants of these explorers discovered all of the scattered island groups of Eastern Polynesia. The last to be colonised were the distant islands of Aotearoa (New Zealand). In about AD 800, the first settlers arrived in this country from either the Cook Islands, the Society Islands or the Austral Islands.

These immigrants were not fishermen who had been blown off course in a storm and cast upon these shores by accident, for fishermen would not have had women on board, nor the useful plants and animals they brought with them. Like most if not all of the colonisers of Polynesian islands, they came on a carefully planned expedition, deliberately setting out to discover a new land. They must have had good reasons for leaving their home; probably there had been overcrowding, and very likely discord and fighting. Ambitious men who had lost a battle or were in disgrace for some reason were quite often sent into exile upon the ocean. On Mangaia in the Cooks, for example, in the seventeenth century a man named Iro plotted with his friends the assassination of the high chief of the island. Their plan was discovered, the high chief's god decreed that they should be exiled, and several months were allowed for their preparations. During this time they built two large double-hulled ships some 9 metres in length, with decks, thatched awnings, masts and sails. They stowed on board all their movable property of value and a good supply of food and water, then when no further excuse could be found, the high chief led them to the beach. They were given a farewell feast by their kinsmen, then as the sun was setting they put out to sea, amidst loud lamentation.

Accustomed to dangerous voyages, the Polynesian explorers faced the ocean with courage and stoicism and an intimate knowledge of its moods. There was no way of knowing whether land lay before them: they had to try their luck. Those who discovered Aotearoa pressed on into cooler seas than any they had known, and were rewarded at last by the sight of land-based birds, and seaweed floating in the water, and a smudge on the horizon. They may have come in a single canoe, but it is more likely that there were several canoes which landed at different times and places. In either case there was at first the unusual situation of a large country with only a very small number of inhabitants. Yet within a few centuries, some of the descendants of these people had sailed on further, discovering the Chatham Islands 860 kilometres off the east coast of the South Island. In this remote place they established a peaceful, isolated society; it was too cold for crops, but permanent colonies of fur seals provided materials for clothing as well as food, and there were sea birds, fish, shellfish and eels, along with fernroot and a few other plant foods such as karaka berries.

Environmental Challenge

In Aotearoa the immigrants had to adjust to much colder temperatures and more pronounced seasonal rhythms, to discover the resources of the country and the conditions it imposed upon them, and to invent new ways of providing themselves with food, clothing, tools and shelter. Many of the birds, fish, plants and insects were new to them, and they had to learn their habits and characteristics. There were some familiar sights, however. Among the birds, the gulls and terns, owls, weka, pigeons and herons were similar to those they had known, and they were named accordingly. The great flightless birds that browsed on trees at the edges of the forests looked like larger versions of the domestic fowls, or moa, that had been left behind in tropical Polynesia, so they were called after them. And the kiwi was called after the tropical kivi, or bristle-thighed curlew, since the two birds have similarly shaped beaks which they use in much the same way: while the kivi digs for marine worms on beaches, the kiwi digs for worms in the forest.

During the first centuries of settlement some crops were grown in the warmest and most fertile places, but people in all parts of the country lived mostly by hunting, fishing and food-gathering. This was no hardship, for they were in an environment that had never before been exploited by human beings, a country teeming with fish and shellfish, moa and other large birds, and seals, dolphins and other sea mammals. At first they spent much of their time near the shore, by river mouths and harbours. The east

Figures incised by Moriori in the bark of karaka trees in the Chatham Islands. They may have marked trees that were tapu, or sacred.
OPPOSITE At first the rhizome of the bracken fern was not eaten a great deal, for there was an abundance of fish and game. Later, when large birds became harder to find and the clearing of some of the forests had extended the areas where bracken could grow, fernroot became a staple food.

Charcoal drawings in a limestone shelter at Frenchman's Gully near Timaru. Drawings in this style are found only in the South Island. They appear to be several hundred years old. Their subjects include birds, fish, lizards, human figures and 'bird-men' such as those above.

coast of the South Island was one of the favoured areas at this time, for the climate was warmer then and the region had abundant moa and seals. But by the early fifteenth century the climate was changing for the worse, moa were disappearing and seals had become less common. The best place to live was now the North Island, and the South Island, despite its greenstone resources, became a place to which tribes migrated after they had lost battles in the north.

The first settlers encountered many new creatures, such as the fur seal (ABOVE LEFT). Others, such as the reef heron (ABOVE), were familiar.

In tropical Polynesia the newcomers had lived close to the sea. Here they were able to continue to do this, for the river mouths and beaches gave them easy access to shellfish, fish and sea mammals. From time to time they made excursions inland in search of other resources.

The earliest carvings that have survived are stylistically related to those of the islands from which the immigrants came. This patu from Lake Horowhenua appears to be very old.
RIGHT Dense, tangled forests covered most of the land.

In the North Island there was at this time an increasing reliance upon horticulture. Though the kumara, or sweet potato, was a sub-tropical plant difficult to grow here, the invention of new methods of cultivation and storage had extended the areas in which it could be grown. Fernroot, the rhizome of the bracken, was being more widely used, in part no doubt because this plant, though it generally grew wild, was often made more productive by being allowed to grow on land that was lying fallow after being used for kumara. Other factors leading to this intensification of horticulture were probably the shortage of large game, and pressure from the growing population. Certainly the change made possible a denser population, and it led to a series of further adaptations and achievements. There was now much competition for the best land, especially when it had been cleared of forest, a most laborious task for a people who could employ only fire and stone adzes. At the same time, the increase in the population led to the full exploitation of areas in which living was difficult. Though horticulture was impossible in inland ranges such as the Ureweras, with their cold winters, even these forbidding regions were made to yield a livelihood by tough, energetic tribes possessing a highly specialised knowledge of their resources.

The men turned over the ground with digging-sticks and the women then broke up the clods of earth. Their wooden tools made this work slow and strenuous, and put limits upon the amount of land that could be cultivated. In the nineteenth century the Maori acquired metal spades and hoes as soon as they could, along with potatoes. These women, recorded in the 1820s, are probably using iron hoes.

The series of cultural changes associated with a greater use of kumara and fernroot began in the northern part of the North Island in about the fourteenth century. Pa, or strongholds, were built to protect possessions and to display them. Usually people spent much of their time elsewhere, but in places with rich resources they were able to live mostly in or alongside their pa. The fertile volcanic soils of Tamaki (Auckland), and its warm climate and the very good shellfish beds and fishing, quickly led to the intensive settlement of the region and a relatively sedentary way of life. These terraced slopes of Maungakiekie (One Tree Hill) were once part of a large palisaded pa, one of a great number built at Tamaki between about 1400 and 1850.

When a tribal people change from hunting, fishing and gathering to horticulture, they settle in one place to protect their plantations and work in them. Having permanent homes, they are able to acquire many more possessions than nomadic peoples, who must carry their goods around with them; and since the women generally do most of the day-to-day work in the fields, the men have more time to devote to such sedentary occupations as house-building, ship-building and sculpture. As well, they have more time for warfare, and possibly also a greater need to demonstrate their bravery and skill at arms now that there are fewer opportunities for them to prove their manhood by hunting animals. Since the practice of horticulture has brought growing pressure for land and an increase in the possessions that can be raided, there are in any case further reasons for war. And warfare is in fact a much more common and highly developed institution in horticultural societies than in those that depend upon fishing, hunting and gathering.

In Aotearoa the change to horticulture was only a partial one, for in the warmest places there had been some horticulture since the first centuries of settlement, and even now other sources of food remained important everywhere. Nevertheless, the greater and more widespread use of kumara

and fernroot led to many other changes in the people's way of life, especially in the north, where a region consisting of Northland, the lower Waikato, and coastal areas in Taranaki, the Bay of Plenty and the East Coast may have supported 80 000 or more people, perhaps as much as four-fifths of the total population. It seems that these cultural changes began in this northern region, and that by the fifteenth century they were having a growing influence upon other areas also. The older way of life is now usually termed the Archaic phase of Maori culture; and the one which finally replaced it, except in the far south, is called the Classic phase. This process of cultural evolution occurred within Aotearoa as a response to changing conditions. There is no evidence to suggest that it was the result of further migrations from other parts of Polynesia.

One of the main innovations associated with this cultural change was the pa, or stronghold. Pa were generally built upon hilltops, cliffs, or other places with natural defences. They were heavily and ingeniously fortified with palisades and sometimes earthworks, and they kept their owners' carved buildings and stores of kumara, fernroot and dried fish relatively safe from enemies. As well, these fortresses were ceremonial centres, places

Motuopuhi, a pa by Lake Rotoaira near Mount Tongariro. It was built on a headland that extends into the lake, so was protected by water on three sides. The other side was guarded by a double palisade, trenches and embankments.

Chiefs were passionate, skilful orators. Near Kororareka in 1828, a war party listen to one of their rangatira as they await a favourable wind. Speeches occupied several days, and 'the animating tones and gestures of the chiefs presented a remarkable contrast with the silent and good-humoured patience of the listeners'.

where meetings were held and where visiting parties from neighbouring tribes were received. Lavish hospitality was offered on such occasions, all the more so because the kumara could be stored for only a limited period, no longer than a year at the most. A chief and his people gained much mana, or prestige, from giving such a feast, and they could look forward with confidence to a time in the future when their neighbours would reciprocate. Most men of rank had several wives, including sometimes slave wives, so that their work in the gardens would produce the stores of food that would enable the family to extend to visitors the hospitality befitting their position.

Maori society was based upon the principle of kinship, the first-born being of the highest rank. Members of a hapu, a tribe or sub-tribe, could trace their descent, in theory at least, from a founding ancestor, often one from whom the hapu took its name. Each hapu had its men of rank, or rangatira. Related hapu would sometimes join forces for large-scale activities such as seine-net fishing or warfare, and the larger of the pa were generally built by several small, closely related hapu under the direction of a leading rangatira. But in Aotearoa even the most able and ambitious of leaders could hope to rule only a relatively small territory.

When tribal societies have evolved into civilisations they have always done so through the centralised control of grain, which will keep for many years; the possession of beasts of burden and metal tools and weapons has also been useful. It is true that on some of the larger islands of tropical

Polynesia, such as Tahiti, exceptionally good food resources and relatively dense populations produced fairly elaborate and hierarchical societies despite the absence of these things, but this was unusual. The inhabitants of Aotearoa did not have such highly productive and easily grown food plants, and their fishing grounds, though usually very valuable, were seldom comparable with those of tropical Polynesia. These other Polynesian peoples, moreover, were crowded on to relatively small islands, whereas the population of Aotearoa was scattered throughout a sizeable country, so could not be controlled in the same way. In each district there were large numbers of leading rangatira, and even these men of rank were not autocratic rulers but depended upon the support of proud, independently minded warriors. Any man who wished to control such volatile followers had to be able to sway them with eloquent words. Oratory became one of the high art forms of the Maori, and many songs took the form of persuasive, rhetorical speech.

The Maori were entirely dependent upon their immediate environment for their survival, and they had a profound knowledge of the resources it offered them. On an intellectual and emotional level, their relationship with their environment was equally close. It shaped the very processes of thought; it led to the development of ideas explaining the origin and nature of the world; and since affinities were felt to exist between all living things, it was a source of images that were applied to human beings. Their songs and narratives express these ideas and employ these images, and in so doing they give us access, to a degree, to their thought and feeling.

In the first half of the nineteenth century, Maori society and thought began to change with great rapidity as they acquired new plants and animals, new technology, new geographical knowledge and a new religion, and as a rival people began arriving in their country. As this happened, much of the traditional culture was in danger of being forgotten; but at the same time, thousands of Maoris were learning to write. By the 1840s, Maori authorities in many parts of the country were recording their myths, legends, songs and proverbs. With later Maori writers, and interested Pakehas who provided support, they laid the foundations of a tradition of scholarship which made the verbal arts of the Maori probably the best recorded of those of any tribal people.

In many ways the ancient system of thought now belongs to the past; and yet much of its spirit survives today. Some of the myths are still powerful, many of the images are employed in oratory on the marae, and there is above all the close relationship which so many Maoris have with the land. They see in it the presence of their ancestors, the continuity of past and present, and they know the land and its people to be inseparable. Though this book is mostly about the eighteenth and early nineteenth centuries, it should not be thought that the story ended then.

Two
WAYS
AND
MEANS

Expecting another island in tropical Polynesia, the ancestors of the Maori came instead upon a land which was very much larger and cooler than the island they had known, and greatly varied in its landscape, soils and climate. Much seemed inhospitable, but in many ways the country offered rich resources. The river mouths and harbours were full of fish and shellfish, with seals nearby, and at first they settled by the coast and lived largely on sea food. There were hardly any land mammals, because Aotearoa has been cut off by a wide ocean for about seventy million years, isolated since before the age of the evolution of mammals; the first immigrants found only two small species of bats which long ago were blown across from Australia. But these people would not have expected to find land mammals here, for nearly all the ones they had known previously — pigs, dogs, rats — were creatures that had been introduced by human beings. And because there were no mammals, the country was full of birds. With no mammals to prey upon them or compete with them, they had taken over the ground as well as the trees, and some species had grown unusually large. In many places the main game birds were at first the different species of flightless moa, which ranged in height from 1 metre up to more than 3 metres.

Some of the settlers' treasured possessions were now useless, or of very limited value. They quickly found that their coconuts, breadfruit and bananas, which in tropical Polynesia had yielded food so abundantly and easily, would not grow in this climate. Their other food plants did survive, but only in the most favourable localities, and even there they were much harder to grow and not as productive; new methods of cultivation and storage had slowly to be evolved. And the paper mulberry tree, which in their former home had produced bark that was beaten into tapa cloth, could no longer be used for clothing; in Aotearoa this tree would grow only in the warmest places, and the climate was in any case much too cold for garments of bark cloth. But as they explored the coastline and the interior they found many new things. It was at once apparent that the tall trees would provide abundant timber, and the flax plant materials for clothing; there were, after all, wild food plants hidden in the forests and the open country; and in the end, after much searching, they found places from which they could acquire the special kinds of stone needed for adzes and chisels. Patiently they experimented with their new materials.

Hunting and Fishing

Nearly all of the 22 species of moa disappeared by about AD 1500, though some small species may have survived longer in areas such as Fiordland which were difficult of access. As well, about a dozen other species of birds were hunted to extinction; they include an eagle, a crow, a pelican, a harrier hawk, swans, geese, ducks and rails. Little is known about the methods used in hunting these birds, but the flightless ones must have been caught with the help of the dogs the immigrants had brought with them. When they disappeared, there remained the flightless kiwi and weka and the nearly flightless kakapo, which were also often caught with dogs. But the most important of the game birds, because they were taken in great numbers, were now the placid, heavy-winged pigeons and the noisy kaka, which grew fat on drupes and berries in the autumn and winter. At this time of year they were taken by men perched in the trees where they were feeding, trees so tall and wide-branching that the fowlers used long, slender, bone-tipped spears as much as 9 metres in length and only about 3 centimetres in diameter. These spears took many months of patient skill to make. The wood used was tawa, which is straight-grained and light. A log would be very carefully split into two or perhaps three lengths, and these would be painstakingly chipped and scraped, then rubbed smooth with pumice. Workmen who were restless to complete some task might be reminded, in the words of an old proverb, that:

Kāhore he tārainga tāhere i te ara!

You cannot make yourself a bird-spear as you go!

When the pigeons had been gorging themselves on the fruit of the miro they became very thirsty, and they were then taken in rows of nooses placed alongside streams and cunningly positioned water-troughs; the birds caught their necks in the nooses as they lifted their heads from drinking, and the fowlers returned and collected them at their leisure. But this method would not have worked with the aggressive kaka, which had powerful beaks and claws to tear nooses apart, so these birds were speared or taken with decoys. The owner of the decoy bird would tie his pet to a suitable tree, hide nearby and tease it with a stick to make it screech. Kaka are gregarious birds, and when the wild ones heard the commotion they would come flying down to investigate. They would edge closer and closer, and at last they would be seized or snared by the man lying in wait.

The big glossy tui were important game birds, and so were the olive-coloured bellbirds, and the kakariki, or parakeets, that flew about in bright, chattering flocks at the edge of the forest. Nearly all birds, however,

Certain trees were famous for the great numbers of birds that were speared in them when their fruit was ripe. A painting on a rafter of Te Whai a te Motu, a meeting-house near Ruatahuna which was opened in 1888.

The light, straight-grained wood of the tawa was used in making bird-spears. A young, soft tree was felled, and cut to a length of 10 or 12 metres. The log was split into two or three lengths, and these were carefully adzed and shaped.

BELOW Everything edible was eaten. Bats lived in large colonies in hollow trees. A smoky fire would be lit inside the lower part of the tree, and after a while the stupefied bats would fall to the ground.

BELOW RIGHT Weka were snared and hunted with dogs. They were especially important in the South Island.

FAR RIGHT The almost flightless kakapo, a large nocturnal parrot, was also hunted with dogs. The birds' moss-green plumage camouflaged them well in the forest. Folklore had it that they would break off fronds of *Blechnum discolor* or crown fern and hold them over their heads to escape detection.

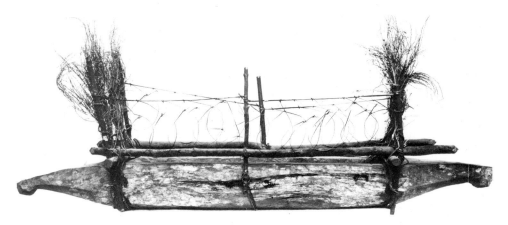

A pigeon feeding on the ripe berries of the nikau palm. Berries and drupes that could not be eaten by human beings were very valuable in providing food for birds.

LEFT A water-trough with nooses, used in snaring pigeons that were thirsty from eating the fruit of the miro.

were caught and eaten from time to time, even small birds, and un-palatable ones such as kokako and bitterns. Much depended upon the locality. In places with many swamps and lakes, such as the Waikato, the Bay of Plenty and Marlborough, ducks were caught in their thousands, especially when they were moulting in the summer and unable to fly; they were then very fat, and easily driven into inlets and on to the shore. Along the coast there were sea birds' eggs to gather and young birds to take from their nests, and the young of the titi or muttonbird were procurable not

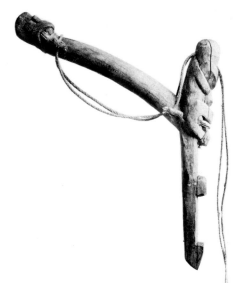

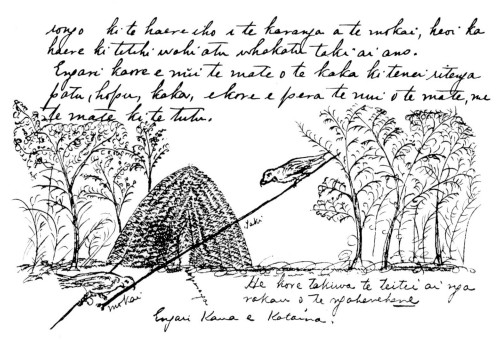

When kaka were fat from eating the fruit of the hinau, tawari and kowhai, they were speared in the same way as pigeons were. On other trees, such as the miro, maire and kahikatea, they were snared by the feet on perches (ABOVE) which were carved from forked branches, and had running nooses attached to them. The fowler, hidden nearby, had a tame decoy kaka with him to attract the wild birds with its cries. Trees where kaka were taken in this way were known as *tūtū*.

BELOW Another method of taking kaka is illustrated by a nineteenth-century Maori writer, Tamati Ranapiri of Ngati Raukawa tribe. A tethered decoy bird pecks and scratches at seeds the fowler has provided for it. A wild bird, having seen this, is edging down a long pole that stretches from the trees to the ground. The man awaits it in a shelter made from branches and the fronds of tree ferns.

Describing this, Tamati explains that if the wild kaka should pay no attention, 'and not come down when the decoy calls, the man will go off and erect his pole somewhere else. But not so many kaka are taken by this method; not so many are killed as when the *tūtū* is used.'

Below the drawing he writes, 'There's no room to show the height of the trees in the forest, but don't laugh.'

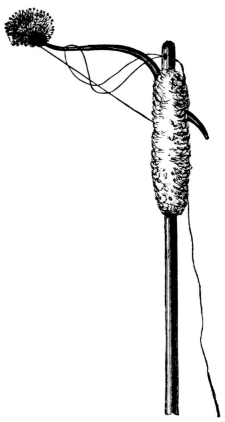

only from offshore islands, as they are now, but from breeding-grounds on high hills far in the interior. In the evening the nesting muttonbirds fly back in flocks to their burrows, and those going inland were caught as they swooped low over the ridges. Men armed with heavy sticks would wait for them in such places, with a strongly-plaited net fixed in an upright position and a fire burning in front of it. When the fast-flying birds made their appearance, they were attracted to the fire and some flew headlong into it, while others dashed into the net, and the men laid about them frantically with their sticks.

All game was treated in the same way. If the birds were to be eaten immediately they were plucked but not cleaned, then steamed in an earth oven or roasted beside a fire. Otherwise they were plucked, cleaned, cooked in water heated with red-hot stones in a wooden bowl, then preserved in their own fat in large calabashes, baskets of totara bark, or containers made from inflated lengths of bull kelp; these big seaweed vessels were especially common in the far south, where calabashes were unavailable because the gourd plant could not be grown. Potted birds would keep for as long as a year, and were one of the most highly prized delicacies at feasts. Birds of different kinds were preserved separately, and the containers placed before guests were decorated with bunches of feathers belonging to the kind of bird to be found within.

Tui feed on berries, fruit, insects and nectar. When the rata were in bloom, these birds were taken in snares baited with rata flowers. A curving piece of supplejack furnished with a noose was fastened to a rod that was camouflaged with moss. Hidden in a shelter, the fowler attracted the tui by imitating their cry of alarm. When a bird alighted on the snare, he pulled a string attached to the noose and entangled its feet.

A gull's nest. Birds' eggs and young birds were taken in season.
BOTTOM Sooty shearwaters, or southern muttonbirds. Their Maori name is titi. Like many related birds, they nest in burrows, laying a single egg. The parents fly far out over the ocean collecting food for their chick, and regurgitate it on their return.

As well as dogs, the settlers had introduced another mammal, a little rat known as the kiore. Despite its small size, the kiore was a favourite delicacy, all the more so because dogs were so valuable that they could be eaten only occasionally at feasts. Kiore lived everywhere in the forests, eating vegetable foods, reptiles and young birds, and growing fat in autumn and winter on beech mast and the fruits of trees such as the miro and tawa. When they moved to new feeding-grounds, they travelled at night in single file along little paths worn smooth by their feet, usually along the tops of ridges. Ingenious traps were laid on these rat-runs, and great numbers were taken. They were plucked or singed, then often preserved in their own fat, like birds.

All hunting and fishing was carried out according to strict rules. Families and tribal groups were careful to confine their operations to their own territories, for there was serious trouble if someone was caught trespassing. Birds, rats and fish were protected for much of the year by a rahui, or ban, which ensured that they were not disturbed when breeding, that their numbers were not unduly depleted and that they were taken only in the best of condition. When the rahui was to be lifted a party of men, women and children would set out for the place in question, the tohunga would perform ceremonies to remove the rahui and to ensure the success

Flax baskets, vessels made from bark, and large calabashes were used for storing food products of different kinds. Smaller calabashes were employed for fetching water and many other purposes. This boy with his calabash belonged to Ngati Mahanga at Whaingaroa (Raglan).

Food was usually roasted over a fire, or wrapped in leaves and steamed in a hangi, or earth oven. Some food items, however, were placed in baskets or bowls before going into the hangi, and water was heated in wooden bowls into which red-hot stones were placed. At feasts, food was occasionally offered to guests in very large wooden bowls. The vessel below is said to have held kumara. It was 2.5 metres in circumference.

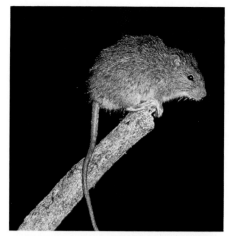

The beech forests were not very productive of food, but they did contain many kiore, or rats.
RIGHT A cunningly balanced rat trap, one of several kinds that were used. When a kiore took the bait, the rod at the top flew up. The kiore was caught in the noose and pulled up against the frame of the trap.

of their venture, and all of them would remain there, living in light shelters, until their task was completed.

These expeditions to different parts of the tribal territory occupied much of the year, especially in summer, when most of the fishing was done. They were much enjoyed, and high spirits prevailed. Usually the men did most of the hunting, while back in the camp the women plucked and preserved the game.

For coastal tribes, catching fish and gathering shellfish were constant occupations. Even in inland waters there were whitebait to be netted and trapped, little galaxias and grayling, lamprey, freshwater crayfish and freshwater mussels. In some places, especially Lake Rotorua, freshwater mussels were so abundant that their importance was proverbial:

Tāne rou kākahi, ka moea.
Tāne moe i roto i te whare, kurua te takataka!

A man who dredges mussels will get himself a wife.
A man who sleeps in his house will get his head thumped!

Eels were a favourite food, and much more plentiful than in the islands the immigrants had left behind; the only places without them were Lake Taupo, where the Huka Falls on the Waikato River barred the way, and Lake Waikaremoana, which is drained by underground channels. They

were bobbed and speared by torchlight, and they were caught in pots, which were often set at large, specially-built weirs. Rivers, swamps and lagoons producing large quantities of eels were greatly valued, especially by tribes possessing no seaboard, and when necessary they were stubbornly defended.

Many traditional fishing grounds are still in use today. Two men netting flounder at Parengarenga Harbour, in the far north.

The manufacture of the different kinds of eel pots and crayfish pots, nets, hooks, and lines required much skill and patience. By far the most ambitious piece of equipment was the enormous seine net used in coastal waters. It was knotted from unscraped flax and was made in many sections, each family group contributing its share. The pieces were joined together, two heavy ropes twisted from cabbage tree leaves were fastened along them, and stone sinkers were tied to the lower edge and floats of whau wood, lighter than cork, to the upper edge. Some of these nets were as much as 1 000 metres long by 10 metres deep. They were owned by all who had worked on them. Under the direction of an expert the great net would be taken out on a platform built across two large canoes that had been lashed together, then when the right shoal of fish made its appearance the expert would shout his instructions, the net would be paid out, and after it had been slowly hauled in by its owners there would be many thousands of fish to be distributed amongst them.

Line fishing was also often a communal activity, especially when the fish were highly prized ones taken in large numbers. In Northland, in Rangaunu Harbour, the Rarawa tribe used to catch the school shark — a fish very like the dogfish but up to 2 metres in length — on only two

A landing net used in catching crayfish. The fisherman felt for the crayfish with his feet, then tumbled it into the net. ABOVE A temporary shelter used by a party of fishermen.

TOP LEFT The small freshwater crayfish were often taken by lowering bundles of bracken to the bed of the lake, allowing them to remain there for a while, then slowly pulling them up with the crayfish clinging to them.

TOP RIGHT Strongly constructed eel weirs were built on many rivers. This one, on the Mokau River, is of a kind not otherwise recorded.

RIGHT Great quantities of eels and water-fowl were taken in swamps.

occasions each year, a night in January just after the full moon and a day two weeks later. Elaborate preparations were made for these events. In the 1850s, when a Pakeha visitor wrote a lively account of them, there were some 50 canoes taking part, each with a crew of about 20 men, and most of the men's wives were working on the shore. On the day before the sharks were to be caught, one of the camps presented a busy and animated scene, with some of the men overhauling their canoes and others bringing in mullet they had netted for bait. Older men were resnooding their hooks, discussing the merits of shape and bend, while many of the women were gathering pipi and drying them for the winter, and some of the older ones were scraping flax fibre and rolling it into twine along the calves of their legs. Meanwhile the young people were amusing themselves with games such as wrestling, spinning humming tops carved from the heartwood of the kahikatea, and playing draughts on a board of flax leaves plaited into squares, with shells and potato slices serving as pieces.

At sunset a signal gun was heard, and the canoes set off at once. They joined the rest of the fleet at the rendezvous, and there was much loud talk and laughter. Then the talking ceased, and there was dead silence as they waited for the tide to turn. As soon as this happened the leader stood up in his canoe and shouted in a stentorian voice, 'Charge!' (*Huakina!*). Then everyone paddled furiously for the fishing-ground, shouting and cheering, racing to catch the first shark. When they arrived they let go the anchors,

A large fishhook, perhaps for shark. It was formed from a twig that had been trained to grow into the right shape. The point is of albatross bone.
TOP Fishermen at Queen Charlotte Sound, drawn by Sydney Parkinson in 1770. They wear feather hats, perhaps as a sign of mourning, and they appear to be setting crayfish pots. The European visitors found that the Maoris were much superior to them at fishing.

A hook lined with paua shell, and used in trolling for kahawai.
RIGHT Pipi, with other shellfish, were eaten in great quantities by coastal tribes.

tied heavy cloaks around their waists and shoulders, threw their baited hooks overboard and almost immediately began hauling in the threshing sharks, using wooden clubs to quieten them with blows on the snout. For three hours there was furious activity, then the deeply laden canoes returned to the camps and the women began the long task of cleaning and drying the fish, and expressing the oil from their livers. Altogether the fleet's annual catch consisted of some 7 000 sharks.

For each kind of fish there was a specialised body of knowledge concerning its habits, the proper times and places for catching it and the right ways of doing so. While the men were responsible for fishing at sea, also for eeling, the women did some fishing in streams and inlets and spent a great deal of time collecting pipi, mussels, toheroa, tuatua, oysters and other kinds of shellfish — though the men did most of the diving for paua, which lie in deeper waters. Enormous quantities of fish and eels were gutted, partially cooked, hung up to dry in the sun and wind, then carefully stored. Shellfish were strung on lines and similarly treated, and whitebait too were dried then stored in baskets. Dried fish and eels were most important foods in that they could, nearly everywhere, be prepared in sufficient quantities to allow them to be eaten regularly in the winter months. Tribes that possessed good harbours, lagoons and inland waterways were especially fortunate.

Often, though, the foods of one area would be exchanged for those of

others. An inland tribe might send a present of potted birds to relatives living by the sea, and in due course the inland people would receive in return a handsome gift of sea food, perhaps dried hapuku or snapper, or moki, or shark.

Kina, or sea-eggs, were eaten raw. They retain their popularity today.

Food Plants

Several of the cultivated plants introduced by the settlers survived in Aotearoa, though only in the warmer districts: yams grew in the northern part of the North Island, taro and gourds as far south perhaps as Nelson, and kumara in suitable places down to Banks Peninsula. These plants were much harder to cultivate here and not nearly as productive as they had been before.

Yams could only be treated as a luxury, something to provide an occasional change. They required the same light, well-drained soil as kumara and often were grown alongside them, but they were far from common and they disappeared soon after the Maori acquired potatoes in the early nineteenth century. Taro were not irrigated as they sometimes were in tropical Polynesia, but were planted in rich, damp ground, often by the banks of streams, with an upper layer of sand or gravel to warm the soil. An early Pakeha visitor described taro plantations on the East Coast which 'looked very neat, the plants being planted in true quincunx order, and the ground strewed with fine white sand, with which the large pendulous and dark green shield-shaped leaves of the plants beautifully contrasted, some of the leaves measuring more than two feet in length, the blade only. Small screens formed of branches of manuka, to shelter the young plants from the violence of the winds, intersected the grounds in every direction.' Taro are perennial and the tubers could be dug up and used at any time, along with the thick, succulent stems of the leaves. They produce many offshoots, and *he puia taro nui,* 'a great cluster of taro plants', was a proverbial phrase used of a tribe too strong in numbers ever to be overcome. Nevertheless they were not very productive in terms of time and effort. Also, they could be grown only in places where the soil and climate were suitable, and these were quite restricted.

Gourd plants grow fast and far, and the luxuriant growth of the gourd

Taro plants require fertile soil, plenty of water and much attention. In Aotearoa they grew much more slowly than in tropical Polynesia, and though their tubers were a favourite food, they were never very plentiful.

was spoken of in poetic metaphor, as when a woman complained of old age and remembered the past:

Ko te wā tonu ia i mua ra, koi tara ana, ē, te hue nei!

Oh, once there was a time when this gourd was shooting!

Many young gourds were eaten like marrows in the summer, the rest being left to mature for use as calabashes and painstakingly trained into the shapes required. The ripe gourds were dried and hardened in the sun and alongside fires, and their spongy contents were removed. Very small calabashes became containers for scented oils or substances such as red ochre, some larger ones were sliced in half and used as dishes and bowls, and others became water containers, these having only a small hole bored beside the stalk. A few of the very largest, which had been trained into an upright position, were made into containers for preserved birds. For this purpose the stalk end was cut off and replaced with a carved wooden neck large enough to admit a person's hand, and the calabash was fitted with three or four legs to serve as supports. These big vessels were looked after

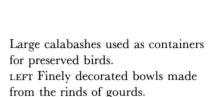

Large calabashes used as containers for preserved birds.
LEFT Finely decorated bowls made from the rinds of gourds.

very carefully and often given names. Some lasted for several generations, being handed down as heirlooms.

The most highly prized by far of the cultivated food plants, and the one most extensively grown, was the kumara, or sweet potato. This sub-tropical plant presented the immigrants with especially complex problems; among other things, they had to devise ways of storing their delicate seed kumara under absolutely dry, temperature-controlled conditions. It was a tapu plant, its cultivation and storage attended by many ritual observances and ceremonial restrictions, and though these elaborate usages reflected the high value attached to the kumara they must also have been felt to be necessary because of the difficulties involved in its cultivation. Only with the greatest possible assistance from unseen powers could the task be successfully accomplished.

Maori horticulture was of the kind known as slash and burn, with an area being cleared with the aid of fire, cultivated for two or three years and then left to lie fallow for several years. Partly this was necessary because the Maori made no use at all of manure, regarding the practice as indecent; they would not touch food from a plant that had grown anywhere near a privy, and in the early nineteenth century they were greatly shocked to see Pakeha missionaries using manure in their gardens. When they cleared new ground they were careful to leave the ash from the burnt trees

Tame black-backed gulls were sometimes encouraged to feed upon the caterpillars of the sphinx moth. These large, handsome caterpillars originally fed only on the bindweed, or New Zealand convolvulus (BOTTOM). Then the Maori arrived with the kumara, a related plant (RIGHT). The sphinx moth transferred its attention to the kumara, and became a major pest.

and undergrowth; often as well they added more ash, and lightened and warmed the soil by the laborious addition of hundreds of basketfuls of gravel and sand. The ground was loosened and broken up with wooden digging sticks and other implements, stones and tree stumps were removed, and light fences were constructed to protect the tender plants from destructive winds. Little hillocks were prepared some 60 centimetres apart, in very neat, regular rows, then the seed kumara were planted with much ritual, each being placed in its hillock facing the rising sun and the tapu land of Hawaiki, the source of fertility.

Afterwards there was the task of weeding, which was done very carefully; many Pakeha travellers remarked upon the neatness and 'minute exactness' with which the cultivations were kept clear of weeds. There was also much work for the women in keeping the plants free from caterpillars, especially those of the sphinx moth, which would suddenly appear in such enormous numbers that it was thought they had dropped from the sky. Usually the caterpillars were picked off by hand, but sometimes they were destroyed with acrid smoke from smouldering kauri gum or wet kawakawa twigs, and tame black-backed gulls might be let loose to feed upon them. Then in the autumn the crop was dug with much ceremony, and there was a time of feasting and rejoicing, with games and dancing.

Occasionally a tribe would hold a great feast for a neighbouring people, usually in return for one that had been given for them some years previously. This flag-bedecked stage, said to have been 25 metres high, was built to display the food presented to the guests at a feast held in the early 1830s, after the acquisition of potatoes and iron spades. In earlier times, such feasts were on a smaller scale. Even so, very large quantities of food were involved.

LEFT Bracken fern growing in good soil produces long, starchy rhizomes. In many parts of the country these were a staple food.

Bracken stalks were used for many purposes. Here a tohunga, temporarily too tapu to feed himself, is fed by an assistant using a stalk as a fork.
TOP The dried fernroot was soaked in water, roasted lightly by a fire, then beaten with a mallet on a smooth stone. The mealy part of the rhizome was then eaten.

Fernroot was regarded as a sustaining food, especially suitable for people undertaking difficult tasks. It was sometimes spoken of as the bones and flesh of Papa, the Earth Mother, which she gave her children.

But kumara were a luxury item, reserved most of the time for important people and the entertainment of visitors. The varieties of kumara that the Maori possessed yielded tubers only about the size of a man's finger, and their wooden spades and digging sticks made cultivation slow and laborious. Furthermore there was another plant which was capable of producing large quantities of food in return for much less effort. This was the common bracken fern, which has a starchy rhizome usually known, inaccurately, as fernroot.

The Maori did not like fernroot nearly as much as the kumara, but bracken grew in most parts of the country and required little or no cultivation. There was virtually no risk of crop failure or loss during storage, and bracken was probably the more productive of the two plants. Certainly kumara grew well in warm, fertile places in the north, but then fernroot did best in these areas too. Even in the Bay of Islands, where the soil and climate were most favourable to kumara, the people cultivated only a limited quantity of kumara, yams and taro, enough to provide for feasts in particular. They must have eaten a good many kumara in the autumn, after the crops were lifted, but on other occasions their usual plant food was fernroot. Elsewhere, in districts not so well suited to horticulture, there was even more reliance upon fernroot. Tribes living in heavily forested areas could make little use of it, and it was not very common on the Canterbury Plains. But most tribes did possess good fernlands, and when they did, fernroot was their staple vegetable food.

Bracken that grows undisturbed in deep, rich soil may be as much as

3 metres in height and will have long rhizomes, up to about 45 centimetres in length and 2.5 centimetres in diameter, with a high proportion of mealy matter to fibre. Such superior fernroot was obtainable only in certain highly prized localities, and people made do with what they could get, but the rhizomes of low, stunted bracken are not edible. Some of the best fernroot came from land that was lying fallow after having had kumara grown upon it; the bracken would grow back, or perhaps be planted there, and some three years later a heavy crop would be ready. The rhizomes would be dug by the men in the spring or early summer, when their starchy content was highest. Those near the surface were stringy and hard, but the ones about 50 centimetres down were much better. They were carried back to the village and placed on storage platforms where they dried in the wind, sheltered from the sun, then after a couple of weeks they were sorted into different grades and stored. Properly treated, fernroot would keep for years. When it was wanted for a meal, the rhizomes were soaked for a while in water, roasted a little in the embers of a fire, then pounded with a wooden mallet on a smooth, waterworn stone. Only the mealy part was eaten, the fibres being rejected. Generally they were eaten with other food, just as bread is, and in most places their usual accompaniment was fish. The beaten rhizomes would occasionally be cooked in a more elaborate way, with the meal being shaped into cakes then steeped in the juice of tutu berries, or nectar collected from flax flowers, or the sweet substance obtained from the stem and root of the cabbage tree.

With so much energy being invested in the procuring and storage of

Kahikatea, the tallest trees in the forest (FAR LEFT), bear small fruit (LEFT) which were much liked. Since they do not fall readily, ladders were lashed to the trees and skilful climbers collected them in baskets which they lowered to those below. The fruit were eaten raw, and were a favourite item at feasts.

ABOVE A number of plants were used for medicinal purposes, among them the kumarahou, or golden tainui, a shrub that grows in the northern part of the country. The leaves of this plant were boiled, and the liquid was used for skin complaints. It was also taken internally, though it is not known whether medicines were employed in this way before the nineteenth century. Until this time it was thought that most internal complaints were due to attacks by spirits, and that the only remedy was for a tohunga to expel the spirit.

The fruits of the karaka (BELOW) and the hinau (BELOW RIGHT) were greatly valued, though they could be eaten only after long, laborious preparation. OPPOSITE The Maori word *nikau* is equivalent to the Tahitian word for the leaf of the coconut palm. The name recognises the fact that the two trees resemble each other mainly in their foliage. Unfortunately, the nikau palm (BELOW LEFT) bears no coconut. Like the coconut, however, it has a tender heart that provides a very good meal, and it could be more readily sacrificed for this purpose than could the coconut.

BELOW RIGHT The upper, inner part of the stem of the mamaku, the tallest of the tree ferns, was steamed in an oven for two days and nights, then eaten cold. When cooked, it could also be dried and kept for future use.

kumara and fernroot, it is not surprising that these plants had important symbolic significance. Kumara were associated with peace, probably because they were a luxury food eaten at feasts, while fernroot was associated with warfare, being regarded as a strong, sustaining food suitable for warriors and other persons engaged in arduous pursuits. This distinction was taken very seriously, so much so that the two plants always had to be kept separate and could on no account be stored or carried together. Another belief was that an amulet of fernroot worn around the neck would protect the wearer from minor afflictions such as headaches and colds.

Many other wild plants provided food. The fruits of a number of trees, shrubs and vines were eaten, though most were very small, and those of the kahikatea, rimu, matai and totara had to be collected from tall trees that were difficult and dangerous to climb. There was a saying that:

He toa piki rākau, he kai na te pakiaka.

A man who is good at climbing trees is food for the roots.

For coastal tribes possessing groves of karaka trees, the kernels of karaka

berries were a favourite delicacy; when raw they are very poisonous, so they were steamed for a long time in earth ovens, then soaked in running water before being dried and stored. The fruit of the hinau tree was very popular with tribes living in the interior, though again it required long preparation; its dark flesh was painstakingly separated from the kernels and skins, then cooked in large cakes. Another forest tree valued for its fruit was the tawa; the kernels are proverbially hard, but they made a useful food item when steamed for long enough. And the rich purple juice of the fruit of the tutu, patiently filtered to remove the poisonous seeds, made a much appreciated drink, the only one apart from water which was procurable in any quantity.

Some plant foods that were much liked were available only occasionally. Lightly cooked or even eaten raw, the heart of the nikau palm is juicy and succulent, with a rather nutty taste, but it could only be eaten by needy travellers or as a special treat, for its removal killed the tree. The frond-stems and trunk of the mamaku, the large black tree fern, yielded a sago-like substance that was very popular, but since the mamaku grows slowly and does not shoot up again when felled, it was of limited value as a source of food. On the other hand the cabbage tree was a useful plant that grows fast, propagates itself very readily and occurs throughout the

The fast-growing cabbage tree was highly valued as a source of food, and its tough, fibrous leaves were used for many purposes.

Cakes made from the pollen of the raupo, or bulrush, were a luxury available in the summer. In times of scarcity, the plant's rhizomes were peeled and eaten raw.

RIGHT Wild celery, or tutaekoau, grows in rocky places along the coast. It is one of a number of small plants that were eaten as greens.

country. Its inner leaf-shoots were cooked and eaten, but it was most highly valued for a sugary, mealy substance extracted from the long taproot and the stem. Young trees were chosen for this, the mature ones being too woody. Some species were much better than others, and at least two of them, the ti pore and the ti para, were planted and cultivated; in fact the ti pore was almost certainly brought to this country by the Maori. These cultivated species grew only in the northern parts of the North Island, and people elsewhere made use of the wild species. On the east coast of the South Island in particular, the roots and stems were eaten at feasts after being dug up in the spring, dried in the sun and cooked in enormous earth ovens.

The young, unexpanded fronds of a number of ferns were eaten in spring and summer, when other foods were sometimes in short supply. Other small plants served as green vegetables all the year round, among them the puha, or sow thistle. The indigenous varieties of this plant are much more bitter than the one introduced in the nineteenth century. Usually it was only their tender young leaves and buds that were eaten, and before cooking the succulent stems were often bruised and washed in running water to get rid of their milky juice. They became very palatable when treated in this way, and were especially liked when eaten with fresh fish. Nevertheless, a person who was complaining about being the subject of gossip might quote a proverb that likens bitter words to the leaves of the sow thistle:

Ka katokato au i te rau pororua!

I keep gathering the leaves of the sow thistle!

In the summer the light, sweetish pollen of the raupo was collected in bark vessels, mixed with water and steamed, producing cakes which reminded one early Pakeha traveller of gingerbread. The starchy rhizomes of the large horseshoe fern and the big, fleshy roots of the rengarenga, or New Zealand lily, were much liked, and these plants were sometimes cultivated. The flower bracts and the fruit of the kiekie were another delicacy. Several kinds of seaweed were eaten, notably the slippery karengo, which grows well on the flat tidal rocks of the East Coast; the early botanist William Colenso remarked that he had 'known baskets of it dried, to be taken inland to Taupo and elsewhere, on the Maoris' backs, as a suitable present, in exchange for the delicacies of the interior forests'. A number of plants were eaten mostly in times of scarcity, among them several kinds of fungi and plants with edible roots such as the bindweed, or New Zealand convolvulus. Though most fungi were not really liked, and it took a long time to dig up enough of the thin, tough roots of the bindweed, they were most welcome when they were needed. Sometimes there was abundant food and sometimes a shortage, but people always knew that seasons of plenty would come again.

Ear fungus is plentiful on rotten wood in lowland forests. It is tough and rubbery, and was eaten with greens to make it more palatable.

ABOVE The sun orchid, like several other kinds of native orchids, has small, edible tubers that were dug up in the winter.

LEFT The rengarenga, or New Zealand lily, was sometimes cultivated for its roots, though it provided only small quantities of food.

Clothes and Ornaments

When flax fibre was required, the leaves of the flax plant were soaked in water, scraped with a shell, then dried. Cabbage-tree leaves are much more durable than those of the flax, so were generally used for articles such as bird snares which were exposed to the weather. As well, in heavily forested ranges where there was little flax, the long, broad leaves of the mountain cabbage tree (BELOW) were woven into heavy capes.

In Aotearoa the immigrants' light garments of tapa cloth had to be replaced at once, and fortunately the flax plant was available. Nevertheless they continued to grow a few of their paper mulberry trees in the warmest places, and what had previously been a necessity now became a luxury valued all the more because of its rarity. Only a very small amount of tapa cloth was produced from the bark of these trees. It was made into thin, white fillets which were worn by chiefs in their hair and ears, it was wrapped around tapu objects in the care of the tohunga, and sometimes it was used in making bird-kites — not the ordinary sort but the fancifully decorated ones that the chiefs and warriors, especially the older men, greatly enjoyed flying.

Flax was very common, growing everywhere except in the dense forests and providing an immensely tough, versatile material which was used in making garments, nets, cordage, floor mats and numerous other articles. There were many varieties. The common kinds were planted near the villages and their green leaves were used all the time for tying things together, for plaited bands around the sides of the earth ovens and for quickly made mats and baskets, including the little dishes that held cooked food and were newly plaited for every meal. Superior varieties possessing special qualities — some notable for their strength, some yielding coarse fibre and some fine — were also planted and cultivated, each having its own particular uses. The leaves of these better plants were always treated before being used. Articles which were plaited, such as sails, mats and baskets, continued to be made in this country in much the same ways that they always had been, with minor modifications to allow for the use of new materials. For clothes, however, entirely different techniques were devised.

The immigrants had no experience of weaving garments, and the first clothes that they made here must have been plaited from flax. The men's loincloths would have consisted of long bands fastened between the legs and around the waist, and the women's skirts were very likely kilts with the ends hanging down loosely; no doubt there were also plaited capes to keep off the rain. In time, though, the women became more ambitious and began to prepare their flax in more elaborate ways, using only the fibrous upper surface of the leaves or scraping them so as to free the fibre completely. Having done this, they had materials from which fine garments might be made; but they also had a problem, for it is very difficult to plait garments from soft fibres without getting the ends in a tangle. So they began to weave their clothes instead of plaiting them, evolving techniques derived from those used all over Polynesia in the making of fish and eel traps.

In Aotearoa as elsewhere, eel pots were constructed from lengths of vine fastened alongside each other by means of parallel pairs of cords

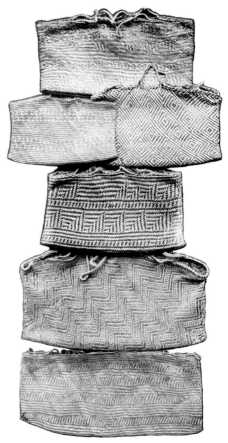

which were twisted between and across them according to a method known as single-pair twining. This technique was similar in principle to weaving in that a warp, consisting of the vines, was interlaced with a weft, and it was now transferred to the making of garments. There was, then, no loom. The warps were suspended between two rods placed upright in the ground and the weavers worked their way downwards, twisting the wefts around the warps with their fingers. The first garments they made were shaggy capes in which rows of overlapping tags were inserted in such a way as to form a kind of thatch that shed the rain. These rain capes became a basic garment, worn by all. They were always taken on expeditions, for one never knew when it would rain, and they were used at night as blankets.

Later there were new developments. As well as being used in making rain capes, single-pair twining was employed in close, tightly twisted rows to form very thick, strong capes that were worn by chiefs as shields in battle. Next, some of these thick capes were covered with differently coloured strips of dogskin, arranged in patterns. Then the dogskin capes came to be further adorned with closely woven borders made with two threads of different colours which were interwoven so as to produce patterns. Afterwards, someone added a third thread in another colour, carrying this along on the underside of the garment and bringing it forward as required. With these three threads, and occasionally a fourth one, the weavers evolved the subtly patterned taniko border.

Finely plaited baskets with ingeniously varied patterns.
TOP The technique of single-pair twining was first employed in the construction of eel pots and similar articles. Later it was used in weaving.
LEFT Women weaving fine garments sometimes made use of four rods instead of two. These weavers are in a house at Porirua. The pole in the foreground supports the ridgepole of the building.

Pu and her sons
Ngati Toa

Mungakahu and his wife
Ngati Tuwharetoa

Te Kawau and his nephew
Ngati Whatua

Paratene Maioha
Ngati Mahuta

Tohi
Ngati Maru

A girl at Pipitea Pa
Ngati Toa

These people were portrayed in 1844 by G.F. Angas. Most of them are wearing their best attire. By this time, garments were trimmed with brightly coloured wool rather than with feathers, as previously. Later in the century, feather cloaks became popular once more.

Paratene Maioha is wearing a parawai, a rare kind of dogskin cloak made by sewing strips of fur to a large cloak made of the finest flax.

These beautiful wide borders were woven in complex geometrical designs in red, white, black, brown or sometimes yellow. To set them off to perfection the weavers invented a new kind of cloak, the kaitaka, which was finely woven from silky, pale yellow fibre, very large and soft, and was quite plain apart from its borders. The kaitaka was made not with single-pair twining but with a new kind of weft consisting of two pairs of threads, and this more intricate technique of two-pair twining was employed on other dress cloaks also. Some of these garments were plain and some were ornamented in different ways. Among them were the korowai, which is a white cloak decorated with black thrums and fringes, and others that were adorned with rolled thrums or flaxen pompoms, or trimmed with dogskin or feathers. A few capes were entirely covered with feathers, either in a

Three children of Te Pakaru
Kawhia

single colour or with differently coloured feathers arranged in rectangular patterns.

Materials other than flax were sometimes used for woven and plaited articles. Fine white mats were made from the leaves of the kiekie, also baskets and strong belts and capes. In the densely forested Ureweras, where there was little flax, people wore very heavy, durable capes woven from the coarse fibres of the mountain cabbage tree; these were dyed black when finished, and they remained waterproof for many years. On snowy ranges and other very cold places, travellers wore sandals plaited from flax, cabbage tree leaves or the leaves of the speargrass, sometimes with moss-lined leggings for further warmth. Specially coloured materials were much sought after. The pingao grass, which is bright yellow when dried, was

TOP LEFT Detail of a wide taniko border attached to an eighteenth-century dogskin cloak. The only one of its kind to have survived, it has a finely worked key pattern on a dark ground.

TOP RIGHT The usual kind of taniko border, with angular patterns in several colours.

LEFT Three children of Te Pakaru, the leading chief at Kawhia in the 1840s. The two girls wear kaitaka cloaks with taniko borders.

ABOVE Two poi covered with taniko.

From the bark of the tanekaha tree the weavers obtained a red dye. First the crushed bark was boiled, producing a reddish liquid. The fibre for weaving was boiled in this, then taken out and rolled in clean, white ashes. After being boiled a second time, it was ready to be hung up to dry.

RIGHT Two men of Ngati Tuwharetoa, on the western shore of Lake Taupo. The chief Tauwhaki wears a korowai cloak. Te Onionga has a heavy cloak of untreated flax that has been dyed black with hinau bark. In his ear are the feathers of a gull.

used for tukutuku panels in houses and for other purposes, and the orange culms of a species of sedge known as maurea were made into ornamental belts and were traded far and wide.

Men sometimes went naked, apart from a string attached to the penis; women did not keep their breasts covered but they always wore a skirt to the knees, sometimes one decorated with thrums. Both men and women usually wore short, heavy capes around their shoulders, and similar garments about their waists. Fine garments such as kaitaka, korowai and dogskin capes were worn by high-ranking men at meetings and festivals, and dogskin capes were worn into battle. Before a festival a chief's long hair would be tied up in one or more topknots, often by his wife, and adorned with treasured plumes and a carved comb of wood or bone. If he had several fine garments he would probably wear them all, fastening one around his waist and arranging the others so that part of each could be seen. Cloaks were sometimes tied on the breast but usually, for a man, on the right shoulder, since this was the male side of the body. Women wore their cloaks tied on the left shoulder.

But in the eighteenth century, women seldom wore dress cloaks. Several European explorers remarked on this, including James Cook: while the chiefs who boarded his vessel in 1769 were in their best attire, he 'hardly ever saw a Woman wear a piece of fine cloth'. A number of passages in Maori literature show that women did sometimes wear fine garments such as kaitaka (though not dogskin capes, which were exclusively for high-ranking warriors). For example, a woman of consequence who had been insulted might retaliate with a song in which she spoke as if she were going on a journey to visit an important kinsman who would honour her by placing a beautiful cloak about her shoulders. One such woman, who lived at Whangaroa in the Lake Rotoehu district, sang that she would visit a relative at Ahuriri (Napier):

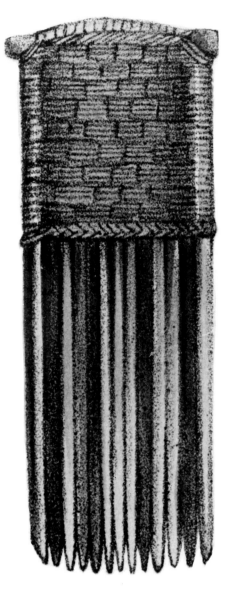

A wooden comb of the kind used by chiefs and warriors. Before battles and feasts, the men's long hair was knotted into one or more topknots. Often it was their wives who did this. Ornamental combs carved from wood or bone were sometimes worn in their hair.

> *Kia hei taku ate i te tau o tana tiki,*
> *Kia tia whakaripa i te kōtore huia —*
> *Kia kahu pūrua i te neko pakipaki,*
> *Ka pai au te hoki ki te koko i Whangaroa!*

Let my heart be hung about with the string of his tiki
And my head adorned on both sides with huia plumes,
Let me be dressed luxuriously in a bordered cloak
That I may look well as I return to the bay at Whangaroa!

She would not have said this if it had not been possible for a woman to be given such treasures, or more probably lent them, but at the same time this was clearly an uncommon occurrence. Generally it was the men who wore the most prestigious garments and highly valued ornaments, such as greenstone tiki and the tail plumes of the white heron, just as it was the men who had elaborate hair styles and much tattooing. However, women and girls of good family did wear plumes in their hair, and beautiful girdles, especially for dancing. Sometimes their girdles were decorated with thrums and taniko, and scented grasses were tucked inside them. In the Marlborough Sounds some women encountered by Cook's expedition had girdles 'very curiously worked' with red kaka feathers, and adorned further with pieces of paua shell 'near the size of a half crown piece'. Since there are only a few red feathers under the wings of a kaka, the making of such garments required much time and patience.

Men painted their faces with red ochre before battles, festivals and funeral ceremonies, and people also painted their bodies to ward off sandflies. Other substances occasionally used as face paints were blue and white clays, powdered charcoal, and a yellow stain obtained from the bark of a tree; an early Pakeha traveller speaks of a man who had a red face with blue circles around the eyes and a black stripe across the nose, and another whose face was fiery red with a bright yellow forehead, nose and

The moko patterns on a woman's lips and chin, as drawn by Renata Kawepo in 1842.
BOTTOM LEFT The facial moko patterns of a chief named Hemoranga, as drawn by himself in 1815.
BOTTOM RIGHT The stiff, spiny leaves of the speargrass provided one of the most highly valued of the aromatic gums used in scented oils and sachets.
FAR RIGHT The species of mountain daisy known as tikumu have leathery leaves that are covered with down on their lower surfaces. The pellicles of the leaves were plaited into headbands, and women and girls ornamented their hair with the white, satiny wool.

chin. The red ochre was collected from deposits on hillsides or from streams and swamps, then mixed with shark liver oil when necessary, but for preference with a fine oil expressed from titoki seeds and scented with sweet-smelling leaves and gum. Girls and women used it as well as men, though less often, and the girls would also sometimes colour their cheeks with ripe, red berries or with pink colouring matter from the feet of pigeons.

Greenstone tiki and pendants shaped from the teeth of sperm whales were the most precious articles worn around the neck, and the least common. Much more often, necklaces were made from the teeth of departed relatives which were worn as talismans, or from the teeth of dogs or sharks, or short lengths of albatross bone, or certain prized shells and seeds; sometimes too a piece of white-feathered albatross skin, or pukeko skin with its brilliant blue feathers, would be saturated with perfumed oil, rolled into a ball and worn as a sachet. People of high rank wore greenstone pendants in their ears, or perhaps the tooth of a mako shark or the head and curving beak of the female huia, but the common ear adornments were the soft downy feathers of the albatross or gannet, human teeth, flowers, the wings or entire bodies of little birds, and curiosities such as dried seahorses. In their hair the chiefs wore especially the plumes of the white heron, huia, albatross and red-tailed tropic bird, but other plumes were valued too, among them those of the gannet, the kakapo and the long-tailed cuckoo, and women and girls sometimes wore wreaths of flowers or sweet-scented leaves. Occasionally a man would fasten the wings of a hawk on both sides of his head. The early artist G. F. Angas remarked that 'the effect of this head-dress resembles somewhat the winged cap of the feathered Mercury; and the forms of the wearers, though more massive, were in point of symmetry not unworthy of the messenger of the gods'.

And as well as such transitory things, men and women wore an

adornment won with much suffering — the lines of their moko, or tattoo, incised upon their faces and bodies with chisels of bone and made permanent with black pigment from the soot of burnt kauri gum or the resinous heartwood of the kahikatea. A man's intricate and beautiful moko proclaimed his status as a warrior, and a woman's moko made her desirable as a wife. Though all else might be lost, these treasures, they knew, would remain with them throughout their lives.

Woodworking

For woodworking and other purposes, materials for tools were of great importance. Implements such as fish-hooks, harpoon heads and needles were often made from the bones of moa and other birds, and shells were used everywhere for many purposes, but the right stone was not to be obtained so easily. Archaeologists have discovered that by the twelfth century, many of the best kinds of stone were

As well as tools, treasured ornaments were shaped from greenstone.
BELOW Ear pendants and neck pendants. Two are hei matau, neck pendants with shapes similar to fishhooks.
LEFT This tiki retains its plaited flax cord and bone toggle.

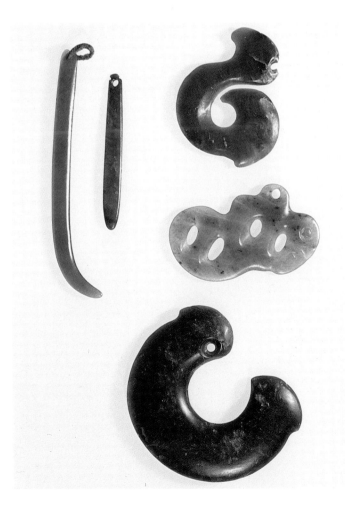

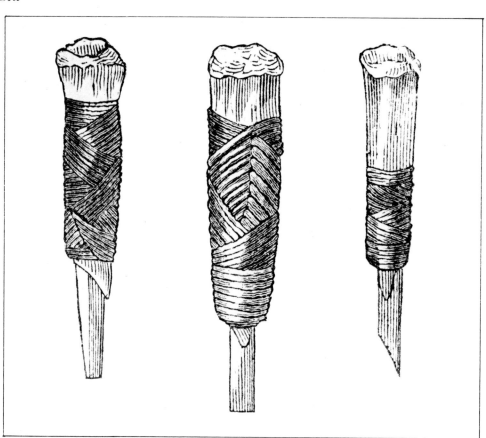

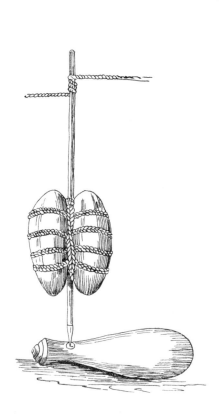

Greenstone could be slowly pierced with drills pointed with sharp flints. RIGHT Hafted greenstone chisels.

being traded over long distances, passing from hand to hand; flaked implements of obsidian from Mayor Island and one or two other places in the north were being used in most districts for cutting and scraping, and adzes of basalt from Coromandel Peninsula and argillite from Nelson and D'Urville Island were widely distributed. Greenstone was employed to some extent in the south, but in these first centuries it was not yet traded throughout the country, for being extremely hard and tough it was very difficult to work. Nevertheless this hardness and toughness made it a most valuable material. In the end, new techniques of manufacture led to its wider use.

Greenstone was obtainable only in a few remote, rugged places on the West Coast, and to a lesser degree in Fiordland and Central Otago. At first the South Island craftsmen worked this stone by using percussion, followed by grinding: they roughed out the basic shape by striking off small flakes, hammer-dressed it to remove unwanted areas of stone, then ground it on sandstone and polished it. This was a sophisticated technique which produced excellent results with other kinds of stone suitable for tools, but with greenstone the difficulty was that it caused much of the best material to shatter in unpredictable ways. So the percussion method was very wasteful, and could be employed only in the few areas where green-stone was readily available. About 500 years ago, it was supplanted in most places by a new technique of abrasive cutting. This was a most laborious method, but it gave the workman precise control over his materials. A slab was slowly sawn off the parent boulder, using thin, sharp pieces of quartzose slate or other suitable stone, together with water and fine, hard sand. If holes were required in the piece, they were painstakingly formed with drills pointed with sharp flints. Then the article was ground and polished in the usual way.

It seems that this technique came into general use at about the time that pa began to be built. The pa brought with them an increased need for woodworking tools of greenstone, for though other tools could have been used in the construction of their high, timbered palisades, the finely carved structures built within them could not have been made without the use of greenstone adzes and chisels. The abrasive cutting of greenstone made possible the remarkable evolution of wood sculpture which now occurred, and from this time on, greenstone became a most precious trade commodity. From the West Coast and a few other places, pieces of raw stone and finished items were carried over the mountain trails that led to the north, then across Raukawa (Cook Strait) and along established routes that took them, ultimately, to every part of the country. Though greenstone remained an uncommon treasure in the north, it was now used whenever possible for tools, weapons, and ornaments such as ear pendants and tiki.

A fine carving might be admiringly described as *ānō me he whare pūngāwerewere*, 'just like a spider-web'. BELOW A waka huia, a treasure box that held the plumes of the huia and other birds. Red was the colour associated with high status, and carvings were painted with a solution of oil and red ochre.

In their tropical home the immigrants had been used to living in large, airy houses, but in Aotearoa they had to learn to build small, thick-walled ones to keep themselves warm in winter. By the twelfth century a rectangular design had evolved with a porch at the front and an internal hearth, and in most areas this became the standard pattern. The substantial ridgepole was supported by posts in the back and front walls and by a central pillar, and it projected forward to form the roof of the porch. Rafters sloped down on both sides, with battens across them. The thick roof was tightly thatched with bundles of grasses and raupo, cabbage tree leaves, the fronds of the nikau palm or the bark of the totara or manuka; the low side walls were similarly covered, and soil was sometimes heaped against them for greater warmth. The doorway with its sliding panel was very small, again because of the need to keep in the heat; it was about 80 centimetres in height, and one entered on hands and knees. The only window was a very small one in the front wall, and the smoke from the central hearth had to escape through this opening and a small vent in the roof. This was not a very comfortable arrangement, but charcoal was used as much as possible, and in cold weather, with the clothes and bedding available to them, the Maori needed warmth above all. For this reason too the houses were very small. They were only about 2 metres in height, just high enough to stand up in, about 2.5 to 3 metres in width and 3 to 5 metres in length.

Raupo leaves, with others, were tied in bundles and used to thatch the roofs of houses. They were cut in March, when they were at their best.

The interiors of these thick-walled buildings were used mostly for sleeping, and then only on winter nights. During the day people often worked in the porch, and in hot weather they generally slept in the open or under light shelters of some kind; often in the summer they were travelling around on seasonal tasks, sleeping in temporary shelters constructed from materials such as nikau and tree fern fronds. They never cooked or ate inside their houses, for these buildings were tapu, not to be profaned with food. All cooking was done in separate, lightly built sheds with open sides, and they ate in the open, or in wet weather in the porches of the houses. Nor could people be born in a house, or die in one. These things had to be done outside, in specially constructed shelters.

Ordinary houses had frames constructed from undressed timber and poles, but in the grand houses of high-ranking families the frames were made partly or entirely from timber that had been shaped by craftsmen using hafted adzes. Surfaces that were to be visible in these houses, especially those of the bargeboards and their supporting posts, the door jambs and the wide slabs along the side walls, were skilfully dubbed in such a way that the adze-marks formed regular patterns. The spaces between the side slabs were filled with bark, with panels made from the culms of toetoe or bracken, or sometimes with tukutuku panels, in which vertically arranged toetoe culms were lashed with coloured flax and grasses to thin, painted, horizontal laths, the different colours and lacing

A small pa on an island at the entrance to Queen Charlotte Sound, as recorded in 1777. The roofs of houses were protected from the wind by open latticework constructed from strong vines. On smaller buildings, manuka rods were used.

The porch of a house which stood at Raroera Pa, in the Waipa Valley, in the early 1840s. Occcasionally, as here, the entrance was on one of the longer walls.

BELOW A house from the same district, erected to commemorate a battle that had occurred in 1836. The figures represent warriors who had taken part in the fighting.

WAYS AND MEANS 57

patterns forming subtle contrasts. The timbers, especially on the outsides of the buildings, were generally painted with red ochre mixed with oil, and the rafters and some other surfaces might be painted with curvilinear kowhaiwhai patterns in red, white and black. Sometimes the facade and the lintel would be carved, along perhaps with the slabs at the sides of the porch, and the figure of an important ancestor would support the central pillar inside the house. Very rarely, the side slabs inside the house might be carved; Captain Cook's expedition of 1769 seems to have seen only one house with carved interior walls, and that, at Uawa (Tolaga Bay), was about 9 metres long, much larger than any other building they found. Most chiefs' houses were small, and adorned mainly on the exterior. Meetings took place on the marae in front of these houses, and only visitors of high rank were invited to sleep in them. The meeting-house as we know it evolved from the chief's house during the first half of the nineteenth century.

But the carvings in these small eighteenth-century houses, while not nearly as large and numerous as in later buildings, were of superb quality.

LEFT The porches of houses provided a sheltered place to work or sit in the sun, and food was eaten there in wet weather. This chief's house stood beside a waterfall at Te Rapa, on Lake Taupo.

BELOW The figure of a tribal ancestor that stood against the base of the central pillar in a chief's house. Human hair was once attached to the head.

Greenstone adzes and chisels were slow to use but they cut very cleanly, and obsidian flakes were valuable for fine work. Tall, straight totara trees provided wood which could be readily split, was soft enough to be easily worked, and was able to take fine detail. Maori sculpture became rich and complex, with sweeping and subtle linear patterns and human figures very freely treated, usually in bas-relief. The ancestors that were portrayed on a chief's house were inseparable from the house itself, lending their powers to its timbers. Part of its very structure, they supported the building and its inhabitants literally and figuratively, guarding them from sorcery and making manifest in their splendour their descendants' power and glory.

RIGHT The fibrous stems of tree ferns formed the walls of cooking sheds and storage pits for kumara. The thick stems of the species known as wheki-ponga were especially useful for this purpose.

FAR RIGHT Totara wood is straight grained, easily worked, and one of the most durable of all timbers.

BELOW RIGHT The flower-stalks of the toetoe form a backing for the tuku-tuku panels that are placed along the inner walls of meeting-houses.

BELOW Tukutuku work in Hotunui, a meeting-house built in 1878 by Ngati Awa of Whakatane, and now in the Auckland Museum.

The storehouses in which the families of important chiefs kept treasured possessions were similarly adorned on the exterior, with some of the carved figures (embracing ancestors, and whales) symbolising the plenitude to be found within. Boxes for storing small, precious things, and many other wooden articles, were finely carved. Sometimes on the death of a great chief a carved monument was erected, and in the pa the enormous gateway and many of the main posts were elaborately adorned. As well as providing places of refuge in wartime, pa were the centres of ceremonial and social life. They may have developed partly as a means

A post depicting an ancestor which formed part of the fortifications of a pa.

LEFT Four storehouses, with other buildings, recorded in the 1840s. They are raised from the ground to keep their contents safe from rats. The woman in the foreground is preparing flax fibre. Pigs had been acquired early in the nineteenth century.

of protecting fine buildings from enemies. According to a much-quoted proverb,

*He whare maihi tū ki roto ki te pā tūwatawata, he tohu no
    te rangatira.*
He whare maihi tū ki te wā ki te paenga, he kai na te ahi.

A carved house standing in a palisaded pa is the sign of a chief,
A carved house standing in an open place is food for fire.

The totara, and the kauri in the far north, provided excellent timber

The figurehead and wash-board of a
small canoe, as seen from the prow.

for canoes, though again the process of felling, hollowing and shaping these great trees was strenuous, highly skilled and slow. The logs were so large that the hulls of even the biggest canoes were hewn from single trees, with topstrakes lashed along the sides and shorter sections forming the bow and stern. Canoes of this kind might be 20 metres or more in length. Finely carved, painted red and adorned with feathers, flying over the water 'like seagulls' as their paddlers bent in perfect time, they were objects of great pride to the tribes that owned them. In the wild landscapes of Aotearoa, where human structures were few and scattered, elaborately wrought vessels, pa and buildings were a powerful assertion of the mana of their owners.

Part of the figurehead of a large canoe that belonged to Te Atiawa tribe in Taranaki.

Three
THE WORLD OF LIGHT

In many traditional societies it has been thought that the sky is male and the earth female. The ancestors of the Maori brought this belief to Aotearoa with them, and they called their first mother by one of her ancient names, Papa, or Foundation. The first father, however, was given a new name; in most of the island groups of Eastern Polynesia he is known as Atea, or Expanse of Light, but here he is Rangi, or Sky. In Aotearoa, as in these other places, the story of the creation of the world begins with the separation of the sky and the earth.

Sometimes there is a list of the ages that preceded them, but often the storytellers begin with the primal parents themselves. They lay closely embraced, and their sons were confined in the darkness between them. After a long time the sons became restless, for they wished for light and room to move. They considered what they should do, and all but one of them agreed that they must part their parents; only Tawhirimatea remained loyal to his father. So one by one the other brothers tried to push the sky up from the earth. None could succeed, until in the end the greatest of the sons, Tane, rested upon his shoulders, pushed upwards with his legs and thrust Rangi into the far distance. Their parents wept and cried aloud as they were separated, and light was seen for the first time in the space between them.

Other separations followed. Angry with his brothers for what they had done, Tawhirimatea followed his father to the realms above; there he reared his children, which are the winds, and from there he still fights today with his brothers, sending winds and clouds down upon the earth and ocean. Trying to escape from Tawhirimatea, the creatures of the sea, who are Tangaroa, and those of the land, who are Tane, went their different ways. And Tu, who represents mankind, now began attacking his brothers upon the earth; for although human beings are related to all living things, they can only survive by overcoming their relatives and making use of them.

This myth explained the origin and nature of the sky and the earth, and the creatures and plants that inhabit it. At the same time, it served to define the characteristics and roles of human men and women, and the nature of the relationship between them. Men are high and tapu, like the sky; women are low, fruitful and profane, like the earth. They are as different in their natures as their first parents.

The Sacred Sky

The sun, moon and stars were said by some tribes to be the offspring of Rangi and Papa, and to have been placed in the firmament by Tane so that they might adorn their father. Apart from this, the mythographers' main interest was in the light of the sun rather than the orb itself. Daylight was associated with life and well-being, and darkness with death and defeat, while as an extension of this idea the rising sun and the east were associated with life, and the setting sun and the west with death. An Englishman named John Savage, visiting the country in 1805, noted that the people sang both at sunrise and sunset: 'On the rising of the sun, the air is cheerful, the arms are spread out as a token of welcome, and the whole action denotes a great deal of unmixed joy; while on the contrary, his setting is regretted in tones of a most mournful nature'. Many of the old laments begin by speaking of the evening as the time when people remember their sorrows. And *he hari no mua,* 'an old song of rejoicing', which must be similar to those that Savage heard each morning, was recorded late last century by an anonymous Maori writer:

Men and women re-enacted the roles of the primal parents. Two ancestors, a husband and wife, from the facade of a chief's storehouse.

E te hihi o te rā e kōkiri kei runga ē,
Tarahaua, ē, pikipiki ake ra, ē,
Ngā moutere tahoratia mai te moana!
Kāore iara, pikipiki ao, pikipiki ao,
Ka puta iara kei tua ē!

The sun's rays that shoot up, stretched out,
Climb up over the islands spread out on the sea!
Oh climb up over the world, climb up over the world,
Reach the other side!

In many ritual performances the tohunga faced the rising sun, sometimes with an arm stretched out towards it. At divination ceremonies it was a good omen if rods fell towards the east, a bad one if they fell towards the west. Houses were generally built facing the east, and the houses of tohunga were situated in the eastern parts of the villages where they lived. Because the mythical Hawaiki was a paradisial land of origin it was generally described as lying in the direction of the rising sun, but when the souls of the dead were being sent on their journey back to this first homeland, it became a land of the dead and could be reached by travelling in the direction of the setting sun.

Daylight and the east were associated with males, and darkness and the west with females. As in all traditional societies, women were thought to be vastly inferior to men, almost another species, so it was natural that this idea should have arisen. Along with the identification of the sky with males and the earth with females, it provided the Maori with a way of aligning the duality seen in the human race — the fact that there are two kinds of people — with the dualities which they perceived in their natural environment. And there were other advantages. Clearly some agent had to be held responsible for the existence of death. It seemed appropriate that women should be to blame, for they after all bring new life into the world, so that one generation succeeds another and nothing is permanent. When Tane had separated his parents and adorned them, he made a woman from the soil of Hawaiki and with her he had a daughter, who was named Hine-titama. In due course he took his daughter to wife also, but she discovered her parentage and fled in shame to the underworld, where she became known as Hine-nui-te-po, Great-woman-of-the-night. She has remained there ever since, dragging her offspring down to death. The trickster Maui attempted to conquer her, but she killed him, and so men die today. If there had been no women, it was claimed, men would have lived forever like the stars in the sky. As it is, human beings disappear but the stars remain:

Sunlight represented life and success, the moon appeared to die but came back to life, and the evening star, like other stars, was greeted with emotion.

The smaller stars were said to be the left eyes of chiefs and warriors who had died and now were atua, spirits. Eyes shining through tears might be compared to stars, and when a beautiful woman was dancing, her flashing eyes were likened to the full moon.

Tātai whetū ki te rangi, mau tonu, mau tonu.
Tātai tāngata ki te whenua, ngaro noa, ngaro noa.

Companies of stars in the sky last forever, forever.
Companies of men on the earth are lost, lost.

Shining in their multitudes in the sacred heights, the stars were thought to be atua, or spirits. The cloud formation known as a mackerel sky, where clouds are broken into long, thin, parallel masses, was said to be a sign that the spirits were planting their kumara, and a meteor was thought to be a spirit visiting the earth — or sometimes, one being expelled for misconduct. It was believed that when a person of consequence died, his left eye became a star. Still today at a tangihanga, a funeral, when the burial has taken place and speakers on the marae are saying their last farewells to the person who has died, they may tell him, *Kua wheturangitia koe,* 'You have risen over the horizon', meaning that he is now a star.

In life, too, valorous chiefs might be spoken of admiringly as stars. Beautiful girls were compared to the morning star, and eyes flashing with rage or misted with tears might be likened in poetry to stars. There was a detailed knowledge of the stars and their movements, and much significance was attached to the more important ones, such as the fiery Rehua, or Antares, a deity that had the power of healing and was a sign of summer, and Poututerangi, or Altair, which with other stars was believed to bring the harvest. The seven stars that make up the faint constellation of the Pleiades were known as Matariki, literally Little Eyes, and their heliacal rising in June marked the beginning of the new year. They

were greeted with tears for those who had died during the past year, and
with joy because the new year had begun:

Tirohia atu nei, ka whetūrangitia Matariki,
Te whitu o te tau e whakamoe mai ra!
He hōmai ana rongo kia kōmai atu au —
Ka mate nei au i te matapōuri, i te matapōrehu o roto i a au!

See where Matariki have risen over the horizon,
The seven of the year winking up there!
They come with their message that I may rejoice.
Here I am full of sorrow, full of sadness within!

Like the stars, the moon lived forever. The difference was that it
seemed to die, then after three days it came back to life. Proverbs and
songs contrasted this apparent death with the one that human beings
encounter:

Me i pēnei te mate ki a koe
Me te mate i te marama, ka ea mai e au!

If your death were like that of the moon
You would rise up again, *e au!*

OPPOSITE Kumara were planted in
neat, regular rows. The cloud
formation known as a mackerel sky
was a sign that the spirits in the sky
were planting their kumara.

The moon was believed to control women's menstrual cycles, and was thought to be masculine. It was said that the marriage of a man and his wife was of no consequence, for the moon was her real husband. People used to greet the new moon by calling, 'The husband of all the women in the world has appeared!'

There was, though, a woman in the moon. Her name was Rona. She had gone out one night with a gourd to draw water from a spring, and when the moon passed behind a cloud she stumbled among the bushes. She was annoyed at this, and she cursed the moon for not giving her light. The moon, enraged, came down from the sky and dragged her back up with him. Rona clung to a ngaio tree, but it was no use, the tree was pulled out by its roots. She was carried up to the moon, and is still to be seen there with her gourd and her tree. It was always dangerous to abuse a person, for the Maori were quick to take offence at insults. Anyone who was running this risk might be told, *Kia mahara ki te hē o Rona,* 'Remember Rona's mistake'.

The mysterious regions of the sky were not to be attained by living human beings, but in the myths one man, Tawhaki, does succeed in going up to this eternal world. Tawhaki is a glorious, tapu chief. Sometimes he climbs a vine and sometimes he goes up on a kite or a spider-web, or he ascends at a place known as the *toi*, 'raised-up centre', the mystical point where the sky hangs down to the earth. He is an archetypal figure, one that presents a pattern to be followed by human beings. Living persons might be honoured by being associated with him, and the dead might be told in songs and in karakia, ritual chants, to mount up on his pathway. The wonderful story of Tawhaki's exploit kept alive the hope that men could make their way up to the tapu skies, though not in this life.

The Earth and its Weather

Just as the high, remote sky with its eternal lights could only be male, so the earth was obviously female, being a most prized resource made productive by men and essential for their sustenance. The importance of land and women was such that they were proverbially the two main causes of strife:

He wāhine, he whenua, e ngaro ai te tāngata.

It is women and land that destroy men.

A tribe's territory was intimately known to its members, with every small feature in the landscape being given its own name. Everywhere the land

held complex associations which came partly from the daily experience of winning a livelihood from it, and partly from a knowledge of events that had occurred in the past. In some places battles had been won or lost, in others there had once stood a village or a pa, or famous lovers had met, or the body of a great chief had lain for a time while being conveyed to its last home. Above all, a tribe's land was dear to them as being the resting-place of the bones of their ancestors. If they had to migrate to new territory they would if at all possible carry their bones with them, so that the living and the dead might remain together.

The earth and the sky were together spoken of as the world, or *ao*, and were often contrasted with the *pō*, or underworld. It is interesting that this word ao means both 'day' and 'world', while po means 'night' and 'underworld'; it is almost as if the sun as it rose each morning was felt to bring

In oratory and proverbs, unhappy circumstances could be likened to cloudy weather.

the world into existence once more, while the night retreated to the nether regions. In songs and karakia, the expression *te ao mārama,* 'the world of light', indicates a state of wellbeing, a successful outcome — often, one achieved after danger and misfortune. For example, a high-ranking child is reminded in a song of the battles his tribe has lost, and the prediction is made that he will grow up to avenge these defeats and preserve the honour of his kinsmen:

Ka puta koe ki te whaiao,
Ki te ao mārama!

You will come forth to the light of day,
The world of light!

Here the light of the sun and the world it shines upon are identified with successful human existence.

The earth's seasons, and the weather, were seen as conveying good or bad omens, or as being in sympathy with human joys and sorrows. A beautiful object might be said to be like a fine day, and it was thought that a child born in fine weather would grow up to be very handsome. Unhappy times might be spoken of as a cloudy day, regret or disappointment

as mist, and a party of warriors, on one's own side or that of the enemy, as strong, relentless winds. The word *hau* means 'breath' as well as 'wind', and these meanings are closely related. Human breath was experienced as the counterpart of the breath of the world, which was felt to possess a kind of life. A light breeze might indicate the presence of a spirit; and a person pining for an absent lover or relative would yearn for a wind from the direction in which he was living, feeling that this would establish a kind of contact between them:

Tēnei ka noho i te puke i Te Tarata,
Kia āta tomo mai he tā uru-mā-tonga:
He kawe aroha mai no Takuira kei te haere!

Here I sit on Te Tarata hill
Waiting for the south-west wind to come.
It is bearing Takuira's love to me!

If a man's wife ran away and he wanted her back, he would ask a tohunga to arrange this for him. The tohunga would wait until the wind was in the right direction, then recite a karakia which would be borne to the woman upon the wind, awakening such a longing for her husband that she would

Human breath, or *hau*, was the counterpart of the wind. A person's *hau* was his vital essence, the life within him. When two people greeted each other by pressing noses in the hongi, they were intermingling their *hau*. For this reason, the ceremony was performed only between persons of similar status.

In this scene recorded in 1844, a party of visitors to a Taranaki pa greet friends and relatives.

at once set out to return to him. And wind could convey a message from the dead, as when the body of a departed relative, lying in state at the funeral, is said to be anointed by dew brought by a wind that blows from the place where his or her ancestors lie buried:

> *Ka tōkia tō kiri te anu o te whenua:*
> *Ko 'e hau tuku mai, ē, ko 'e hau tuku iho*
> *I runga o ngā puke kai ō mātua ē,*
> *Kai ō tūpuna e moe noa mai ra —*
> *Te tini o te tāngata, te tini o te tāngata!*

> Your skin is anointed with cold from the land
> By a wind come towards us, a wind come down
> Over the hills from your elders,
> From your ancestors who are sleeping there —
> The multitude of men, the multitude of men!

Clouds being carried by the wind towards an absent loved one might be greeted as establishing a link with him, while a brightly glowing sunset was a sign that a battle had been fought that day. Rain was sometimes felt to be falling in sympathy with human tears; still today it is thought to come

down heavily at funerals. A waterspout might be thought to be conveying water to the spirits in the sky, for water is needed up there just as it is here below. A rainbow was a good omen when seen on the right, and a bad one on the left; if it were pale, someone was going to die. Shining through misty rain, a rainbow could signify a noble chief surrounded by a multitude of followers. Sometimes it was a pathway for spirits descending from the sky, or for the souls of departed chiefs who were making their way upwards. In the South Island, it was the path that had been taken by the mythical Roko-i-tua when he arrived from Hawaiki in the early times bearing the kumara as a gift for mankind.

The Underworld

Light and the underworld were closely associated, and both were called by the one word, *pō*. Like most traditional peoples the Maori feared the darkness and the spirits that moved about in the dark, and they would not venture out at night if they could possibly avoid it. When forced to do so, they would talk or sing loudly to scare away the spirits, and often they would carry cooked food

After the death of an important chief, a tribe's canoe might be broken as a sign of mourning, and part of it set up as a monument. This cenotaph was erected at Pipiriki, on the Whanganui River, in about 1824.

with them, for the spirits, being very tapu, feared contact with this profane substance. The nights were full of strange, ominous sounds. Owls hooted from tapu places or from crossroads, and there were mysterious crashing noises in the distance, and the whistling cries of spirits. Travellers camped in the forest always lit a fire as protection against the night, and even at home a fire was essential. An early missionary wrote that 'when it is dark they consider the absence of light to be a torture, they are not willing to abandon themselves to sleep without lighting a fire nearby or, if their intention is not to sleep but to converse, they must have a light. According to them, the faculty of speech cannot be separated from the faculty of sight. If it happened by chance that they could not light a fire you would see them, full of distress, muttering, but without the courage to speak. But suddenly give them light in such upsetting circumstances and they will cry out in expressive speech: "Now we can start living".'

The visions that come at night were thought to belong to the underworld. If someone dreamt about another person, the explanation was that in sleep his wairua, or soul, had left his body and gone to the underworld, and there met the soul of the other person. In many songs a woman separated from her lover complains that she embraced him down there, thinking it was in this world, then woke and found him gone. And a person might meet in sleep the souls of kinsmen who had died:

Takoto rawa iho ki te pō,
E huihui ana mai ō tātou wairua
Kia piri, kia tata mai ki taku taha.
Matatū tonu ake, ka maranga kei runga.
Whitirere ki te ao, tirotiro kau au:
A, me he wairua atua te tārehutanga iho!
E te manawa i raro, kapakapa tū kei runga!

As I lay, down in the underworld
Our souls were crowding about me,
Coming near, coming close to my side.
Suddenly I woke, and sprang up.
Thrust back into the world, I stared about in vain —
Ah, like spirits they had faded away!
O my heart at rest, rise up, beating!

Though the souls of distinguished men were sometimes said to go up to the sky, and orators often spoke of their return to the homeland of Hawaiki, the usual belief was that the souls of the dead made their way down to the underworld, entering it at a place known as Te Reinga, The Leaping Place. This was in the far north of the North Island, in the region known as Muriwhenua, Land's End. On the rocky cliff-face of this headland there grew an ancient pohutukawa, and from this tree the souls leapt to a cave in the waters below.

The souls came at last to Te Reinga (Cape Reinga), in the far north. From an ancient pohutukawa similar to this one, they leapt into the water and down to the underworld.

Often when a man was near death he heard the souls of his departed relatives calling to him to join them. At the funeral his kinsmen wept and wailed for him, and they spoke and sang their farewells, bidding him set out for Hawaiki and the underworld. After three days the soul left the body and began its journey. Sometimes its passage was felt as a light puff of wind.

In funeral laments the soul may be described as pausing on a hill at the boundary of the tribal territory and gazing back:

> *Ka eke ki runga ra,*
> *Ka tangi ki te whenua nā ī:*
> *'Hei konei ra, i te ao-tū-roa!*
> *Ka haere tēnei ki te pōuriuri,*
> *Ki te pōtangotango*
> *Ki tua o Paerau, i pepehatia ai nā ī.'*

> When you reach the summit
> You will weep over your land:
> 'Farewell, remain in the enduring world!
> As for me, I go to the gloomy shades,
> The intense darkness
> Beyond Paerau, of which men speak.'

The souls were sometimes thought to travel by land and sometimes by water. In a song from the Lake Rotoehu district a mother tells her son to dive into the Waitahanui, a stream that rises near the lake and flows into the Bay of Plenty, then to make his way through the ocean, passing the Moehau Range and the islands beyond. When he reaches the tapu moun-

The islands of the Hauraki Gulf, as seen from Mount Moehau.

tain of Rangitoto, he is to call a greeting to a kinsman whose bones lie in
a cave there:

E hopu tō ringa ngā rimu rapa nui, hai whakatau ringa.
E tae koe ki Moehau, titiro tō kanohi ngā motu whakatere —
Ko Rangitoto pea nge! Whakaoho tō reo!
Tēnā tō matua te whakamoe mai na
Kai roto i te whare kōhatu!

Grasp the kelp with your hand, to steady yourself.
At Moehau, let your eyes gaze at the floating islands.
Rangitoto is there! Lift up your voice!
Your elder is sleeping in his stone house!

'The floating islands' is a beautifully exact way of describing the islands
of the Hauraki Gulf. In some lights they do seem to be floating.

The souls brought with them leaves and twigs of the plants that were
most common in the districts where they had lived, and they left one in
each of the places where they rested on the way. These tokens were known
as *whakaū*, a term used also of a similar custom followed by living people
when they visited a district for the first time. Fearful of inadvertently

The lava caves of Rangitoto Island
were a resting-place for the bones of
ancestors.

trespassing upon the tapu places in that unfamiliar locality, they would placate the spirits by offering them a twig or a handful of grass, reciting a karakia as they did so.

On a hill near Te Reinga the souls paused to gaze back and weep, sending a last farewell to their kinsmen and the world:

In the water, the souls made their way down through the seaweed to a cave beneath.

BELOW A puriri moth, largest of the moths of Aotearoa. Souls returning to visit the living often took the form of moths or spiders.

E tae ki Te Rerenga, tahuri mai ki muri, mihi mai i konā
Te riu ki te whenua, ē. Tēnei, e te hoa,
Ā tāua kura i waiho i muri i tō tua.
Ma wai hoki ra e pupuri ringa rua?
E here ana mai te taura o te pō hai kukume ki raro ra ē!

When you come to the Leaping Place, turn back and greet
The vale of the land. Friend, these are our treasures,
Which you are leaving behind your back.
Who can hold them forever in his hands?
The rope of night binds us, and will drag us below!

They left all their tears on this hill. Then they passed along the steep, narrow ridge, and down to the pohutukawa tree that clung to the cliff

above Te Reinga. Perched upon its branches they looked down into the watery cave below, waiting until the waves washed aside the long seaweed growing about its entrance. Then they made their descent:

Tirohia iho ra te timunga o te tai:
Ka māwhe ngā rimu, ka tuku ai i a koe
Ki te rua e mutu ai tō kite mai i te iwi,
I te toka tū iho i runga i Tīrau,
I te wai kaukau i Taupō rāia,
He tīherunga hoe na Tūwharetoa.

Look down, and wait for the tide to ebb.
When the seaweed subsides, it will take you down
To the abyss where you will no more see your people,
The rocky peak high up on Tirau
And the waters of Taupo where the people bathe
And Ngati Tuwharetoa bail their canoes.

In some districts, such as Rotorua, it was believed that the souls had then to cross a stream known as Te Wai Ora a Tane, The Living Waters of Tane. A guardian spirit took them across in a canoe, or sometimes placed a plank across the stream for them, though occasionally he would refuse to admit a person, sending him back to the world of light. Even when the soul reached the underworld he could sometimes return, provided he did not eat any of the food down there. This food was of two kinds. There were plenty of kumara and taro, the plant foods that were best liked, but there were also flies, and what the early Pakeha writers on this subject call 'filth': the reverse, that is, of what was acceptable in the world above. There were many tales about people who had met relatives in the underworld who had urged them to go back up. One woman was told by her father that she must return because his grandchild still needed her care; he warned her not to accept any food, she followed his advice, and in the end she succeeded in returning to the world. It was sometimes thought that the souls experienced a series of further transformations in the underworld, ending up as earthworms, and that when a worm died a soul finally ceased to exist. Dogs made their way down there, though they followed a different path, and food and crops that had been destroyed might also be said to have gone down to the dark world.

The souls of the dead kept their concern for the relatives they had left behind, and often they visited them. They came sometimes in dreams and seances, they returned as spiders or moths, they spoke through the voices of little birds inhabiting the tapu groves where their bodies lay, and their figures, given substance by the carvers, were on the facades of the chiefs' houses and storehouses and the palisades of pa. This was not mere decoration. Through their powers these ancestral figures protected their descendants and ensured their well-being, threatening the enemy and turning aside the evil effects of sorcery. Above all they proclaimed the unity of the living and the dead.

The bones of ancestors were concealed in remote caves, and in the north they were sometimes placed inside carved chests. This figure of a chief holds one of his descendants.

The High Places

Close to the sky, raised above human habitations and difficult of access, the mountains inspired fear and awe, and often were thought to be the homes of spirits. As well, each tribe had a special relationship with one particular mountain within its territory which it regarded as tapu, and to which it looked for signs foretelling the future. Many high mountains served this purpose, and so when necessary did smaller, less imposing ones. Usually the bones of high-ranking men and women were laid to rest in well-hidden caves on their tapu mountain, and in some areas these mountains and their burial caves were invoked in karakia to strengthen warriors of the tribe before they went into battle. From time to time the tohunga would make their way up the mountain to communicate in secret with the spirits and fairies that lived there, but generally they would not infringe its tapu and risk their lives by climbing right to the top. There were many stories about terrible spirits that lived on the peaks of these mountains, and it was said that their summits could not be reached. In the Rotorua district it was claimed that when men attempted to climb the slopes of Mount Tarawera, the mountain grew higher above them.

Burial caves were in hidden places difficult to reach. Cliffs on Taranga (Hen Island), off the east coast of Te Tai Tokerau (Northland).

Nevertheless, there are a few accounts of people climbing to the summits of tapu mountains. One such concerns the tribe of Ngati Awa, whose mountain is Putauaki (Mount Edgecumbe), in the Bay of Plenty. We are told that the bones of most men and women were placed in caves at the foot of the mountain but that the remains of people of especially distinguished descent were carried to the very summit, where they were lowered into a deep chasm at the top of the higher, eastern peak, known as Te Tatau o te Rangi, The Door of the Sky. The other pinnacle, towards the west, was called Te Tara ki 'Tauaki, 'Tauaki Peak, and the central crater with its lake was Te Matapihi o Rehua, The Window of Rehua. This Rehua was a well-disposed and most tapu deity who was identified with the star Antares and lived in the highest of the skies.

Often in laments for departed chiefs it is said that the peak of the dead man's tribal mountain is fallen down; apparently the chief is being honoured by being identified with his mountain, though it may be that the mountain itself is seen as bowed down in mourning. On the other hand, on a famous occasion when the people of Taranaki won two great battles in one day, their mountain Taranaki (Mount Egmont) swelled so much with pride that all could see it had grown taller.

The banks of mist that swirled about the peaks of these tapu mountains were often thought to represent the fairy people who lived there, and

Mount Tarawera, the tapu mountain of Ngati Tuhourangi in the Rotorua district.

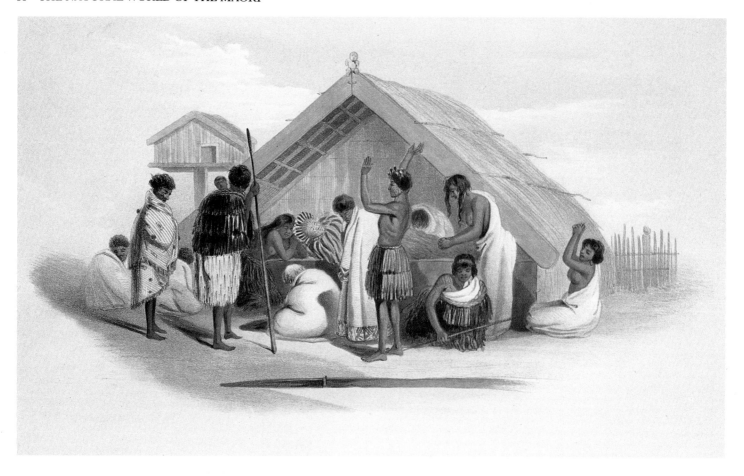

Erected near the East Cape in the
1830s, this platform bore the body of
a leading chief.
TOP A tangihanga, or funeral
ceremony, recorded in the 1840s. The
body is adorned with huia feathers.

their houses and fortifications. Sometimes, though, the mist revealed visions of things to come. When the people of the Lower Waikato were waiting to fight the British troops before the beginning of the Waikato War in 1863, they looked over one morning to their mountain, Maungaroa, and as the sun's first rays shone upon the mist about its summit they saw a great battle in progress, with armies pursuing and retreating. There was a steamboat in the mist; and it was soon after this that the first steamboat, a British gunboat, entered their river. And the people saw the towns, with houses and forts, that the Pakehas later built upon the lands they seized.

Lightning flashing over a tapu mountain was also a portent, its meaning depending upon the direction in which it struck. If it pointed towards another tribe it was a good omen for the local people, though a bad one for the other tribe, but lightning that came straight down upon the summit of a mountain warned of a defeat in battle or the death of a chief:

Terā te uira e hiko i te rangi,
E wāhi rua ana ra runga o Tauwhare!
Kāore ianei, ko te tohu o te mate!

See the lightning flashing in the sky,
Splitting in two over Tauwhare!
Oh alas, it is the sign of death!

Thunder over such a mountain could be the voice of an ancestral spirit. In a legend, a hero named Tu-whakairi-ora, setting out to avenge the death of his grandfather, visits for the first time his kinsmen at Whareka-hika (Hicks Bay on the East Coast). The chief of these people, a man named Te Aotaki, performs a ceremony acknowledging their relationship, in this way committing himself to Tu-whakairi-ora's cause. Then, facing his tapu mountain, Pukeamaru, he invokes an ancestress named Rangi-popo: 'Old lady, old lady, arise, arise, arise! Announce your son, give voice!' Before long she speaks with the voice of the thunderclap, first to the tribes on the near side, then to those on the far side; three times her voice is heard by the tribes in the far distance, and on the third occasion they exclaim, 'It must be for a matter of great importance that Te Aotaki is tearing apart his mountain Pukeamaru! Tomorrow we will hear the news.'

The Waikato tribe claimed for their Mount Taupiri priority over all other mountains, saying that in the beginning, when Maui fished up the North Island, it was the first land to rise above the waves. Exactly the same thing was said by the East Coast tribe, Ngati Porou, about their mountain, Hikurangi, though in this case they also believed that Maui's canoe, turned to stone, was to be seen upon the summit. This name Hikurangi is an ancient one that occurs in mythology; in the paradisial land of Hawaiki there is a mountain named Hikurangi which the light rests upon, a place of eternal life where death is unknown. In Aotearoa many prominent peaks were called after this first tapu mountain, with the mythic Hiku-rangi and the local one being closely associated or perhaps completely identified. Certainly this happened with Mount Hikurangi on the East Coast, which was said to have been the first land to rise up to the light of day; furthermore this event is constantly repeated, for at dawn each day it is the first place in this part of the country to be touched by the sun's rays. In the 1830s a Pakeha trader travelling near this mountain found

Taranaki (Mount Egmont), the tapu mountain of the Taranaki, Te Atiawa and Ngati Ruanui tribes.

that the countryside round about was so seldom traversed as to be pathless, its only inhabitants innumerable birds and lizards that were believed to be spirits. As well, the summit was thought to be the home of a solitary moa, which stood there on one leg and fed only on the wind.

This word *moa* was originally used by the ancestors of the Maori in speaking of the domestic fowl, which they had possessed in tropical Polynesia but did not bring to Aotearoa with them. In this country they applied the term to the large, flightless birds known as *Dinornis* which they found here, and which disappeared in most places some 500 years ago, hunted to extinction. There is a proverbial expression *mate-ā-moa,* 'lost like the moa', which means 'lost utterly and hopelessly'. Though this expression could in theory refer to the loss of the domestic fowls left behind in tropical Polynesia, it must instead refer to the much more serious loss of *Dinornis.* The first immigrants could not have worried too much about the loss of their fowls, having gained instead the meaty *Dinornis,* but their descendants must have suffered very considerably when these big birds finally became extinct.

In Maori tradition, moa appear as remote creatures possessed of supernatural attributes; they stand alone on high mountains, they are similar in appearance to human beings, and they drink the wind. So a sparing eater might be called *he moa kai hau*, 'a moa that feeds on air', and a girl in love who had lost her appetite might sing,

Kia tū tonu au, ko te moa i Hikuran[g]i
E taufiaki nei ia!

Let me stand here always, the moa
That watches at Hikurangi!

A moa stood on Mount Whakapunake, inland between Gisborne and Wairoa, and another lived with giant lizards upon the icy heights of Taranaki. When a geologist named Ernest Dieffenbach was climbing Taranaki in 1839, his two Maori guides stopped at the snowline and would go no further; very much afraid, they sat down, took out their prayer books and began to pray. To the Maori, Dieffenbach wrote, 'the mountains are peopled with mysterious and misshapen animals; the black points, which he sees from afar in the dazzling snow, are fierce and monstrous birds; a supernatural spirit breathes on him in the evening breeze, or is heard in the rolling of a loose stone.'

In the centre of the North Island there stand the three volcanic peaks Ruapehu, Ngauruhoe and Tongariro. These last two are close together and were formerly regarded as being a single mountain, Tongariro, so that what is now Ngauruhoe was formerly the peak of Tongariro. This mountain, an active volcano, was the tapu peak of Ngati Tuwharetoa tribe in the Taupo region; its fires were said to have been placed there by their ancestor, Ngatoro-i-rangi, and the people spoke of the mountain itself as their ancestor. Many spirits lived upon it, in a house called Te Haruru o

OPPOSITE Kaitotehe Pa, in the lower Waikato, lay at the foot of Mount Taupiri, the tapu mountain of the tribes in that region.
OPPOSITE BELOW At dawn on the East Coast, Mount Hikurangi is the first place to be touched by the rays of the sun.
BELOW A nineteenth-century drawing of a moa, with kiwi at its feet.

te Rangi, The Roaring of the Sky. When flames and smoke burst from Tongariro, Ngati Tuwharetoa thought that its spirits were commanding them to make war. The neighbouring tribes would also see this sign in the distance, and they would know to expect an invasion.

Mount Ruapehu, some 14 kilometres to the south, was the tapu mountain of the tribes of the upper Whanganui River. It used to be called Ruapahu, and was spoken of in poetry as Para-te-tai-tonga or Pare-te-tai-tonga. Because it is always snow-capped this mountain could symbolise extreme cold or misery, as when a poet abandoned by her lover complains,

> *E hōmai ana koe, e te kōkōraro,*
> *Te mate o te aroha, ka eke kei te kakī.*
> *Kei ngā puke au ki Para-te-tai-tonga.*

> North wind, you are bringing me
> The pain of longing, it rises to my throat.
> I am on the peaks of Para-te-tai-tonga.

Mountains were often thought to be male or female; Tongariro, for instance, had two wives, the smaller peaks Pihanga and Hauhungatahi.

Mount Ruapehu, with the headwaters of the Tongariro River. To the Maori the Waikato River begins at this point, rather than at its outlet from Lake Taupo.

Sometimes the Maori themselves arranged for mountains to be married, as a way of ensuring peace between tribes. After there had been fighting for a long time between the Tuhoe tribe in the Ureweras and Ngati Kahungunu of Heretaunga (Hawke's Bay), the men of Ngati Kahungunu wished to make peace. So a high chief told his people that he would give his daughter in marriage to a leading man of Tuhoe, and they agreed to this. Then another chief proposed that as the equivalent of this human marriage their mountain Kuha-tarewa should become the wife of Tuhi-o-Kahu, a high hill overlooking Lake Waikaremoana in the Ureweras. Both tribes accepted this idea, the marriage took place, and ever afterwards there was peace between their peoples. It was the union of the two mountains which made the peace a lasting one.

By the 1850s the tribes had become alarmed at the ever-increasing numbers of Pakehas arriving in their country in search of land, and many wished to elect a king who would oppose the further sale of land to the foreigners. To this end a great meeting of chiefs from different areas was held in 1856, its purpose being to bring together all their power and prestige, their mana, so that it might be bestowed upon the man who was to be king, Potatau Te Wherowhero: possessed of this, Potatau would have the right and the power to forbid the sale of land. The chiefs met in a

Mount Ngauruhoe, regarded as the peak of Tongariro. This volcano, the tapu mountain of Ngati Tuwharetoa, was regarded with the greatest awe and dread.

village on the shore of Lake Taupo, in the centre of the island and close to Tongariro, the most dreaded and venerated of all the tribal mountains. Te Heuheu, the high chief of Ngati Tuwharetoa who had called the meeting, had caused a tall flagstaff to be erected in this place. At its masthead there flew a copy of a flag which the king of England had presented to a northern confederation of tribes at a time when the country had not yet come under British rule, and beneath this, at intervals down the mast, there were long ropes of plaited flax, their ends hanging loose. When the tribes were seated in companies around the flagstaff Te Heuheu announced that it represented Tongariro, and that each of the dangling ropes was the tapu mountain of one of the tribes assembled before him. Under his direction the leading chiefs rose one by one and fastened their ropes to stakes which they drove into the ground. At last all the ropes were taut, and the land was united. Then its mana was passed to Potatau.

Many mountains and hills were the homes of patupaiarehe, or fairies. These were spirits, yet they were different from other spirits, for they had bodies like those of humans and they hunted and fished, wove garments, fought and made love just as humans do. Their skins were white, though, and there were other differences as well. Being spirits they were very tapu, so they ate only raw food, and they greatly feared cooked food, the steam

Lake Waikaremoana, in the Ureweras. The people of this district and those of Heretaunga (Hawke's Bay) established a lasting peace by agreeing that their mountains should be married.

from earth ovens, and even fire. And as spirits they shunned the light, being encountered mostly at night-time and in misty places such as the hilltops at daybreak. They were a handsome people, much given to dancing and singing, and the sweet sound of their men's flutes, heard in the high hills, greatly excited human women. Sometimes a fairy and a human would meet in the forest, and sometimes a fairy would enter a house by night and visit a human there. Erotic dreams might be explained in this way, and a further proof was the occasional birth of albino children, whose pale skins, fair hair and inability to stand the sunlight were obviously inherited from fairy fathers.

Existing at the margins of human experience, in dreams and wild places, the fairies occupied an intermediate, ambiguous position between the human and the spirit worlds. Often they were frightening figures, or at the very least a race of strangers who lived apart, but occasionally they were concerned for human welfare. Sometimes they were thought to have been living in the land before the arrival of human beings and to have been displaced by them, but sometimes it was said that they had been placed in the hills by the powerful tohunga, Ngatoro-i-rangi, after his arrival from Hawaiki. Fairies often lived on the peaks of tribal mountains, and their presence there, while certainly alarming, must have been felt to reinforce the sacredness of these peaks; indeed, it is known that tohunga sometimes presented offerings to them and sought their assistance. Such tapu mountains inhabited by fairies included Pirongia in the Waikato,

Mount Pirongia in the 1860s. This mountain was a famous haunt of the patupaiarehe, or fairies.

Rangitoto in the ranges north-west of Lake Taupo, Ngongotaha by Lake Rotorua, Te Aroha near the Hauraki Plains and Moehau at the extremity of the Coromandel Peninsula.

Some mountains and hills, also headlands and islands, were the sites of massively palisaded pa, or fortresses. As well as being strongholds these were the centres of social life, the places where guests were received and feasted, where chiefs and warriors debated tribal policy and finely carved buildings could be admired. The larger pa were divided by low fences into a number of areas which were each under the control of a small hapu, or sub-tribe, and which contained several buildings grouped around a marae, or courtyard; naturally enough, the area belonging to the relatives of the leading chief was upon the highest ground. Other pa were much smaller. In 1769, the British explorer Joseph Banks saw at Te Whanga-nui-o-Hei (Mercury Bay on the Coromandel Peninsula) a pa, 'the most beautifuly romantick thing I ever saw', which was built upon a steep rocky island that was in the form of an archway, and only large enough to hold five or six houses. These miniature pa were refuges in times of war and, like the larger ones, objects of great pride and prestige to their owners.

The poetry of every tribe is full of references to the mountains, hills and headlands that its people held dear. Travellers making their way along a ridge would rest when possible at a lookout place, and often as they sat there they would sing old songs about events that had occurred in the hills and valleys spread out before them. Sometimes, too, a person would climb to a lookout place just to gaze upon the scene below. A man forced to abandon his ancestral lands might ascend a hill to look upon them for a last time and farewell them in song, and a woman yearning for an absent lover might sit weeping and singing in a place from which she could glimpse the hills near his home:

> Taku taumata tonu ngā hiwi teitei kei 'Tauaki ē,
> Mārama te titiro, pae ka riakina kai Rāwhiti ē.
> Kai raro a Tawhiti — te awhi tipu a tō wahine ē!

> My lookout place is always the high ridges of 'Tauaki
> Where I can see clearly the hills lifted up in the east.
> Tawhiti is below there — you whom your wife embraces!

Always the mountains were the most significant of landmarks, their physical presence inseparable from their human associations.

OPPOSITE Te Puta o Paretauhinau, Paretauhinau's Opening, the pa at Te Whanga-nui-o-Hei which the Pakeha visitors admired in 1769. On the island, someone waves a garment in welcome.

OPPOSITE BELOW Some tapu mountains had pa on their lower slopes. One such was Tokatoka, a volcanic cone on the east bank of the lower Wairoa River, near the Kaipara Harbour.

Four

SHAPING THE LAND

It was Maui who fished up the land. He was a trickster, a man who broke all the rules and got away with it, a youngest son with amazing powers who invented the eel pot and the bird-spear, and turned his brother-in-law into the first dog, and bound the sun to make it go more slowly, and won fire for mankind. Maui made such a nuisance of himself with his tricks that one day when he wanted to go fishing with his brothers they would not agree. But he hid under the decking and went anyway, only showing himself when they were too far out to return. He persuaded his brothers to go further still, then after they had tried their luck with no success he brought out his own hook, which was the jawbone of his ancestress Murirangawhenua. No one but Maui would have dared to profane the tapu bone of an ancestor in this way. He flung his magic hook into the water, and he caught his great fish. His terrified brothers begged him to let it go, but he kept pulling on his line, and in the end the fish rose up through the water. Then they saw that there were trees and houses on it, and fires burning, and people walking about.

That fish is now Aotea, or Aotearoa (the North Island); often it is called Te Ika a Maui, Maui's Fish. Its head is in the south, with the mouth forming Te Whanga-nui-a-Tara (Wellington Harbour), and one of the eyes Lake Wairarapa. The heart is Lake Taupo, or so say Ngati Tu-wharetoa; in the Ureweras, the Tuhoe people claim that their mountains are the heart. The fins are Taranaki and the East Coast; the tail is Northland; and Maui's hook is the sweeping curve of Hawke Bay, the barb having turned into Mahia Peninsula. When the fish was caught, Maui told his brothers to watch over it while he went back to Hawaiki to find a tohunga who would remove its tapu; he warned them that in his absence they must do nothing to interfere with it. But as soon as he was gone the greedy brothers forgot their instructions and began hacking up the fish. It was not yet dead, and in its pain it writhed and twisted, making mountains and valleys. If only they had left it alone, the land would have stayed smooth and flat.

The brothers' canoe, which was called Mahunui, became the South Island; in oratory and poetry this land is known as Te Waka o Maui, Maui's Canoe, and as Mahunui. The anchor stone became Stewart Island, which is still sometimes called Te Puka o te Waka o Maui, the Anchor Stone of Maui's Canoe. And the thwart against which Maui braced himself while hauling up the fish turned into the Kaikoura Ranges, which are still known today as Te Taumanu a Maui, Maui's Thwart.

The first person to visit these islands was Kupe. He was a precursor, a man who prepared the way for the human beings who were to follow. According to one story, Kupe came from Hawaiki and overtook the land as it was floating along on the ocean; he found that the ground was soft and trembling, and his first task was to make it firm and stationary. Some said that Kupe cut Aotearoa off from Hawaiki, to which it was then joined; and others that it was he, not Maui's brothers, who jumped upon the back of the fish and sliced it up, making it twist into hills and valleys. Often he was said to have cut the strait that separates the North and South Islands, forming as he did so a number of landmarks, in particular Kapiti, Mana and Arapawa Islands, which still bear witness to this exploit. He was thought to have sailed around much of the coast of Aotearoa, especially the west coast of the North Island, and to have left behind him many possessions turned to stone, such as his sail, his fishing net, his bailer, his dogs and his footprints. The two small islands in Te Whanga-nui-a-Tara (Wellington Harbour) are Kupe's daughters, Matiu and Makaro, whom he left there. Even at Lake Waikaremoana, far from the sea, an upright, fissured rock is called Nga Hoe o Kupe, Kupe's Paddles, and a sunken rock nearby is Te Waka o Kupe, Kupe's Canoe. It has turned to stone along with the crew, and on a calm day you can look down through the water and see the men seated at their places holding their paddles.

Kupe was also associated with the rough seas and heavy surf found on the west coast of the North Island: sometimes he was said to have encountered these obstructing seas on his way here, and sometimes to have raised them behind him when he was being pursued from Hawaiki by a man whose wives he had stolen. Similarly, he was often said to have introduced to this country the prickly bush lawyer, the thorny matagouri and the stinging tree nettle, which so often barred the way for travellers in the forest. Because he was a forerunner, a precursor, he returned to Hawaiki when his task was completed. Often it was said that he left from Hokianga in Northland, and that this district gained its name, literally 'Place of Returning', from this event. When he was asked in Hawaiki if he would go back again, he replied *'E hokihoki Kupe'*, 'Will Kupe keep returning?' This remark is a proverb which is quoted by those who would indicate indirectly but firmly that they will not return to a place.

The Ancestral Canoes

Some tribes believed that their ancestors had lived here always. Many of Ngati Porou on the East Coast traced their descent from Maui himself, while in some places the original ancestor was a certain Toi, who was sometimes believed to have been Maui's descendant but often was said simply to have been the first man, and to have lived here from the beginning. It was thought that Toi ate only wild

Maui and his fish, carved about 90 years ago by a Rotorua artist. OPPOSITE Lake Taupo is often said to be the heart of Maui's fish.

plant foods such as fernroot and the pith of the mamaku, and that he did not possess fire, but ate his food raw; in one story he acquires the kumara from two men who arrive from Hawaiki bearing this cherished food. Toi is, then, a transitional figure who lacks the normal human possessions of fire and the kumara. His name is suggestive, for in the Maori language the word *toi* can be used in a mystical way of people who are the first ever to live in a land. His association with the fernroot and the mamaku was proverbial, and sometimes he was said to have provided these plants for his descendants. Thus an East Coast poet, complaining that the crops have failed, says that his people must now rely upon wild plant foods:

E tama mā e! E ahu ki uta ra
Ki ngā kai a Toi, i mahue i muri ra —
Te aruhe, te mamaku, te pou o te tāngata e!

Men, make your way inland
For the foods of Toi, who left behind him
The fernroot and the mamaku, sustenance for mankind!

OPPOSITE Among the obstacles left behind by Kupe were the high seas on the west coast of the North Island, and two formidable plants. The matagouri (FAR LEFT) is a spiny shrub or small tree found in open tussock and dune country. The tree nettle or ongaonga (LEFT) grows up to 3 metres high and can inflict a most painful sting. People trying to make their way through thickets of ongaonga have been badly poisoned and even killed. BELOW Hokianga Harbour, from which Kupe is said to have returned to Hawaiki.

The ancestors' migrations from Hawaiki were often depicted in meeting-house paintings in the late nineteenth century. One of these voyages may be the subject of this painting in Hinetapora, a meeting-house near Ruatoria.

Some tribes in Northland traced their origin rather similarly to a man named Tumutumu-whenua, who was not from this world but came up out of the ground. This man married a woman who did belong to this world, though she was a fairy, not a human.

But most people believed that the founders of their tribes had come from a place called Hawaiki which lay in the direction of the rising sun. This paradisial land was the stage upon which the dramas of the myths were enacted, the place where the very first men–Maui, Tawhaki, Whaka-tau and the rest of them–had had their archetypal adventures, establishing social patterns by creating precedents for their descendants to follow. And Hawaiki was also the source of most forms of life. Some kinds of birds flew from there; the little kiore swam in a long line, each holding the tail of the one in front; and all the fish in the sea came from the spring at Rangiriri, which is close to Hawaiki. Of the tribal ancestors who made the journey, most came by canoe but some arrived in other ways. One came on a rainbow, and another on the back of an albatross; a man named Tara-whata rode with his two dogs on a taniwha that took the form of a piece of firewood; a man named Manawa-tere glided over the ripples of the waves; a woman called Wairakewa, who had been left behind, caught up with her family by speeding across the ocean seated upon a manuka bush, then planted her tapu bush when she reached Whakatane; an ancestor named Paikea travelled on the back of a whale, chanting a powerful karakia, spell, as he came; and two ancestors floated here on calabashes, one of them, a man named Maia, introducing in this way the seeds of the gourd plant.

Many of the ancestors who came in canoes were escorted by taniwha and other supernatural guardians, and their captains recited potent karakia to calm the waves and speed their progress. Nevertheless, several of the crews found themselves in perilous situations upon the ocean. During the voyage of the Arawa canoe, from which the peoples of Taupo and the Rotorua district trace their descent, the powerful tohunga Ngatoro-i-rangi discovered that his wife had been seduced by the captain, Tamatekapua. In his fury he called up the winds and drove Te Arawa towards the throat of Te Parata, the monster at the edge of the sky which controls the ebbing and flowing of the tides. It was only when they were about to sink into the ocean — the realm of the mythical Tangaroa — that he relented, bringing them up to safety with a karakia that ends with the words

Eke, eke, eke Tangaroa,
Eke panuku!
Hui ē, tāiki ē!

It mounts, mounts, mounts Tangaroa,
Mounts up, and moves on!
Oh unity, oh victory!

The lifting up of Te Arawa is one of the many archetypal events which occur in these myths. Traditionally, Ngatoro-i-rangi's famous karakia was recited to round off speeches of welcome when people of Te Arawa were receiving visitors from other, related tribes; the final words, shouted in chorus by everyone present, asserted that all would be well with those who were gathered together. The chant was also recited by orators when they considered that their tribe was facing a grave danger from which it must

On top of the porch of Whitireia, a meeting-house at Whangara on the East Coast, Paikea rides the whale that brought him from Hawaiki. It was at Whangara that he settled after reaching Aotearoa.

Tamatekapua, captain of the Arawa canoe. He had been forced to leave Hawaiki because of a feud with another chief, and at one stage in this quarrel he had used stilts to steal fruit from his enemy's tree. In this carving he is depicted with his stilts.

be saved. Identifying themselves with Ngatoro-i-rangi, they symbolically brought up from the depths the Arawa canoe — that is, those who claimed descent from it — thus persuading their hearers that the danger was a real one, and at the same time affirming that it would be overcome.

A similar story was told of the Aotea canoe, from which the people of southern Taranaki and Whanganui trace their descent. While the Aotea was on the ocean, a man named Potoru insisted that they were sailing in the wrong direction. For a time the crew followed the advice he urged upon them, but his course led to disaster, and soon the canoe began to sink into the throat of Te Parata. At the last moment, when eight of the thwarts were under water and it seemed that all was lost, the captain, Turi, chanted a karakia which drew the Aotea up from the depths and back to the world of light. This karakia, and a number of others recited by Turi, were treasured by the tribes that claimed him as an ancestor. The best known of them is a long chant that he recited to calm the ocean and encourage the paddlers:

Nguaha te kakau o taku hoe nei,
Ko Kautu-ki-te-rangi, ki te rangi, hikitia!
Ki`te rangi, hāpainga!
Ki te rangi tū torona atu,
Ki te rangi tū torona mai,
Ki te rangi tū te ihi, ki te rangi tū te koko,
Tū te mana, tū te tapu!
E tapu tēnā te ara!

The shaft of my paddle, Kautu-ki-te-rangi,
Thrusts fiercely to the sky, lift it up!
To the sky, raise it up!
To the sky stretching away from us,
The sky stretching towards us,
The dreadful sky, the fearful sky, the mighty, the tapu!
Tapu is the path before us!

On canoe voyages the men of southern Taranaki and Whanganui used to recite this chant when calling the time for paddlers. It is still sung today by seated dancers who re-enact and celebrate the voyage of their ancestral canoe, their swinging poi taking the place of paddles.

On the Takitimu canoe, from which tribes in Heretaunga (Hawke's Bay) and many other places trace their descent, the captain and his tohunga had to quell a great storm which had been sent to obstruct their path by enemies who had left before them. With the Tainui canoe, the main impediment to its progress occurred after it had landed at Tamaki (Auckland) and was being dragged across the isthmus there before sailing down the west coast. The men hauling on the ropes found that the canoe would not move, and the tohunga finally established that the fault lay with one of the chief's wives who had had an affair with a slave. After her adultery had been revealed and the necessary rituals performed, the Tainui once more moved forward. The chant that was sung by the crew as they pulled on the ropes was thought by the Tainui tribes to have special powers, and it was employed by them on important occasions. When the meeting-house which is now in the Auckland Museum was being erected for the first time, the heavy ridgepole at first could not be raised. Then the chant for hauling the Tainui was recited, and it was at once lifted effortlessly into its place.

Many of the crews travelled along the coast after first reaching land. On these voyages of exploration their leading men gave names to many of the headlands, rivers and plains that they passed, and with their extraordinary powers they created landmarks — as when a man on board the Tainui thrust into the ground at Awhitu a paddle made of karaka wood, and it took root and became a tree from which sprang the large groves of karaka that used to grow there. Finally, each of the ancestral canoes came to its last resting-place. The Arawa was burnt by enemies — a dreadful act, soon avenged; but nearly all the other canoes turned to stone, and are still to be seen today.

Maunganui Bluff, a famous landmark on the west coast of Te Tai Tokerau (Northland). The Mamari canoe, turned to stone, is said to lie nearby.

The Aotea, for instance, lies beneath the waters of the Aotea Harbour; the bow and stern of the Tainui are at Maketu near Kawhia; and the Takitimu is now the Takitimu Mountains in Southland. The Mamari canoe was wrecked near the Riripo beach just south of the Maunganui Bluff on the west coast, and is now a reef there; or, according to the Hokianga people, it was turned to stone and lies keel upwards at the entrance to the Waima River. As well as the canoes themselves there are often objects associated with them, such as the anchor and the bailer. In the Hokianga district these stone landmarks include the bailer of the Mamari and the buoy of its anchor, the footprints of the captain Nuku-tawhiti and his dog, the dog itself, and the baskets the captain had used in a feast. On a rocky face north of the Hokianga Heads the crew of the Mamari are to be seen in the act of pulling in a fishing net; and a tapu stone at the head of the Hokianga Harbour was brought there by Nuku-tawhiti after one of his exploratory journeys in order to show his great strength. Long after the Maori became Christian, people passing this spot continued to pay reverence to this stone by reciting a propitiatory karakia and making an offering of a twig of rangiora.

In the South Island, the entire crew of the Araiteuru canoe turned into mountains, hills and pillars of rock. As they sailed down the east coast, several of the men on board plunged into the sea, swam ashore and became mountains there; among them are Maukatere or Mount Grey in the upper Awatere valley, Mount Tapuaenuku in the Inland Kaikoura Range, Tawera or Mount Torlesse inland from Christchurch, and Te Kiekie or Mount Somers in from Ashburton. A violent gale swept the Araiteuru on as far as Matakaea (Shag Point, near the present town of Palmerston some 45 kilometres north of Dunedin). There it was wrecked, and it turned into a reef along with the captain, Hipo; the cargo was swept ashore nearby at Moeraki, where big spherical boulders and other, elongated boulders are the petrified eel pots, calabashes and kumara that the canoe was carrying. The Araiteuru was hurled to destruction by three great waves followed by a cross-wave, and these waves also turned to stone: they are known to the Pakeha as Old Man Range, Raggedy Range, Rough Range and Horse Range.

When the crew of the Araiteuru struggled ashore they were very cold, so they set out that same night to look for firewood. It was only to be found far in the south, at the mouth of the Matau (the Clutha River). A woman named Puketapu made her way there and returned with a bundle of sticks, though as she came back some of the sticks dropped from her bundle and grew into forests. When she got to Waihemo (Palmerston) she was overtaken by daylight, and she turned into a conical hill that stands close by. Her bundle was tied with a string of flax and a withe of toetoe stalks, and these bands can still be seen in the two gullies on the hill: one filled with nothing but flax bushes, and the other with nothing but toetoe plants.

Aonui, who was responsible for the party's drinking water, went looking for water with his two kelp bags, and travelled all the way to the Matau or, as some say, the Mataura River, near the present city of

OPPOSITE Te Punga o Tainui, a tapu stone said to be the anchor stone of the Tainui canoe. It used to lie in shallow water near the Mokau Heads, where it was regarded as the mauri, or life principle, of the fish that were to be caught there in abundance. In the 1920s some of Ngati Maniapoto wished it to be given to a museum for safekeeping, but most of the people were unwilling to lose their mauri. To keep it safe, they conveyed it to the tribal cemetery at Awakino and embedded it in a cement model of the Tainui canoe which marks the grave of the chief Tamati Kingi Te Wetere.

OPPOSITE BELOW Big round boulders at Moeraki, north of Dunedin, are said to be the kumara, calabashes and eel pots carried by the Araiteuru canoe, which was wrecked there.

A woman named Puketapu was collecting firewood when she was changed into the hill near Waihemo (Palmerston) which bears her name. Her bundle was fastened with flax and with toetoe flower stalks (RIGHT), and these two plants now grow on the hill. BELOW Kakiroa (Mount Sefton), which was once a man.

Invercargill. He started back with his water-bags, but day came and he turned into a tall pillar of rock, with kelp growing on either side, which stands on the Tokomairiro beach. Another man, Kaitangata, had brought painting materials with him, and when the sun rose he became a hill bearing deposits of red ochre which stands near the present town of Kaitangata. But Pakihiwi-tahi or One-shoulder, who carried the whet-stones, went no distance at all. As he left the canoe he fell and broke his right arm, and he is now a lopsided hill between Waihemo and the sea.

Altogether there are about 150 mountains and ranges in the South Island which are said to have been people who arrived in the Araiteuru, then were turned to stone. Some went south, some inland and others far to the north, where they turned into some of the highest peaks in the land, such as Horokau (Mount Tasman), Kakiroa (Mount Sefton) and Aoraki or Aorangi (Mount Cook). Some storytellers said that Aoraki had been a man, and others that he had been a small boy who was being carried along on a relative's shoulders, so was taller than anyone else when the sun rose and he became a mountain.

Aoraki or Aorangi (Mount Cook), the highest of the mountains.

Things Brought from Hawaiki

Many treasured and remarkable objects were said to have been brought from Hawaiki. In a sense this was true of the mountains in the South Island which owed their origin to the Araiteuru canoe, for though these arrived as people they soon acquired their present form. Mauri, the tapu objects which embodied the life principle of a food resource — a kumara crop, birds in a forest or eels in a river — were often thought to owe their potency to their having been brought here by the ancestors. Any specially valued possession might have its origin explained in this way; for instance, in the Rotorua district this was said of a deeply-grooved block of sandstone which lay beside a stream and had been used as a whetstone by many generations of workmen. When its owners were asked how such a heavy stone could have been brought in the Arawa canoe, they replied that it had originally been light but that it had become heavy from having been tapu for so long.

Greenstone had come from Hawaiki. Usually it was said to have been a fish named Poutini which lived in Hawaiki with its owner, Ngahue, until one day it was attacked by a woman called Hine-tua-hoanga, or Sandstone Woman. (This is not surprising, for sandstone is used in shaping greenstone, so is its natural enemy.) Ngahue and his fish fled from Hawaiki and came to these islands, ending up at Arahura on the West Coast, where the fish remained; it is still to be found there, in the form of greenstone. As for Ngahue, he tore off one side of that fish, carried it back to Hawaiki with him and there shaped it into adzes, neck pendants and ear pendants. In this way greenstone came to be located in Aotearoa, and at the same time Hawaiki became the source of the first articles to be made from greenstone, pieces which provided the patterns and the mana for all the things that have been made from it since. Some of these archetypal pieces were brought here by the ancestors and remained in the possession of high-ranking families. Among them was a famous ear pendant called Kakau-matua which was originally the property of the captain of the Arawa canoe, and afterwards was passed down in the Te Heuheu family for many generations.

Because greenstone was really a fish, it was said that boulders of this stone were taken like fish from the rivers where they lay. James Cook, visiting the country in 1777, was told that 'this stone is originally a fish, which they strike with a gig in the water, tie a rope to it, and drag it to the shore, to which they fasten it, and it afterwards becomes stone'. In the 1830s an early trader, J. S. Polack, was told this story on several occasions by tohunga who would enact the scene they were describing. Taking the part of a fisherman, and with a stick to represent the fish, they would go to take a bite from their victim and discover to their dismay that in its anger at being taken from the water it had turned itself to stone.

In another story, greenstone came to the Arahura Valley when a man

Among some tribes the mauri, or life principle, of the kumara crop took the form of a stone figure said to have been brought from Hawaiki. This figure is from the Taranaki district.

named Tama arrived from Hawaiki in search of his three wives, who had deserted him; because his slave broke a tapu restriction, the wives were turned by spirits into the different kinds of greenstone now to be found there. Further south at Piopio-tahi (Milford Sound), there is a translucent, softer kind of greenstone known as tangiwai which is sometimes said to be one of these wives. The name tangiwai means 'weeping tears', and the marks like water drops which are often seen in this stone are the tears shed by Tama when he discovered the petrified body of his wife.

Greenstone was treasured for its beauty, hardness and indestructibility: though the generations came and went, it lasted forever. Pendants and tiki that had been worn by departed relatives were venerated because of their associations with the dead, and mourning kinsmen would sometimes address them by the names of their previous owners as they wept and caressed them. There were endless stories about the magical properties of treasured pieces. Sometimes in a legend the dull appearance of a greenstone mere warns of a coming disaster, or a piece loses its lustre when taken from its rightful owner and then shines once more when returned to him. Objects which had been seized or lost in foreign parts were thought to

The great Taupo chief Te Heuheu Tukino, with his brother Iwikau. Te Heuheu wears a greenstone tiki and holds a mere. The long greenstone pendant in his right ear must be Kakaumatua, a treasure said to have been brought from Hawaiki. In 1846, two years after Te Heuheu sat for this portrait, he was overwhelmed with 60 of his people in a huge landslide said to have been caused by a taniwha. He was wearing Kakau-matua at the time. His body was recovered and interred on Mount Tongariro. Kakaumatua was also found, but it was lost again in about 1880, when one of Te Heuheu's grand-daughters was swimming in Lake Taupo and it slipped from a ribbon around her neck.

The praying mantis (ABOVE), the stick insect (TOP RIGHT) and the green gecko (RIGHT) are among the creatures said to have been brought from Hawaiki by Wheketoro. He came from the east, so the island of Whanga-o-keno was the first land that he reached. Since it was the closest place to Hawaiki, it was appropriate for this island to be tapu, and the myth provides a reason for its being so.

grieve for their homes, and travel back like fish along the waterways.

The most ancient of all the heirlooms brought from Hawaiki was an adze called Te Awhio-rangi, or The Sky-encircler. This was Tane's adze, which he had used in the beginning to cut poles to place between his parents the Sky and the Earth. Some said that from Tane it passed down a line of eldest sons to Turi, captain of the Aotea canoe; others denied this, saying that it was brought here by Tamatea, captain of the Takitimu, and that on the ocean he used it to cut through the great waves of a storm sent by enemies to bar their way. In 1887, at a place near Waitotara in southern Taranaki, a woman who was gathering fungus in the forest, and was a stranger there, accidentally trespassed upon a tapu place. Inside a hollow tree she saw something shining, and it frightened her. She ran away, crying, and there was a terrible thunderstorm, with much lightning and a fall of snow. One of the old men knew that someone had trespassed upon a tapu place; he lifted up his karakia, and the storm ceased. When the people were assembled they heard what the woman had found; they went and looked at it, and they recognised it at once as Te Awhio-rangi. It had been hidden there by one of their ancestors seven generations before, and had been guarded by two lizard spirits, Tutangata-kino and Mokohiku-aru. Then karakia were recited, the adze was taken from its hiding-place, and all the people wept over this tapu relic of their ancestors.

Many creatures and plants were brought in the ancestral canoes. The Aotea, for instance, was spoken of proverbially as *Aotea utanga rau,* 'the heavily laden Aotea', having arrived with kumara, taro and gourds, kara-ka and paper mulberry trees, kiore, pukeko and kakariki. One of the ancestral canoes on the East Coast was the Mangarara, which came under the leadership of a chief named Wheketoro and brought with it the different kinds of lizards, the tuatara, certain kinds of insects such as centipedes, stick insects and crickets, and the oystercatcher and the pipit. When the canoe arrived at Whanga-o-keno (East Island off East Cape), Wheketoro put his creatures on shore and they spread all over the island. To protect his pets he made the island tapu, and he blocked with a high cliff the only place where there was easy access to it. He caused a spring to flow on the rocky beach, then leaving most of his reptiles on the island in the charge of the pipit and the oystercatcher he sailed off towards the mainland. But his canoe capsized near the shore, and though the men and the reptiles still with them pulled on it together, day came before it could be shifted. The canoe turned to stone, the reptiles retired to the shelter of overhanging banks and vegetation, and Wheketoro and his companions settled in the East Cape district and became ancestors of Ngati Porou.

Nearly every tribe claimed that their ancestors had brought the kum-ara first. Often a woman named Whakaotirangi was held responsible for its introduction: when other people had eaten their seed kumara on the way, she had prudently kept hers tied in a corner of her kit. Many tribal areas claimed Whakaotirangi as an ancestress, and altogether she was said to have come in five different canoes. According to the Tainui traditions she was the senior wife of the captain, Hoturoa. During the journey the

captain's second wife, Marama, disgraced herself by having an affair with a slave, and because of this her plants went wrong: her seed kumara grew up as bindweed, her gourd seeds came up as a weed known as mawhai, or the bur cucumber, and her paper mulberry tree turned into the whau, which resembles the paper mulberry but has bark that is useless for cloth. The seeds brought by Whakaotirangi, however, flourished in Aotearoa.

Some of the ancestors acquired the kumara by making their way to Hawaiki from this country, then returning with their prize. Pourangahua, for example, sailed there in a canoe of bark and albatross skins, then flew back on a great bird owned by Tane. The Horouta canoe, also on the East Coast, made a voyage which was re-enacted each spring during the elaborate rituals that accompanied the planting of the seed kumara. According to this story the Horouta set out from Aotearoa, reached Hawaiki and sailed alongside the cliffs of that land, which are composed entirely of kumara; a tohunga on board the vessel recited a karakia, the kumara tumbled down into the canoe, and then they returned. The hidden meaning of this myth becomes apparent when one learns that in the kumara storehouse the heaped-up baskets of seed kumara were sometimes called 'the cliffs of Hawaiki', and that each year in the planting season a tohunga re-enacted this story by making his way ceremonially to the storehouse to acquire the kumara from the cliffs of Hawaiki, just as the crew of the Horouta did in the beginning.

The ancestress Whakaotirangi with the basket in which she kept her seed kumara during the voyage from Hawaiki. Since the kumara plant (RIGHT) was highly valued, there were many myths explaining its origin. OPPOSITE The kakariki (BELOW), the pukeko (TOP LEFT), the pipit (TOP RIGHT) and the oystercatcher are among birds said to have been brought by ancestors from Hawaiki.

Ngatoro-i-rangi prepared the way for his descendants by putting fish into Lake Taupo. These men are catching the little fish with a fine-meshed seine net, driving them into it with a pole which is about 6 metres in length and has bunches of grass fastened to the end.
OPPOSITE Thermal activity at Waimangu, south-west of Lake Rotomahana.

Volcanic activity also had its origin in Hawaiki. It was brought here by the great tohunga, Ngatoro-i-rangi, who arrived on the Arawa canoe and set out with his slave, Ngauruhoe, to explore the countryside. When he reached Lake Taupo he climbed Mount Tauhara, by the north-eastern shore, and from its summit he cast his spear into the water; it turned into the trunk of a tall totara tree which stood there for many generations. He then descended to the shore of the lake. Finding there were no fish in it, he performed a ritual, then shook his cloak over the waters. From the strips of flax that fell from it there sprang the inanga and the banded kokopu, two species of galaxias which now inhabit the lake.

When Ngatoro-i-rangi arrived at Taupo it was dark and stormy, but suddenly the clouds parted and he saw Mount Tongariro — that is to say, the two neighbouring peaks which are known to the Pakeha as Mount Tongariro and Mount Ngauruhoe. At once Ngatoro-i-rangi determined to climb to the far, white summit of the mountain. As he and his slave made their way upwards they were attacked first by wind, then by rain and sleet and lastly by snow, but they would not give up, and in the end they stood upon the topmost peak. It was icy cold and they were in danger of freezing to death, so Ngatoro-i-rangi shouted to his two sisters to bring him fire.

The sisters, who were back in Hawaiki, heard his call and set out at once. They rested and lit a fire at Whakaari (White Island), which is now an active volcano in the Bay of Plenty, and then they made their way underground to Tongariro; sparks fell from their fire at Waiotapu, Ohaki, Rotokawa, Tapuaeharuru, and Tokaanu, creating the hot springs, geysers and boiling mud pools now to be found in these places. At Tongariro the sisters' fire warmed Ngatoro-i-rangi but came too late to save the life of his slave, Ngauruhoe; the crater of the mountain became his tomb, and its peak is known by his name. Then Ngatoro-i-rangi took the fire and hurled

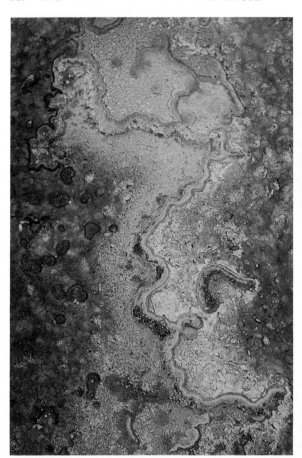

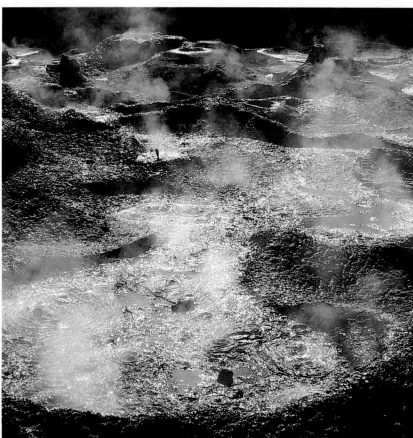

it into the crater, where it still burns. His sisters returned to the Bay of Plenty, again going underground and this time travelling further to the north and initiating as they went the thermal activity at Waimahana, Whakarewarewa, Ohinemutu and Tikitere. Some say that the fiery subterranean channels they formed are still in existence.

The Explorers

After the arrival of the canoes, many of their chiefs and tohunga set out to claim land for themselves. On these journeys of exploration they defined the boundaries of the tribal territory their descendants were to possess, they created landmarks, and they had adventures that are perpetuated in place-names. Sometimes they encountered rivals on their travels, and overcame them. Ngatoro-i-rangi, for example, met at Taupo a man named Tia and another called Hape-ki-tuarangi, who were seeking land for themselves; he got the better of them both, tricking Tia into thinking he had a prior claim and over-whelming Hape with a snowstorm. Then as he was returning to the Bay of Plenty he was confronted near Mount Tarawera by the original inhabitant of that place, a demonic, man-eating being named Tama-o-hoi. So Ngatoro-i-rangi stamped upon the mountain, forming a great chasm, then forced Tama-o-hoi inside and closed the ground over him. Tama-o-hoi remained imprisoned there until he burst free in 1886, causing the terrible eruption of that year.

OPPOSITE The hot springs, geysers, mudpools and silicate deposits of the thermal region were thought to have been brought from Hawaiki, which lay to the east. Ngatoro-i-rangi's sisters created the active volcano of Whakaari (White Island), then established other areas of thermal activity on their way inland. In the centre of the island their fire lit the volcano of Ngauruhoe.

LEFT Swimmers at Orakei Korako, with a geyser in the background. Villages were often built in thermal areas. The warm pools were popular bathing places, and food was easily cooked in baskets lowered into hot pools.

The Tarawera Eruption of 1886 was thought to have been caused by a demon named Tama-o-hoi, who long before had been imprisoned in the mountain by Ngatoro-i-rangi. The eruption devastated a large area, rendering in uninhabitable for many years. In the village of Te Wairoa, the meeting-house Hinemihi was one of the few buildings that survived that night. Many people took shelter within it.

As Ngatoro-i-rangi walked about the country he established his claim to the land by setting up tuahu, shrines, in the places he visited. Another tohunga who did this was Rakataura, who came on the Tainui. From the Manukau Harbour he and his followers explored the interior, setting up tuahu and also distributing mauri which he had brought from Hawaiki. These tapu objects were hidden in hills throughout the territory of the Waikato and Ngati Maniapoto tribes, thus ensuring that the pigeons, kaka, tui and other birds would remain in the forests and not fly away to new homes. Because of Rakataura's work these hills continued to yield abundant game, with the forested ranges owned by Ngati Maniapoto (in the territory now known as the King Country) being especially famous for the enormous quantities of birds taken there each year.

On the East Coast the Horouta canoe was under the command of a man named Paoa. On its return from Hawaiki it capsized and was damaged at Ohiwa, near Whakatane. Some of the men on board remained to repair the canoe, others set off to catch birds for the workmen (thus initiating the rituals appropriate to this task), and a third group went inland with Paoa to fell a tree from which to obtain a new haumi, or bow-piece for the canoe. They found a suitable tree on a high mountain which they named Maunga-haumi, Haumi-mountain, and after felling and adzing it they looked for a river down which it could be floated to the sea. There was no river, so Paoa recited a karakia and urinated, in this way creating the Waioeka River, the Motu River and the Waipaoa River; this last name means 'Paoa's water'. Paoa and his men found on their return that the Horouta had gone on without them, so they made their way overland, with Paoa naming places and creating landmarks as they went. At Wharekahika (Hicks Bay) he left his child Maroheia, turned to stone; he created the Waiapu River in the same way he had the others; at Turanga (Poverty Bay) he left his dog, turned to a white cliff known as Te Kuri a Paoa, Paoa's Dog (the Pakehas call it Young Nick's Head); and finding himself threatened by a giant named Rongokako he laid a trap for him just north of Tokomaru Bay, on a hill known as Te Tawhiti Nui a Paoa, Paoa's Great Snare. The trap consisted of a huge tree, bent down and tied to the ground. Rongokako approached with enormous strides, leaving footprints in the rock behind him, but then he spotted the trap and he set it off. The debris flung up by the uprooted tree formed the high peak known as Mount Arowhana, and the tree itself flew all the way to the Waikato district and became the ancestor of the forests there.

Some early ancestors were associated with particular possessions. Taramainuku, who is generally said to have been a grandson of Tama-tekapua, captain of the Arawa, is said to have owned an enormous seine net which his followers had made in preparation for a feast. According to one story the floats of his net are now the islands in the Hauraki Gulf; others say the net is the dangerous bar at the mouth of the Manukau Harbour, with the rocks nearby; and others again that Te Kupenga a Taramainuku, Taramainuku's Net, is a name for the stars that the Pakehas call the Milky Way. The phrase is used proverbially of formidable obstacles and inescapable traps, as when, in the funeral orations of Te Arawa, a person who has died is said to have been caught in Taramainuku's net.

There is also the famous Tamatea, who is often associated with fire. Tribes in many parts of the country claimed him as an ancestor, and each had their own account of an exploratory journey he had undertaken in their territory. Usually he was said to have been the captain of the Taki-timu canoe, and often he was called Tamatea-pokai-whenua, Tamatea-who-encircled-the-land. He had other names as well. On the Tamaki isthmus he was Tamatea-o-te-ra, Tamatea-of-the-sun, and he lived in the volcanic cones there; occasionally he would leave his home to visit other districts, where his presence would be disclosed by earthquakes and other underground activity. His canoe is said to lie turned to stone in Opoe (Doubtless Bay), in the far north, and it is also said to have turned into a mountain range in Southland, three other ranges nearby being the petrified forms of the waves that swamped it.

The southern story is that after this disaster Tamatea walked up the east coast of the South Island, creating landmarks as he went. Several of these are marked by his fire, such as an island in Foveaux Strait which is called Te Kauati a Tamatea, Tamatea's Firestick (Green Island), and a red cliff near Chalky Sound known as Te Karehu o te Ahi a Tamatea, The Ashes of Tamatea's Fire. But Tamatea lost his fire at Oamaru, for it sank into the ground and continued to smoulder there. So by the time he and his party reached Banks Peninsula, they were very cold. He climbed a steep peak there which became known as Te Poho o Tamatea, Tamatea's Chest, and with the aid of karakia he called to the tohunga Ngatoro-i-rangi, asking for his assistance. Ngatoro-i-rangi was just then standing on the peak of Tongariro, having established the volcanic fires that burn there, so he collected up some of his fire and sent it south to Tamatea. The fire passed over the surface of the land, digging out the gorge of the Whanganui River, then when it reached the sea it rose into the air and made straight for Banks Peninsula. A piece dropped off on the way, forming the hot springs at Hamner, and another piece created the landmark in the Port Hills which is known as Te Ahi a Tamatea, Tamatea's Fire. (To the Pakehas, this wall of lava rock is The Giant's Causeway.) The fire warmed Tamatea's party, and it guided their footsteps. They continued north, then they walked across the sea to the North Island and went on towards a meeting with Ngatoro-i-rangi at Taupo.

Many of the mountains in the South Island had their origin, as we have seen, in the wreck of the Araiteuru and the transformation of its crew. The great lakes on the east coast of the South Island were created by

Takapo (Lake Tekapo), believed to have been excavated by Rakaihaitu with his digging-stick.

Rakaihaitu, who came with his son Te Rakihouia in the Uruao canoe. They landed in the north of the island and set off southwards, Te Raki-houia sailing along the coastline and Rakaihaitu exploring the interior. Thinking that the country needed lakes, Rakaihaitu dug them at intervals with the digging-stick he carried with him. He began with Lakes Rotorua and Rotoiti, then went on to dig Hokakura (Lake Sumner), Whakamatau (Lake Coleridge), Oturoto (Lake Heron), Takapo (Lake Tekapo), Pukaki, Ohou (Lake Ohau), Hawea, Wanaka, Whakatipu-wai-maori (Lake Wakatipu), Te Anau, and Roto-ua (Lake Manapouri). The hardest one to dig was Whakatipu-wai-maori, because of the high mountains surrounding it; much effort and many karakia were required. Then Rakaihaitu went on to Foveaux Strait and met his son with the canoe. Together they returned northwards, with Rakaihaitu completing his task by digging Waihora (Lake Ellesmere) and Wairewa (Lake Forsyth), along with other, lesser lakes. Most of the South Island lakes are of glacial origin. They clearly have been excavated by some agency, and it was only reasonable to suppose that this had been done by the first man to arrive from Hawai-ki. In poetry and oratory, the collective name of these lakes is Ka puna-wai karikari a Rakaihaitu, The water-pools dug by Rakaihaitu, and some-times this name is given to the entire South Island. Sailing along the coast, Te Rakihouia had discovered high cliffs where sea-birds breed. These

Ohou (Lake Ohau), another of the great lakes created by Rakaihaitu. At the right times of year, his descendants took eels and waterfowl in them.

places, which were precious for the eggs and young birds taken there, became known as Ka whata tu a Te Rakihouia, Te Rakihouia's vertical food-stores.

The Burrowing Taniwha

Taniwha are dragons, creatures with great powers that can travel through the earth and the water. In the beginning there were taniwha that created harbours and lakes by burrowing through the land and thrashing about. Te Whanga-nui-a-Tara (Wellington Harbour) was formed in this way by two taniwha who were trying to reach the sea, and Hokianga Harbour was made by a female taniwha named Araiteuru and her eleven children, each of whom formed an inlet. Lake Waikaremoana was created by a woman named Haumapuhia who lived with her father, Mahu, until one day he asked her to fetch

Certain ancestors were said to have become taniwha after their death. Sometimes they are depicted in the form of marakihau, figures with long tails.

RIGHT Lake Waikaremoana in the Ureweras, believed to have been formed by Haumapuhia after she became a taniwha.

water for him, and she refused. This angered Mahu so much that he threw her into the water, and she became a taniwha. She struggled to reach the sea, making the branches of the lake as she did so, then in the end she thrust down into the ground, forming the underground channel where the water leaves the lake. But daylight came, and she was turned to stone and lies there still. Mahu was so upset at the loss of his daughter that he travelled to the ocean and from there sent back shellfish and lamprey as food for her. The lamprey are still in the lake, and the shellfish are turned to stone. (There is, in fact, much shell conglomerate in the rock strata by the lake.)

There were many stories of man-eating taniwha that had been challenged and conquered by heroic ancestors. One concerns a taniwha named Kaiwhare that lived near the Manukau Harbour, in an underwater cave and blowhole just south of Piha. He regularly set out from there to visit the Manukau and receive offerings from the people; a small portion of meat would be placed in a miniature house on a little raft, then set adrift on an ebb tide, and if the food was gone next day the people would know that Kaiwhare was satisfied and that there would be plenty of fish.

But after a while Kaiwhare began killing and eating people who were out fishing in canoes or spearing flounder on the mudflats. It became too dangerous to go out on the harbour, and its rich fishing grounds could not

Just south of Piha in the Waitakere Ranges, the taniwha Kaiwhare lived by the shore in a cave which Pakehas call The Gap (BELOW). Often he could be seen spouting through a blowhole connected to his home (BELOW LEFT).

The volcanic crater of Whakaari (White Island), which was thought to have once lived with other prominent islands and mountains in the centre of the North Island.

BELOW Taranaki (Mount Egmont), seen in the distance from Ruapahu (Mount Ruapehu). After the mountains quarrelled, Taranaki went far to the west. He was near the coast when he was stopped by the rising sun.

be used. The Manukau tribes were desperate, until they heard of a man named Tamure who lived at Hauraki and who possessed a greenstone mere with special powers which could kill any taniwha if only it could be brought close enough. They sent a messenger to Hauraki, and Tamure agreed to help them. He arrived very quickly, for he could stride from hilltop to hilltop, stepping over rivers as he went. At Awhitu the Manukau people welcomed him and told him of their sufferings; he listened to them, then gave them his instructions.

On a fine evening soon afterwards Tamure hid himself close to Kaiwhare's den, having first sent some men out flounder-fishing with spears and torches. When Kaiwhare saw their lights in the shallows he began to stir, and as his head emerged from his den Tamure struck him on the head with his mere. Kaiwhare writhed and lashed about, sweeping away cliffs with his tail, and Tamure made off inland to escape the falling rocks. The taniwha was so badly wounded that he had to content himself ever afterwards with the crayfish and octopuses that were to be had near his cave, and the level stretch of rock which he cleared in his struggles can still be seen today.

Most taniwha, however, had a stable relationship with the tribe with which they were associated. Quite often they were ancestors who had assumed this form after their death. The tohunga of the tribe made them offerings, and had the power of summoning them when he wished to do so. Taniwha did sometimes cause landslides, and people who broke the laws of tapu were often dragged into the water and drowned by them, but those who respected them were usually safe. Sometimes, indeed, a person who was in trouble at sea, having been thrown from his canoe in a storm, would appeal to his taniwha ancestors and be brought safely to the shore.

Pohaturoa, a steep, rocky hill at Atiamuri, is said by Ngati Awa to be one of the wives of their mountain Putauaki (Mount Edgecumbe).

Mountains that Moved About

Some mountains were thought to have taken up their present positions under cover of darkness. Once there stood in the centre of the North Island a group of mountains with Tongariro as their chief, but the male mountains quarrelled over the females and they went their different ways. Taranaki (Mount Egmont) rushed off to the southwest, his great bulk digging the gorge of the Whanganui River, then he turned northwards and made his way along the coast until the sun's rising put an end to his travels. Other mountains went eastwards, and ended up in the Bay of Plenty; among them were Whakaari (White Island), Moutohora (Motuhora Island), and Putauaki (Mount Edgecumbe), who did not get as far as his companions because one of his wives stopped to cook food on the way. In the Ureweras it was said that Maungapohatu and his wife Maunga-kakaramea (Rainbow Mountain) used to live with their children by the southern sea, and that when they set out on their travels they quarrelled as to the way they should go. Daylight found them in the positions they now occupy, their children being steep hills and large rocks situated in different parts of the Bay of Plenty.

Another mountain that moved up from the south was Kakepuku, a volcanic peak near the present town of Te Awamutu. He was searching for his father, but when he reached the Waipa Valley he caught sight of Kawa, a smaller, rounded volcanic hill who stands nearby, and is herself the offspring of Mount Pirongia and Mount Taupiri. Kakepuku at once forgot his father and fell in love with Kawa, and when he found she was already married he fought with her husband, Karewa, and defeated him. Karewa fled in the night, and now stands in isolation in the sea off Kawhia, where the Pakehas call him Gannet Island. When the mist comes down over Mount Kawa and the land breeze blows it in long streamers towards the ocean, Kawa is sending her mihi, her sorrowful greetings, to her lost husband Karewa.

In Northland a group of volcanic hills was said by some to have arrived one night from a home across the western ocean: Manaia, the

From the Whangarei Heads a natural causeway extends some distance into the harbour. According to one story, Manaia's daughter built it with stones in order to fish from it, but was stopped by spirits from completing her task. In another story, Manaia himself tried to construct a causeway across the harbour mouth so that he could more easily visit a woman on the other side.

largest and strongest, travelled the furthest before daybreak and is now a bold peak forming part of the Whangarei Heads; Tokatoka and Maungaraho, the tallest of his companions, were transfixed near the Wairoa River. Others told the story differently, saying that Manaia was a chief who came from Hawaiki in ancient times and along with his family was turned to stone by spirits; on the Whangarei Heads he and his wife, his two daughters, his slave and his dog are all to be seen as projecting rocks. As for Tokatoka and Maungaraho, they and other rock formations were followers of Manaia whom he had sent away in a fit of rage, and who turned to stone as they fled.

In another tale, Rangitoto Island used to stand at Karekare in the Waitakere Ranges until it was lifted up, leaving steep cliffs behind, by a fairy tohunga who objected to its blocking his view. With this burden on his back the fairy strode across the ranges, intending to carry Rangitoto out beyond the Hauraki Gulf, but it was winter and the water was cold, so in the end he left it quite close to the shore.

Stories such as these explained the existence of many isolated and dramatically shaped hills, rocks and islands. There had to be reasons for their presence, and it was natural and most satisfying to assume that motives and passions similar to those of human beings had been involved in their creation.

Mount Manaia, the highest part of the Whangarei Heads, was said by some to be a mountain that had arrived one night from over the sea. Others said that a group of jagged rocks near the summit are Manaia and his family, turned to stone.

Five

THE REALM OF TANGAROA

It was thought that the land and its creatures belonged to Tane, and the sea and its inhabitants to Tangaroa. Between these two, and between their children, there was endless strife. Men in canoes set out to attack Tangaroa's children, catching them with nets and lines, and Tangaroa rose up and consumed the children of Tane: canoes were lost at sea, and land, trees and houses were swallowed up by the waves. It had been this way from the beginning, ever since Tangaroa became angry when some of his children, the lizards and the tuatara, abandoned the water and made their homes with the children of Tane.

The land was experienced as the familiar, human realm and the ocean as the unstable, dangerous place where men ventured at their peril, winning from it the great catches of fish necessary for their survival. Daring the wrath of Tangaroa, they went out to display their endurance and skill in a trial of strength that was all the more significant because there were no large animals for them to hunt. Fishing expeditions were surrounded with careful ritual observances, and women were not permitted to go on them; such restrictions helped to placate Tangaroa, and the absence of women had the further effect of preserving this high adventure for men alone, making it an assertion of manhood. The women's part was to greet the men on the beach, singing and dancing for joy when the catch was good, then prepare the fish and cook them, or dry them for the winter.

The meaning of such scenes in the Maori imagination can be better understood in terms of the poetic imagery derived from them. People conquered in war are often spoken of as fish caught in a net, and in the love poetry a woman may be a canoe and her lover a paddler. This ancient symbolism, which existed in other parts of Polynesia as well, took its meaning not only from the forms and functions of canoes and paddles but also from the complex roles played by the sea in the people's life and thought.

Since the ocean lay beyond the human, 'normal' realm, it was often associated with enemy forces. In a lament for departed chiefs, a poet likens them to men calling the time for paddlers, their canoe symbolising the tribe:

Ka ngaro hoki ra, ē, ngā waha kī, ngā hautū o te waka
I hoea ai te moana hei whakapuru atu ra, ē,
Mo ngā tai kino, mo ngā tai marangai ka puta ki waho ra!

Oh they are gone, the speaking mouths, the fuglemen of the canoe
That was paddled across the ocean to confine
The evil seas, the stormy seas that came from outside!

Several myths tell of heroes who set out to avenge the death of a father killed by enemies; against great odds they succeed in this sacred task, setting examples to be followed in later times by all men facing similar situations. The interesting thing is that most of these archetypal heroes – Whakatau, Rata, Tawhaki — have had their fathers slain and their mothers enslaved by a people who live in the sea — which appears, then, as an appropriate and natural home for the enemies of mankind.

Yet there were treasures to be won from these enemies. In an East Coast story the art of wood-carving is discovered when a man named Rua-te-pupuke goes looking for his son, and finds he has been stolen by Tangaroa and set upon the gable of his house to serve as an image. Approaching the house, Rua sees that its posts are carved into figures; those in the interior can talk, and those on the outside cannot. He burns the house, and he brings away his son, and some of the carved posts as well. Because these posts come from the exterior of the building, carvings now cannot speak.

Always the sea was the unknown, the mysterious. The watery wastes were a fit home for taniwha, frightening and unpredictable spirits which sometimes assisted people but drowned those who broke the laws of tapu. Water itself, usually the moving water of a stream, was employed in many ceremonies, the underlying idea seeming to be that a person who entered in ritual that formless, ever-changing element was renewed and made different. This of course is a widespread human belief. Another ancient idea is that which associates water and women. In Maori mythology it appears in the story of the archetypal woman, Hinauri, who swims across the ocean for many days to reach the man she wishes to marry.

In oratory a marae might be spoken of as the land, so that approaching visitors would be told, *Haere mai, haere mai ki uta,* 'Come forward, come forward to the land!' The implication was that the village and marae were the central, truly human place, surrounded by the ocean. When tribal land was lost through warfare or sales to Pakehas, it could be said to have been taken by the waves: a song of protest blames the missionaries and the governor for the parts they played in the sale of Maori land, and ends by lamenting that *Kua riro te whenua, e tere ra i te moana,* 'The land is gone, drifting out to sea'. In the nineteenth century a number of sayings identified the Maori with the land and the encroaching Pakehas with the sea, or sea winds:

I naianei kua hā te hāhā tai.

Now the sound of the waves has gone far inland.

Some shells were worn as ornaments. This boy's shell had been brought from the coast to his home at Te Rapa, on Lake Taupo.

On the shore, the rising and falling of the tides was explained by the belief that in the deepest part of the ocean there is a huge monster, a son of Tangaroa, who breathes twice every twenty-four hours: in at ebb tide, and out at flood tide. This monster was called Te Parata. The ebb tide was associated with misfortune, and in figurative speech a person who had unexpectedly met with great trouble might be said to have fallen into the throat of Te Parata. It was thought that dying persons left this world when the tide was on the ebb, and if in a desperate battle a warrior saw a comrade lying wounded he might take leave of him with these words:

Haere ra, e tama e!   Mōu te tai ata,
Mōku te tai pō!

Farewell, friend! The morning tide is for you,
The evening tide will be for me!

Breakers sounding more loudly than usual might be thought to bring a message from the dead or tell of troubles to come, or they might be said to be weeping in sympathy for human misfortune, 'greeting mankind'. Poets' tears were often likened to crashing waves. And when the mourning was done and it was time to dry one's tears, again a comparison might be made:

Kāti te tangi, āpōpō tātou ka tangi anō.
Apā ko te tangi i te tai, e tangi roa, e ngunguru tonu.

We have cried enough, for soon we will cry again.
It is not like the crying of the waves, which ever cry, ever sound.

The shore itself, between the land and the sea, was thought of as a kind of no-man's-land, an area where those things that rightfully belong to the sea are cast up and lie stranded, out of their element. Poets might liken themselves to stranded sea-foam or driftwood, or to seaweed, which once did have a home in a place far away that no man could discover. A woman who had been abandoned by her lover might compare herself to a broken canoe lying on the shore, and a well known proverb refers to the passing of the generations and the renewal that accompanies it:

Ka pū te ruha, ka hao te rangatahi.

The worn-out net lies in a heap, the new net goes fishing.

In songs and proverbs, people in unhappy circumstances are likened to driftwood, seafoam, and seaweed cast up on the shore.
BELOW Men venturing out on the ocean were entrusting themselves to the spirits of the winds and the sea. For this reason, two long streamers of feathers floated behind the carved stern-posts of the great war canoes. The upper one was a resting-place for the spirits of the winds. The lower one, which often trailed in the water, belonged to the spirits of the ocean.

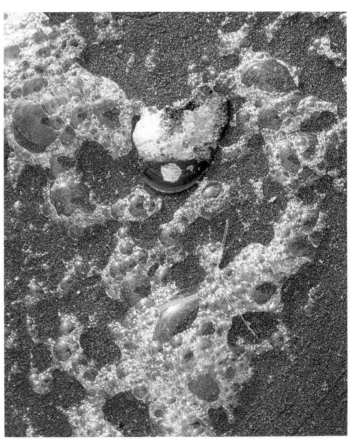

On the East Coast the moki was a very tapu fish, and many restrictions were placed upon the fishermen and their families. The season began in the middle of June, when the moki, it was believed, arrived at Whangaparaoa (Cape Runaway) from Hawaiki. At the end of August the fish returned to Hawaiki.

BELOW Hapuku, or groper, are caught in deep water near sunken rocks, some of them far out to sea. These fishing grounds were much prized, and very tapu. The fishermen recognised them by aligning landmarks on the shore, such as hills and headlands.

Creatures of the Sea

It was the special role of fish to be caught and put to use, the very reason for their existence. The land itself had been a fish, brought up from the depths by Maui and made a home for men. Another resource in the form of a fish was greenstone, which swam all the way from Hawaiki followed by its owner, Ngahue, and finally turned to stone at Arahura, where it is now to be found. And people who were victims were very often spoken of as fish.

Most human 'fish' were the victims of warfare. It was an inflexible rule that any person who crossed the path of a war party must be killed,

A fishing party encamped on Rangitoto Island, probably in the 1840s. Fish that have been cleaned and partly cooked are hanging up to dry in the sun and wind. By this time the Maori had acquired tarpaulins, used here for sails and tents.

for it would be unlucky to spare him, and such a person was called *he maroro kokoti ihu waka*, 'a flying fish that cuts across the bow of the canoe'. In a battle, the first enemy to be slain was *te mātaika*, 'the first fish'. Young warriors would eagerly contend for the honour of killing him, and sometimes in laments they would be blamed for having been too anxious to win fame in this way:

Tē ai he mahara ki te ao,
Whakarere rukaruka te moenga i te wahine,
Rere-ā-manu tonu ki te hui mātāngohi
Kei hoki te ingoa, kia tārewa ki runga ra.

You gave no thought to this world,
You hastily abandoned your wife's bed
And flew like a bird to catch the first fish
Lest your name be lost — so it would be raised on high.

Sharks were seen as fighters. There was a warriors' proverb:

Kia mate ururoa tātou, kei mate-ā-tarakihi!

Let us die like white sharks, not tarakihi!

A finely carved ceremonial knife. The blade is formed from the many-pointed teeth of the seven-gilled shark, or tuatini.
RIGHT Dried shark and other fish, with basketfuls of kumara and potatoes, displayed at a feast at Matata in the Bay of Plenty. Putauaki (Mount Edgecumbe) is in the background.

Enemies, on the other hand, could be said to be small, harmless species of sharks, as when a poet reminds a neighbouring tribe of the time his people defeated them, and they were 'carried like bundles of dogfish along the shore at Ohope'. One could also insult one's enemies by calling them small fry. When Ropata Wahawaha attacked the people of Whakatane in 1870, and they furiously paddled up their river to escape him, he laughed, and called them a shoal of whitebait, tiny fish that dart from the fishermen's nets.

Whales were the chiefly fish. The sperm whale was especially impressive because of its teeth, and its strength was proverbial:

Anā tā te uaua parāoa!

Here's the strength of a sperm whale!

Another proverb noted that:

He rei ngā niho, he parāoa ngā kauae.

If you have a sperm whale's teeth,
You must have a sperm whale's jaws to carry them.

Since chiefs were feasted when they went abroad, good food would be found by those who travelled *i muri o te tira parāoa*, 'in the retinue of a party of sperm whales'. Chiefs who had been killed in battle were often spoken of as sperm whales stranded upon the shore, for this image enabled a poet or orator to praise his kinsmen, and at the same time mourn their deaths and the defeat they had suffered.

Though small species of whales such as blackfish were sometimes driven into shallow waters so that they beached themselves, whales usually became stranded without human involvement. These great fish appeared to come ashore of their own accord, presenting their finders with enormous quantities of meat and oil, also whalebone, from which many kinds of implements were made. Not surprisingly, they were symbolic of rich food and abundance. In a general way this idea lies behind the poetic images in which chiefs are identified with whales; and in the wood sculpture, stylised whales were depicted in some parts of the country on the facades

LEFT A panel in a meeting-house, Te Mana o Turanga, which stands at Manutuke, south of Gisborne. Carved in the early 1880s, it probably depicts Tinirau, lord of all the fishes in the sea, with his pet whale, Tutunui.

TOP Some eighteenth-century chiefs wore the tooth of a sperm whale shaped into a pendant, with inset eyes. These rei puta were valued as highly as greenstone tiki.

ABOVE A necklace of imitation whalebone teeth, made from moa bone in about the twelfth century. The first immigrants brought with them a liking for whale-tooth necklaces, and they made copies of them from the plentiful moa bone they found here. The fashion for wearing a single whale tooth as a pendant developed much later, after the moa had disappeared.

of elaborately adorned storehouses which held special food and other precious things set aside for the use of high-ranking families. In these buildings the whales are carved in bas-relief on the two barge-boards; their heads, turned to spirals, occupy the lower ends, figures representing supernatural beings are superimposed upon their bodies, and above, controlling them, there is the figure of an important ancestor. They speak of the riches within, and at the same time they ensure by magical means that there will indeed be an abundance of treasures.

The two foods said to be found in the paradisial homeland of Hawaiki were whales and kumara, for these were the most prized of all. Several accounts tell of a tribal ancestor who arrives with his followers from Hawaiki and settles in a place where he has found a stranded whale, clearly because this is a sign of plenty. In the story of the Tainui and Arawa canoes the whale is stranded at a place which is known today as Whangaparaoa, Sperm Whale Bay, and the two canoe-loads of immigrants quarrel over it, each claiming to have discovered it first. In the same way the leader of the Tokomaru canoe finds a stranded whale, quarrels about it with the occupants of other canoes that land soon afterwards, then loses the argument and goes on to settle in Taranaki. Further along the East Coast, the leaders of the Takitimu canoe sail southward searching for the right place to live. Finding it at last at Te Mahia (Mahia Peninsula), they perform a ritual to attract whales to them there, pouring out a small quantity of sand which they have brought all the way from Hawaiki. This sand becomes the mauri, or life principle, of the whales, and the very next day one of them is seen lying on the beach. Ever since that time, whales have been in the habit of casting themselves ashore at Te Mahia.

A barge-board from the facade of a storehouse that once stood at Te Kaha in the southern Bay of Plenty. One spiral represents the eye and the other the mouth. On the building this head was at the lower end, so that the whale's body, with stylised figures superimposed upon it, slanted up towards the top of the porch. A similar barge-board occupied the other side. This intricate masterpiece was carved some years before 1814.

This custom of theirs was attributed also to the powers of another tapu mauri which took the form of a hillock by the shore which was in the shape of a whale, its spout being a mapou tree that grew upon it. However far the whales might roam, they never forgot this mauri. Always they attempted to reach it, and often they succeeded in doing so.

Sometimes a special whale would be a guardian spirit. Several of the ancestral canoes were escorted on their voyage from Hawaiki by such whales, and one famous ancestor named Paikea arrived on the back of a whale — or, in some versions of the story, became a whale himself. And there were many family groups with their own guardian whale. For example, a white whale with a taniko band around its middle was the ancestral guardian of a family group living on the Coromandel Peninsula; when they glimpsed it in the distance while they were out fishing, they knew it was watching over them. If a man with such a guardian whale got into difficulties out on the ocean he would call to his ancestor, and the whale would hear him at once and bring him safe to shore.

When a whale was stranded on the shore, a tribe suddenly found itself the possessor of great quantities of meat and oil. This was all the more welcome as the Maori, with no large land mammals, possessed only limited sources of meat.

Spouting whales might be thought of as weeping, and an unhappy person might associate himself with them:

Ka whano nei au ka nunumi,
Ka riro ngā roma, ka riro ia
Ki tawhiti, haere atu ra ki te moana
I tere ai te pakake!   Waiho nei ki ahau,
Ka taute noa au i konei!

Soon I will be lost to sight,
Carried away on the swirling currents,
Carried far away, going out on to the ocean
Where the whale swims!   All that is left to me
Is to spout endlessly!

There were some other sea creatures to which chiefs could be likened. Though the turtle is uncommon in this country it is occasionally seen off the coast of Northland, and in one poem a chief successful in battle is called *he honu manawa-rahi*, 'a great-hearted turtle'. The kingfish could also be regarded as a chief. Because mullet flying from predacious fish jump out of the water, they were known poetically as *ngā tama korowhiti a Tangaroa*, 'the leaping sons of Tangaroa'; sometimes they escaped from the nets, so a chief or valorous warrior was *he aua rere kaha runga*, 'a mullet that leaps the upper rope'. There are two kinds of mullet, the grey mullet and the smaller, yellow-eyed ones sometimes called herrings, and *he aua mata whero*, 'a yellow-eyed mullet', was yet another term for a fighting chief. But this is not the whole story, for the word *whero*, translated here as 'yellow', was used in fact of a range of colours, from yellow through to orange, red and reddish-brown. These were the prestigious colours, those associated with chieftainship. The 'yellow' or 'red' eyes of this fish showed its chiefly character, and may also have been associated with warlike anger.

A creature's habits were often more important than its size; even the

A large trumpet shell fitted with a wooden mouthpiece and a toggle of birdskin. These ceremonial instruments were used to assemble the people and to announce visitors. In some tribes they announced the birth of a first-born son.

lowly sandhopper could be identified with avenging chiefs because of its high leaps. Large size was significant, however, when it served to distinguish a species from related ones, as in the case of eels. As one might expect these were proverbially slippery, and someone might complain that 'the eel has slipped through my hands'. As well, the large species of eel known as paewai could represent an important man:

He ika paewai anake hei tomo i roto i te hinaki.

None but paewai will enter my eel pot!

Many sea creatures were associated with particular habits and characteristics. Slander and malicious gossip could be likened to the dangerous sting of the sting-ray, and an invalid complains in a song that

Whano ake ka korikori kai te hopehope
Whai e koni ki te tāhuna one.

I writhe like the fins of a sting-ray
Thrashing on the beach.

Something that was caught fast and could not be shifted was *etia me te wheke e pupuru ana,* 'holding on like an octopus', a man or a tribe threatening to attack was *me te waha kahawai,* 'like a kahawai's mouth', and a person who travelled a great deal was *me te ihe,* 'like the garfish', which moves about fast on the surface of the sea. Because the butterfish is active at night, someone committing murder in the dark was *he rarī-kai-pō,* 'a butterfish that feeds at night'. Tattoo markings, among other things, could be compared to the mottled bars on the mackerel, and beautiful, pale objects were likened to cockle shells, or the belly of a trevally. Determined warriors might be spoken of as mussels or paua clinging tightly to rocks, or crayfish that will not be dislodged from their holes. Since crayfish turn red very fast when put on a fire, a person who was easily defeated could be compared to one, and so could a man who quickly grew red-faced with rage and rushed into unnecessary fights. Flounder lie on the sea bed in

An eel pot made from the thin, wiry stems of the mangemange, a climbing fern. Eel pots set in rivers had a single entrance, but those used in lakes were often double-ended.
LEFT The giant kokopu, a freshwater fish found in overgrown streams and lake margins. Like other species of *Galaxias,* it was admired for its markings.

shallow tidal waters and dart away when attacked, stirring up the mud as they do so; when someone had got into trouble in a place and was unlikely to return there, the question was asked,

E hoki te pātiki ki tōna puehutanga?

Will the flounder go back to the water it has muddied?

In most inland waters the important fish were eels, but there were also lamprey, whitebait, grayling and the small kokopu or galaxias. This has markings that were much admired, and an object might be praised as being *me he kōrinorino kokopu,* 'mottled like a kokopu'.

Birds of the Sea and Shore

Explanations as to the origins of birds varied somewhat from tribe to tribe, but generally they were regarded as the descendants of Tane. In some districts, such as the East Coast, a figure named Punaweko was immediately responsible for land birds and Hurumanu was the parent and personification of sea birds. Since the birds of the sea and the land belonged to different realms, they were opposed to each other.

Once there was a great battle between them, which began when a shag from the coast was invited by a shag from the interior to visit his

Some kinds of shags, or cormorants, live by the coast, while others spend much of their time inland. The pied shag is mainly a coastal bird.

home. The coastal shag discovered that the inland shag had a much better food supply, with plenty of eels, and he determined to seize its territory. Returning to the shore he summoned all the birds of the ocean, and they agreed to attack and kill the birds of the land. Meanwhile the land birds were preparing for the fray. It was a spectacular sight when the two armies came together, each bird behaving in its characteristic way. After fierce fighting the sea birds were overcome, and fled in confusion. So it was a great victory for the land. The muttonbird and the black petrel were captured as they tried to escape, and because of this they now rear their young inland.

Shags are conspicuous birds with remarkable habits, and they were often spoken of in the folklore. The guardian spirits that watched over family groups frequently took the form of shags, special ones usually seen when they brought a warning that someone had died. Chiefs could be compared to them, as when a man wearing his finest raiment was likened to the black shag of inland waters. And the bird's tenacity was proverbial:

E kore te kawau e neke i tōna tumu tū.

The shag will not move from its stump.

Because it is a powerful diver with a voracious appetite, a triumphant warrior could be likened to a shag claiming its prey in the water. It is a strong, unswerving flier, so a traveller who could not be distracted from his purpose was *me he kawau ka tuku ki roto i te aro maunga,* 'like a shag making for a mountain face'. Before taking flight it stretches its long neck before it, and the saying *ka mārō te kakī o te kawau,* 'the shag's neck is stretched out', signified that a travelling party was about to depart. In war dances and battles a strong forward movement by men in close formation was termed *he kawau mārō,* 'a stretched-out shag', and the bird was referred to in karakia to speed a runner, or to bring a canoe to land as it flew before a storm.

On the East Coast there was a myth about a woman named Houmea who was really a shag. This woman was very greedy, so much so that when her husband returned from fishing she would sometimes swallow his entire catch, then pretend the sea fairies were to blame. One day she gulped down her two sons, thus becoming that well-known figure in mythology, the Devouring Mother; but fortunately her husband, who now understood her nature, recited a karakia that made her bring them up again. In the end she was killed, but she did not really die. As an old storyteller explains, 'she is to be seen now in the form of a shag. Houmea's activities are still in this world ... the name Houmea is given now to evil and thievish women'. With her insatiable hunger, Houmea was fittingly identified with the shag. She was also held responsible for karakia that were thought to have the power of swallowing up an enemy's crops.

The big black-backed gulls are among the most conspicuous of the birds that live on the shore, and they are quite often mentioned in folklore.

A pied shag prepares to swallow a flounder. Fish traditionally represented victims.

Though they sometimes travel inland they were associated especially with the coast, so that a person accustomed to live beside the sea could be called *he karoro inu tai,* 'a black-backed gull that drinks the tide', and it was thought to be a bad omen when one was seen in a valley far from the sea. With their loud, melancholy-sounding cries they were sometimes said by poets to be mourning for a person who had died:

Tangi amio ana te karoro i te awa,
Ngā tohu o te ipo unuhia noatia.

The black-backed gulls circle the channel, crying.
They are a sign my beloved is taken from me.

Black-backed gulls are scavengers. More than one tribal defeat was named *Kai Karoro*, 'Seagulls' Food', because it was so disastrous that the black-backed gulls fed upon the remains of the dead.

The red-billed gulls and black-billed gulls, which are much smaller, are only occasionally referred to in poetry and history. There is, though, the story of the time the Ngapuhi tribe attacked the Arawa tribes, who were gathered on Mokoia Island in the middle of Lake Rotorua. This was

Red-billed gulls (BELOW) live mainly on the coast, and black-billed gulls (OPPOSITE BELOW) feed largely by rivers and lakes. Both species, however, have colonies by Lake Rotorua (OPPOSITE ABOVE), where they were once held sacred.

in 1823. Te Arawa thought themselves safe on the island, but Ngapuhi had laboriously dragged their canoes in from the coast, and early one misty morning they attacked Mokoia. They would have taken its people completely by surprise if it had not been for the red-billed and black-billed gulls, which have a colony on the lakeside; the gulls saw the canoes, and cried a shrill alarm. Even so, many were killed. Then when peace came once more, Te Arawa remembered how the little gulls had tried to save

A pied stilt. These birds, like pied oystercatchers (RIGHT), feed on marine organisms on tidal flats. Standing on the beaches, such wading birds seemed comparable to human beings.

them, and their tohunga recited karakia over the birds, making them tapu so that no one would touch them, for they had acted as if they were human beings. It was thought that the souls of the men who had fallen fighting against Ngapuhi, and those killed on later occasions as well, entered the bodies of these gulls.

The wading birds which search for shellfish and other creatures on beaches and mudflats, and stand in flocks waiting for the tide to fall, were seen as walking about as people do. The stilt, with its very long legs, is mentioned in a legend in which a high chief, on his way to pay a formal visit to a neighbouring tribe, is said to tower above his retinue like a pied stilt. And sometimes in a prophetic song a poet would speak of a time when a land would be devastated by enemies and lie deserted, its only inhabitants the little wading birds:

> *Ko wai rawa te tāngata hei noho mo tō whenua?*
> *Ko Turiwhatu, ko Tōrea, ko ngā manu matāwhanga o te uru!*

> Who will be the people to live in your land?
> Dotterel and Oystercatcher, the birds of the western shore!

With godwits the main point of interest was the migratory journey they make in the autumn. The Maori of course did not know the godwits' destination, which is the tundra lands of the northern hemisphere, where they rear their young. But they were well aware that there was a mystery,

and in Northland, where the birds set off on their journey, a proverb asked, 'Who can tell of the nest of the godwit?'

Also in Northland, the godwits' seasonal departure was sometimes associated with the journey to the underworld made by the souls of the dead. In a lament for a young kinswoman a Hokianga poet speaks of the birds that are preparing to migrate, their journey presaging the one that the girl's soul must make:

Godwits, with other wading birds, were netted and taken in snares. In some places they were an important food item.

> *Rārangi noa ra te rāngai kūaka,*
> *Kia tauhikohiko he pari tū waho.*

> Flocks of godwits are gathering,
> Moving restlessly on the seaward cliffs.

Out on the ocean, great flocks of shearwaters and petrels dived for fish and squid. They came to land only to breed, and the Maori encountered them on coastal hills and off-shore islands, where they nested in burrows and in high, creviced rocks. The young birds were taken just before they were ready to fly, when they were very fat; in the south they were mostly sooty shearwaters and in the north grey-faced petrels. These birds, with one or two related species, are now known to the Pakeha as muttonbirds. Their Maori name is *tītī*, a word imitative of their cries.

Several proverbs refer to muttonbirds. Because each pair of birds rears a single chick, an only child might liken himself to the offspring of

Not surprisingly, chiefs and warriors were often likened to the handsome terns. These black-fronted terns wear the black caps that all terns acquire in spring, in the mating season.

he tītī hua tahi, 'muttonbirds, that lay only one egg'. Someone who could go a long time without food, or a person claiming to have little to eat, might speak of *he tītī kainga tahi,* 'a muttonbird, that is fed only once', for as the chick gets bigger its parents fly far over the ocean, returning every few nights to give it an enormous meal of regurgitated fish. Because the chick waits so long for its meals, perhaps also because of the distance its parents can fly, a person with great powers of endurance might be said to have *he manawa tītī,* 'the guts of a muttonbird'.

A related bird, the black petrel, was occasionally mentioned in laments when departed chiefs were identified with it. Other birds seen as resembling chiefs were the elegant terns, with their graceful flight. Since terns fly in flocks, an assembly of high-ranking men might be said to be *he pōkai tara,* 'a flock of terns', or *he tāhuna-ā-tara,* 'a sandbank of terns', but a single individual could also be praised by a poet as 'my flock of terns'. And chiefs were often identified with gannets, mollymawks and albatrosses. The one word *toroa* could be used of all these great birds, particular species being indicated by the use of distinguishing epithets. Their plumes were treasured ornaments for the hair, their soft white down was worn in the ears, and bunches of their feathers adorned the sides of large canoes and hung in streamers from the high sternposts. A chief who had died might be called *taku pōhoi toroa ka rehua e te kohu,* 'my bunch of albatross feathers drenched in mist', or he might be spoken of as the bird itself:

Gannets were valued for their white plumage, and tattooing chisels were made from their bones. Expeditions to catch these large birds were made to the remote islets where they breed.
BELOW The white, downy feathers of the albatross and the gannet were worn in the ears by people of rank. This chief is the famous warrior and poet Te Rangihaeata, of Ngati Toa.

Waiho kia whana atu ana,
He toroa awhe nui e topa ana ia ki te uru!

Let him set out on his journey,
An albatross that travels far away, soaring to the west!

In a beautiful image, a man who neatly and compactly arranged his flowing garments was *me he toroa ngungunu*, 'like an albatross folding its wings'. And the albatross was seen as a wanderer, always travelling on-wards over the water. If someone was far from his home and was thought to be homesick, people might quote the proverb:

Ka pā te muri, ka tangi te toroa
Ki tōna kāinga i waho i te moana.

When the north wind blows,
The albatross weeps for its home far out on the ocean.

The albatross's tears must be the salty secretions from its tubular nostrils. Like many related sea-birds they take in large quantities of salt with their food, more than their kidneys can deal with, so they have nostrils in the form of tubes from which a concentrated saline solution is excreted.
      One other sea-bird was treasured for its plumes, though it is not

Soaring and gliding over the vast ocean, the albatross was seen as a wanderer far from its home. The bird rids itself of salt by excreting a saline solution through its tubular nostrils. When it did this, it was thought to be weeping for its distant home.
BELOW Roimata toroa, or albatross tears, is the name of a pattern employed in tukutuku, the lattice-work that decorates the walls of meeting-houses.

normally seen in this country. Occasionally in the far north an amokura, or red-tailed tropic bird, is driven ashore after an easterly gale, and people living there still search their beaches after storms in the hope of finding a dead or exhausted bird. The two tail plumes are red with black shafts, very narrow, and about 35 centimetres in length. Because of their colour and rarity they were prized above all others, and they were traded for precious pieces of greenstone with neighbours to the south. In a few songs from Northland a chief is called *taku hau amokura*, 'my red-tailed tropic bird's plume', but it seems that elsewhere they were so rare that they were not mentioned in the poetry.

Reptiles

Lizards, and to a lesser extent the lizard-like tuatara, were thought to have supernatural powers and were regarded with fear and awe. These attitudes were assumed by many early writers on the Maori to go back to some dim, distant time when the ancestors of the Polynesians encountered crocodiles, perhaps in Melanesia, and became frightened of them; ever afterwards, according to this theory, they dreaded all creatures resembling crocodiles, however small they were, and they told tall stories about giant, lizard-like monsters. But this is not how human thought operates. People have had a dread of lizards in many societies, believing them to have supernatural powers; snakes, too, have often been regarded in this way. When lizards are feared it is because they are seen as creatures which resemble fish yet have legs as well, and live on the land rather than in the water. Since they cannot be classified and understood in the normal way they are anomalous, and because of this they are uncanny and dangerous, a threat to ordinary life.

They do, however, fill a necessary role. In real life the ordinary, ideal patterns of existence are disturbed at intervals by the intrusion of disease and death, and these must be explained somehow. To the Maori the lizard was the immediate cause of these troubles, and as such it performed an essential function, though in the nature of things an unpopular one.

The most feared and hated of the lizards were the green and brown geckos. Their tree-climbing habits may have seemed especially unnatural in fish-like creatures, and the dilation and contraction of the pupils of their eyes may have been unnerving. Certainly they were especially dreaded when they lifted their heads and emitted chattering sounds that were thought to be laughter. When a green gecko laughed at someone, it was a terrible omen.

It was these two geckos in particular that were believed to bring illness and death. All diseases were thought to be caused by ancestral spirits who punished in this way those of their descendants who broke the laws of tapu, for example by improperly entering a sacred place, or allowing persons of inferior rank to eat their food or wear their garments. It made no difference if the action were accidental, or if the person had been tricked into breaking his own tapu by an enemy; all that mattered was the act itself, and the consequent insult to the family ancestors. At once a green or brown gecko was sent to punish the wrongdoer by gnawing at the exterior of his body, or by crawling through his mouth or nose while he was asleep, and settling in his stomach. Once a gecko had begun to devour a man's stomach his life could be saved only if a tohunga performed the proper ceremonies to placate the offended spirit and expel the creature from his client's body.

As well as explaining the existence of illness and death, this belief in avenging spirits was occasionally the cause of them. If someone in perfect health discovered he had broken an important tapu he would very likely become genuinely ill, and sometimes he would die. Several early Pakeha travellers described with amazement how they saw this happen.

When a person saw a gecko before him on a path, he knew that it threatened death to himself or a close relative. To avert this fate he had to kill the lizard, then find a tohunga to destroy the powers which the dead creature still possessed. In some places these rituals involved burning its body, then sprinkling the ashes over food and eating them; elsewhere a woman would step over the lizard, depriving it of its mana; or the tohunga would cut up the body and throw the pieces to the four winds so that the evil would be visited upon other tribes than his own.

The brown gecko, like the green one, was dreaded as an agent of evil. Geckos are small, with loose, soft skin. They are inactive during the day, emerging at dusk from their hiding places. In bright light the pupils of their eyes appear as vertical slits, while in darkness they become large and round.

In extreme circumstances a man might be faced with the ordeal of swallowing a gecko. This ceremony was the supreme test of a person's resolution and powers and was performed only in special circumstances such as the initiation of a sorcerer, or sometimes the proclamation of war. There is a story about a beautiful girl in the Waikato district who eloped with a chief who had come visiting from Rotorua. Later she returned home with her husband and sought her people's forgiveness. In doing so, she boasted of her husband's prowess: there was, she claimed, no feat he could not accomplish. At this her elders consulted together, then placed a large lizard before the husband and dared him to eat it; he reluctantly did so, winning much fame and receiving a new name, Ngarara Nui or Great Lizard. In Rotorua carvings this hero is shown eating his lizard, a symbol of the triumph of human powers over the forces of evil.

Lizards were occasionally depicted in the sculpture to warn that an area was tapu, or to guard a threshold. In the Auckland Museum there is a finely carved chest in the form of a lizard which was made early in the nineteenth century to protect a burial cave near Hokianga. The cave is a very small one, in a cliff-face in rugged country; it was packed with skeletons, and the chest was placed in the narrow entrance. When it was taken to Auckland, a man belonging to the tribe that owned the cave explained that 'the lizard was endowed by the incantations of our forefathers with powers of evil. It was placed as a guard over the bones of the dead, to prevent interference'. He also said that his grandfather had once gone to the cave to deposit the bones of a relative, and in entering it had stepped over the lizard. 'He must have been confused; he did not go round as was the custom. He stepped back again over the lizard, and was bitten by the spirit of the lizard. He felt sick when he got out; went home, and died.'

Usually, lizard guardians were live ones. A gecko would be captured, then ceremonially released to watch over a burial cave, a boundary stone, or a stone representing the mauri or life principle of a tree where birds were speared; it was thought to stay there forever, down through the generations, and occasionally it would be glimpsed gliding from its home. Similarly, a lizard would sometimes be buried beneath a pillar in an important building to protect the welfare of those within.

Spirits might manifest themselves as geckos, birds or spiders, and those that took the form of geckos were especially feared. As well as the spirits of ancestors there were atua kahukahu, spirits that had their origin in aborted foetuses or still-born children; these owed no allegiance to the human race, not having survived to become members of a kinship group. Sometimes, though, the powers of these malicious spirits could be channelled. In the Ureweras in the early nineteenth century, an ambitious man named Uhia became the medium of such a spirit, which was named Te Rehu o Tainui. It appeared as a lizard, and Uhia would reveal it to the people as it lay upon his hand with its tongue flickering from side to side — an action regarded as a good omen. With Uhia as the interpreter of its oracular utterances, Te Rehu o Tainui embarked upon a career as a war

A chest carved in the form of a gecko which guarded a burial cave at Waimamaku, near Hokianga. It could 'bite' in both directions, for there is a head at the tail end as well. The lizard's tail forms the nose of this second head.

god. For some years, the battles fought in the name of this god were so successful that its fame was great. Later it lost its powers, and the people were defeated.

The tuatara was not regarded with quite so much dread and awe, though there are a few accounts of spirits in the form of tuatara that guarded tapu places. This ancient reptile is much larger than the lizards, up to 60 centimetres in length, and has rows of spines on its head and back which it can erect in an alarming manner. So it could well have seemed more terrifying than the lizards. But at the same time its size made it well worth eating, and it was in fact eaten regularly: by assigning the major role in religious belief to the small gecko, the Maori were able to control their fear of the tuatara sufficiently to make use of it as a food item. However, there were restrictions placed upon their approach to these creatures. When men went out with baskets to capture them, the people left behind in the village had to refrain from eating, as the tuatara would otherwise become angry and attack the hunters. And women never ate tuatara, presumably because they did not have the mana to allow them to do so with safety. It was said that if a woman ignored this prohibition, all the tuatara would come and kill her.

In a few passages in poetry a chief is spoken of as a tuatara, and once or twice there is even an identification with a lizard, or *moko*, probably because this word, a general term for lizards, was also used of tattoo patterns: in some way the two were connected. Since the nature and extent of a man's tattoo patterns depended upon his status, this adornment must have been felt to possess a fearsome aspect, and so to be associated with the lizard.

According to a well known story, lizards and tuatara are the descendants of Punga, whose children are all ugly. At first they lived in the sea, then they became dissatisfied and they moved to their present home. Before going, they discussed their situation with other inhabitants of the ocean. There were two versions of these dialogues, which were chanted by the storytellers. In one of them, the shark and the lizard debate as to which is the safer place, the land or the sea; they disagree, and go their different ways. In the other dialogue, the debate is between the tuatara and the gurnard:

tuatara:	*E te kumukumu, ka haere tāua ki uta.*
kumukumu:	*Kāhore, haere koe ki uta.*
tuatara:	*E, haere mai, ka pau koe i te tāngata!*
kumukumu:	*Kāhore, e kore au e pau.*
	Ko koe anake te pau!
tuatara:	*E kore au e pau!*
	Tuku aku tara, rarau aku peke,
	Mataku te tāngata, oma ki tawhiti!

The ancestor Ngarara Nui, as depicted at the apex of the barge-boards of a meeting-house at Whakarewarewa. He is eating his lizard, thereby overcoming the forces of evil.
OPPOSITE The pet lizards owned by Kurangaituku, a dangerous bird-woman who was finally overcome by a hero she had captured. Detail from a carving made in about 1905 by the Arawa artist Tene Waitere.

The gurnard (BELOW) and the tuatara (BOTTOM) were seen as counterparts, and a story explains how the tuatara once lived with the gurnard in the sea, then left to live on the land. Because of this association, Ngaiterangi tribe in the Tauranga district used to regard the gurnard as tapu, and would not eat it.

tuatara: Gurnard, let us go to the shore!
gurnard: No, you go to the shore!
tuatara: Come with me, or men will destroy you!
gurnard: No, they will not destroy me,
It's you who will be destroyed!
tuatara: I will not be destroyed!
I will erect my spines and stick out my claws
And men will be frightened, they will run far away!

Such tales helped to explain why the tuatara and the lizard looked so disturbingly like four-legged fishes. The gurnard must have been seen as the tuatara's counterpart because it has feeler-like processes associated with its side fins, its two dorsal fins look rather like the tuatara's rows of spines, and its head is somewhat similar in shape to that of the tuatara.

Another story explains the migratory journeys of the long-tailed cuckoo by saying that the lizard (or in some versions, the tuatara) periodically goes back to the water and enters a cocoon, emerging as a long-tailed cuckoo — a bird which is at enmity with all other birds, has markings rather like those of lizards, sometimes perches lengthwise on branches rather than crosswise, and has the habit of rearing its head as reptiles do. The shining cuckoo's origin was sometimes explained similarly.

Traditional tales tell of great monsters called ngarara which used to inhabit the land and threaten human beings. These ngarara were enormous reptiles. Sometimes they are said to have lain in wait for humans and devoured them, but in the usual story a woman alone in the forest is kidnapped by a ngarara and made his wife. She lives with the monster for some time, then finds a way of escaping back to her village. When her brothers hear what has happened, they devise a plan. The woman goes back to the ngarara with an invitation to visit the village, and in due course he does so, being welcomed in the proper manner — though in one version of the story he becomes angry when the woman's brothers address him as a fish. He is taken into a large, specially built house, and while he sits waiting for the feast he is burnt to death. Sometimes his scales or his tail escape the fire and turn into lizards.

Such stories are never told about the taniwha, that other monster which was thought to live mostly in the water and might resemble a shark, a whale, a lizard or tuatara, or indeed a log of wood. Though taniwha often attacked human beings they generally had a close relationship with them. The ngarara on the other hand had no relationship with people, except insofar as it was the embodiment of evil, and for this reason it was a ludicrous and exciting idea that a reptile should attempt to marry a human woman and visit her brothers. The inevitable climax to the story, when the brothers' pretence of hospitality comes to an end and the ngarara is destroyed, must have been felt to be a satisfying victory for the human order against its ancient enemy.

Long-tailed cuckoos, arriving from over the ocean, were sometimes thought to be reptiles which had returned to the water, entered cocoons, then emerged in this form. BOTTOM Lizards were sometimes carved on tapu objects in order to proclaim and protect their sacredness.

Six

THE CHILDREN OF TANE

Tane was the creator of life, the source of the fertility of the land. In the beginning he tried to separate the sky and earth with his shoulders, but he could not do so. Then he lay upon his mother the earth, he stretched up his legs, and he succeeded at last in parting his parents. This is why the trees, which are Tane, have their legs in the air and their heads to the ground.

After pushing up the sky, Tane set the sun, the moon and the stars in their courses. Then he went looking for a female. At first he found females who were not human, and with them he had children that were plants and birds. In this way he had the totara with Mumuwhango, the rata and other climbing plants with Rere-noa, the tui with Para-uri, the weka with Haere-awaawa, and so on. He also met Punga, the parent of ugly creatures, and with her he had the insects. But still he wanted a human woman. In the end he modelled the figure of a woman from the soil of Hawaiki, then covered her with his garments and breathed into her mouth. She came to life, he took her as his wife, and their children were human beings.

Tane's name is a personification of the word *tāne,* the ordinary term for a male, or a husband or lover. He represents the fertilising energy of the human male, which was thought to be the active element in the creation of life. All forms of life on the land were said to be descended from him, so that all were related. At the same time, these children of Tane might themselves be spoken of as Tane, as when the name was applied to an important species of tree or bird. The creator was thought to be present still within the plants, birds, insects and men that he had created.

Because the birds and trees were Tane, and because they were the elder relatives of human beings, they could be attacked only after Tane's tapu had been ceremonially removed. The bird-snaring season was marked by careful ritual observances, with many restrictions upon the behaviour of those involved. And while the lesser trees were cut down without ceremony, elaborate rituals were performed over the important ones. In the Ureweras a man went fasting to his tree at dawn and struck it first with a token adze made from a small, leafy branch. He then took one chip from the tree with a real adze, and deeper in the forest he kindled a fire and burnt it, reciting as he did so a karakia addressed to the spirits of the forest. Later, when many chips had been cut from the tree, the chips were burnt at the base of the trunk so that its tapu would be removed and Tane would be prevented from punishing the workmen by breaking an adze or causing an accident. There were more rituals when Tane fell at last, and the stump was covered with fern.

Long ago, a man named Rata wished to fell a tree and hollow out a canoe so that he could make a voyage to avenge the death of his father. But he did not perform the necessary rituals, and the day after his tree had fallen he found it standing upright once more. Again Rata felled the tree, and again next day it was standing there. So he hid himself, and he discovered that the spirits of the forest had restored the tree to life because, as they told him, 'You did not consult us, so that we might know and consent to your cutting the neck of your ancestor Tane'. The spirits taught Rata the proper ceremonies, which people have performed ever since. Then after he had done the right things they magically completed his task for him. In the morning the canoe lay finished in the forest.

Plants and People

Detail of a wall painting in Rongopai, a meeting-house at Patutahi in Turanga (the Gisborne district).

Some special trees were so tapu that they served as shrines. In the Ureweras, a famous old hinau tree was believed to have the power of making a woman conceive: possibly it seemed suitable for this purpose because the hinau fruits very heavily. Under the direction of a tohunga a woman would approach the tree blindfolded, and embrace it; if she went to the east side she would have a son, if to the west a daughter. There were trees that had rituals performed before them, such as an ancient pohutukawa at Kawhia which was employed in ceremonies relating to warfare, and had under its arching roots a shallow cave where the tohunga used to sit. And sometimes a tree or a rock was thought to be inhabited by a spirit, and people passing by would pluck a twig or fern frond as an offering. Strangers were especially careful to do this, but usually everyone did so, as there would otherwise be rain. As they threw their twig before the tree, they humbly addressed the spirit of the place:

Ka ū ki Mata-nuku, ka ū ki Mata-rangi,
Ka ū ki tēnei whenua, hei whenua.
He kai māu, te ate o te tauhou.

I come to Point-of-earth, I come to Point-of-sky,
I come to this land for it to be my land.
The stranger's heart is food for you.

Green twigs and small branches were employed in many ceremonies, especially the branches of the mapou, rangiora, koromiko, karamu and kawakawa. Sometimes there was a mystical relationship between a person and a tree, as when at the birth of a chief's son the umbilical cord was buried, and a tree planted above it; the tree's growth, either vigorous or weak, foretokened that of the child. In death, too, there was a close association with trees, for the dead were often placed in them. Hollow puriri trees were frequently chosen for this purpose, and sometimes for this reason the foliage of the puriri was worn in mourning. Kawakawa leaves were also worn at this time, or sometimes the kidney fern or the flowers of the clematis.

In the forest the Maori saw a hierarchy of trees similar to that in human society, and they spoke of the grandest of them as *rākau rangatira*, 'chiefly trees', as opposed to *rākau ware*, 'common trees'. Because their wood was the most valuable, and because they towered above their fellows, they were the lords of the forest, not to be cut down without ceremony. It is not clear exactly which trees were the chiefly ones, and ideas may have varied somewhat in different places, but the totara and the other large conifers such as the kauri, kahikatea and rimu were among them, and so were trees such as the rata and the maire. A man who was told he was becoming grey might reply that moss grows only on chiefly trees, meaning by this the long, grey moss often seen on different species of conifers.

Occasionally a tree symbolised a tribe, but much more often it represented a person, as when a childless man was said to be *he tangata māmore*, 'a branchless man'. And in poetic metaphor, people might be compared

The kidney fern was one of the plants which were worn in mourning.
RIGHT The koromiko was often used in ritual. Because this shrub sometimes grew alongside houses, a stay-at-home might be called *he kōkōmuka tū tara-ā-whare*, 'a koromiko standing by the wall of the house'.

to trees that were fallen, or destroyed in some other way. Women who had been abandoned by their lovers or husbands sometimes composed songs lamenting their fate — for there was no point in trying to conceal the story, everyone knew it already, and a clever, vigorously worded song did much to relieve the poet's feelings and save her face. When one of these women compares herself to a tree she does not mention any particular kind, presumably because it would have been presumptuous to have identified herself with an important tree and ridiculous to have named a lesser one. Instead, she makes her image specific in some other way:

Kei whea ko te tau i whāia e au?
Ra ka tuku atu ki te kiri e kakara —
Nāu, e hine, i toko kia mamao!
Waiho ki te tinana ko te kōiki kāpara
E tū ki te ngahere o Te Tipi kei tua.

Where is the lover I pursued?
There he goes, to the body that smells sweet —
It was you, girl, who took him far away!
My body is left like the burnt heartwood
That stands over there in the Te Tipi forest.

The flowers of the clematis vine were sometimes worn in mourning, though it is hard to believe that Nga Toenga of Ngati Maru is wearing them for this reason. The date is 1844. Her straw hat is of foreign manufacture.

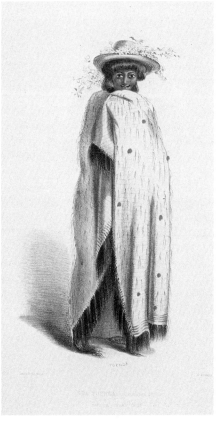

The honoured dead, however, were compared in poetry and oratory to trees of particular kinds. The huge rata was often mentioned, and so were the totara and the kahikatea. After a battle near Taupo in 1829, a woman praised in this way a chief named Te Wharerangi and the men who had died with him:

Ehara i te tangata koe, māhuri tōtara!
He wao kahikatea i rutua e te hau,
Pae ana ki te one, ngā tuakirikiri i waho Wairehu.

You were not a man, you were a young totara!
A kahikatea forest uprooted by a gale
Lies cast up on the sand, on the gravel beaches beyond Wairehu.

Occasionally the kauri occurs in these comparisons, but not very often, since it grew only in the north of the North Island. And these, it seems, the totara, kahikatea, rata and kauri, are the only large forest trees to which great men were likened. Even the rimu was of lesser importance.

The noblest of all was the totara, a tall, slow-growing conifer with straight-grained wood, easily worked and very durable, which was the preferred timber for carved objects and canoes, chiefs' houses, and other major structures. Since red things were associated with chieftainship, it

As well as yielding excellent timber, the totara provided sheets of thick, stringy bark. These were stripped from the tree and ingeniously folded into large baskets that were used for storing preserved game and water. BELOW A fallen kauri.

must have seemed appropriate and indeed inevitable that this wood should be reddish in colour. The best timber is found within a forest, not on its borders, and in this respect also a chief was likened to a totara: his proper place was in the midst of his people. As for the kahikatea, the tallest of the trees, its soft wood is subject to attacks from the huhu grub, which can ultimately destroy it. So there was a proverb used of a project that required persistence:

He iti hoki te mokoroa, nāna i kakati te kahikatea.

The huhu grub is very small, but it chewed through the kahikatea.

Kahikatea usually grow in swampy areas, and on the East Coast there is a myth to explain this. A man named Pourangahua flew here from Hawaiki on the back of an enormous bird that had been lent to him by Tane, and as he neared his home he ill-treated the bird, pulling some feathers from under its wing and throwing them into the sea. There they turned into kahikatea trees that today are still bearing fruit under the ocean. A branch from one of these wonderful trees was cast ashore at Turanga (the Gisborne district), and from it there grew a forest of kahikatea. Because of its association with water the kahikatea likes swampy places, and in its feathery shape one can see the plumes from which it had its origin.

FAR LEFT The rata usually begins life as an epiphytic plant growing high in the branches of another tree. It gradually encloses the trunk of its host, and finally becomes a tall, hollow tree. Occasionally the rata grows on the ground, and it then has a short, usually crooked trunk. The Maori explained this by saying that the tree had once been trampled down by the moa (*na te moa i takahi te rātā*). LEFT The kahikatea tree is attacked by the huhu grub (BELOW), which bores into both live and dead timber.

The best known story about the kauri tells how the whale once tried to persuade this giant tree to join him in the ocean, then when it would not do so, induced it to exchange skins. This is why the kauri's bark is so thin, and why it is as full of resin as the whale is of oil.

Folklore about the rata is mostly concerned with its crimson flowers. According to some they took their colour from the blood of Tawhaki, when that glorious hero fell to his death from the sky; others called them the eyes of Tawhaki. And when someone was growing angry for no good reason, he might be told,

Kei whawhati noa mai te rau o te rātā!

Don't keep plucking the flowers of the rata!

When the wind blows away the stamens of these flowers, they fill the air and cover the ground. The man growing red-faced with anger was seen as imitating this situation.

The pohutukawa, which fringes the beaches and clings to coastal cliffs in the northern part of the North Island, is related to the rata and in summer is covered with red blossoms. Again these were said to be the

Flowers of the rata (BELOW) and the pohutukawa (RIGHT). These trees are related. Both were said to owe their brilliant flowers to the mythical hero Tawhaki.

blood of Tawhaki. They are mentioned also in the myth of the ancestral Arawa canoe. When its crew were approaching the shore after their voyage from Hawaiki, they saw ahead of them groves of pohutukawa in full bloom. The immigrants mistook these scarlet masses for red feathers, and thought in their excitement that in this new land such wonderful things were obtainable everywhere. No longer would they need the red plumes that they possessed — so taking them from their hair and ears, they cast them into the sea. Too late they discovered it was flowers they had seen. The real treasures had floated away.

Many trees were associated in proverb and metaphor with a single quality for which they were best known. The hard wood of the maire made wedges for splitting timber, so a warrior who split the ranks of the enemy might be called a wedge of maire wood. And there is a war song in which the dancing warriors, working up their courage, shouted:

E kore te whakamā piri ki ahau,
E kore te whakamā piri ki ahau!
He maire au ka pūkengatia,
He maire au ka pūkengatia!

Shame will not cling to me,
Shame will not cling to me!
I am taught by the maire tree,
I am taught by the maire tree!

The pikirangi, a species of mistletoe, usually grows on beech trees. Its name means 'climb to the sky'. In the South Island it was said that when Tane created the forest, the pikirangi was the last plant remaining in his basket. Gazing at it fondly, he said, 'I cannot let my youngest child lie on the ground.' And he put it up on the trees, close to the sky.

Another hard wood is the kanuka, or white manuka. Under favourable conditions this develops a straight-grained trunk which could be readily split, and it was used for spears, paddles and tools. A man who was short in stature but nevertheless tough might have it said of him that

He iti, he iti kahikātoa.

Though he is small, he is small like manuka.

On the other hand the pukatea and kohekohe trees have wood that quickly becomes waterlogged, so that canoes made from their timber would be heavy and slow. Cowards were called canoes of pukatea and kohekohe, and a Taranaki man lamenting the death of his younger brother blamed him for having been prepared to fight alongside unreliable allies:

Nāu i eke atu i te waka pukatea,
I te waka kohekohe ra.
Kura tongarerewa!

It was your fault, for going aboard,
A pukatea canoe, a kohekohe canoe.
What a great treasure!

Insects and similar creatures are usually said to be the children of Tāne and of Punga, whose children are all ugly. Each had its own character and significance in folklore. Ancestral spirits sometimes assumed the form of spiders when they visited the earth, while a man with hidden intentions might be likened to a spider in its web. The stick insect (ABOVE) was seen as related to the praying mantis, and if either of these insects alighted upon a woman it was a sign she was pregnant. Weta were proverbially ugly, above all the giant weta (RIGHT), which was known for this reason as *te wētā Punga*, 'Punga's weta'.

When a cabbage tree is cut down, new shoots grow from the stump. This power of renewal was the subject of proverbs:

Ka whati te tī, ka wana te tī, ka rito te tī.

When a cabbage tree is broken it shoots up.
And grows a new head of leaves.

Perhaps because the tree has this remarkable capacity, and possibly also because the stem and taproot have a sweet sap that made them a prized delicacy, it is mentioned occasionally in laments:

E hine kaitu, e hine kairere,
E hine kaikapo i te ranga-awatea,
I te hihi o te rā, ko'e tī ka ngaehe
Roto o Awapoka, ō takanga tonu!

Girl who is far distant, who fled,
Went so fast in the light of day,
The rays of the sun, you were a rustling cabbage tree
At Awapoka, where you used to roam!

The fuchsia tree loses its leaves in winter, and the early spring was the

time when the ground had to be dug for crops. So laggards could be asked,

I whea koe i te ngahorotanga o te rau o te kōtukutuku?

Where were you when the fuchsia leaves fell?

But like many proverbs, this had more than one application. Sometimes the leaves represented kinsmen fallen in battle, and the question meant, 'When your people were killed, where were you? Absent, or in hiding? Is it for you to boast, or find fault?' At such times, as William Colenso tells us, it was 'a very cutting sarcasm; often causing intense feeling'.

When two things resembled one another it was thought, naturally enough, that there must be a connection between them. The open seed-pods of the rewarewa tree look like Maori canoes, complete with prows and sternposts, so they were said to have been the original model for the canoe. In a story from the East Coast, a boy who is seeking his father makes a magical voyage seated in one of these seed-pods, and is taken straight to his destination.

Two trees which look rather similar are the whau and the paper mulberry, which is not an indigenous tree but was brought here by the ancestors of the Maori, then died out in the last century. These trees were valuable in different ways: the whau has very light wood which was used for fishing floats, and the bark of the paper mulberry, in some favoured localities, was made into small pieces of cloth which were worn in the hair

Many fishing nets had among their floats of whau wood a carved figure that brought good luck. This one belongs to the Rotorua district. It represents either Tangaroa or a tribal ancestor.

FAR LEFT The seedpods of the rewarewa tree resemble canoes, so they were thought to have provided the model for the first canoe.

LEFT The wood of the whau tree is much lighter than cork. Its leaves were seen as resembling those of the paper mulberry, which was brought to this country from tropical Polynesia.

and ears. A chanted dialogue depicts the two of them as agreeing to occupy their respective places:

whau:	*Hei konā koe, tū ai hei parepare!*
aute:	*Haere koe ki te moana hei whau kupenga,*
	Ka mutu, hei pōuto kupenga!

whau:	You stay here, to make headbands!
paper mulberry:	You go out on to the ocean to be whau for nets,
	Floats for the nets!

The rangiora and the kawakawa were also sometimes contrasted. The rangiora is a small tree or shrub with very big leaves, silvery white on the under-surface, which were used for covering and wrapping everything from babies to parcels of food; since a person who was ashamed was thought to go pale rather than blush, it might be said that *me rau whārangi te kanohi*, 'he has a face like a rangiora leaf'. Probably because the white colour of these large leaves was felt to be auspicious, the rangiora was associated with life and wellbeing. The name rangiora means 'living sky',

In many situations the kawakawa (BELOW) was associated with death and the rangiora (BELOW RIGHT) with life and prosperity.

but there are other names for it also, and it seems that it came to be called rangiora after it had acquired its symbolic meaning.

The kawakawa on the other hand was associated with death, and was worn on the head as a sign of mourning. In a ngeri, a dance song sometimes performed at funerals, these two trees were set against each other. The singers were in two rows, one group wearing chaplets of kawakawa and carrying its twigs, and the others wreathed in rangiora and holding it in their hands. At first those with the kawakawa were in front, and they sang of death. But in the last stanza the singers with the rangiora came forward:

> He aha te tohu mo te ora?
> He rangiora!
> E tuku ki runga kia ora,
> E, kia arahia!

> What is the emblem for the living?
> The rangiora!
> Lift it up, that all may be well,
> Oh lift it up!

In the Land Wars of the 1860s, a haka addressed to the Governor, who was held responsible for the government's actions, spoke of him as a cow, or bullock, that was eating up the rangiora. While it is not great poetry, it is most meaningful when one knows what the rangiora symbolises.

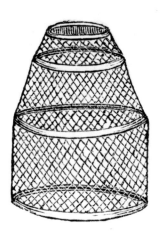

The mamaku, the largest of the tree ferns, is another plant associated with sorrow. Its drooping fronds were sometimes said to be bent with grief, and a poet's tears could be likened to *he pua kōrau e ruia, e tipu i te waru*, 'spore of the mamaku spread around in summer'. Much the same thing was said of the flax:

The tough pliant stems of the supplejack, with other, thinner vines, were used in making fishing pots and many other articles.

> Ko te rite i aku kamo ki te pua kōrari.
> Ka pupuhi te hau, ka maringi te wai ē!

> My eyes are like the flowers of the flax.
> The wind blows, and down comes the nectar!

And a beating heart could be compared to trembling flax leaves.

With unpopular plants, an explanation was required. Why was it that the entangling supplejack, the stinging tree nettle, the prickly bush lawyer and the thorny matagouri barred the way and threatened the passer-by? At least the vines of the supplejack were useful for lashing palisades and making crayfish pots, but most of these obstructing plants had few uses — though matagouri thorns are so hard that they were employed as tattooing needles when other materials were unobtainable. Why, then, should these

In the South Island, tussock and other grasses were said to have grown from the cloak of a man named Tama, who came seeking his wife.

undesirable plants be growing here? The answer was that in the early times they had been deliberately brought from Hawaiki to serve as obstructions. In many parts of the North Island this was said to have been done by Kupe, because he was being followed by the husband of a woman he had abducted. In a similar story told in the South Island, the man responsible was Tu-te-koropanga, who stole the wife of a man named Tama, fled with her to this country, built himself a house and planted around it the tree nettle, the bush lawyer and the matagouri so that the pursuing Tama should not be able to reach him. As for Tama, in his frantic search for his wife he ran up and down the West Coast, and his cloaks were torn to pieces as he did so. The cloaks had been made from the undressed leaves of flax, tussock and other rough grasses, and when they were torn apart these plants grew up behind him.

Obstructing plants were sometimes said to grow in tapu places, and they were then impassable. When a buried treasure was said to lie in a place guarded by a lizard and overgrown with nettles, this statement was accepted literally but it was known also that these were no ordinary nettles, and that they could not be overcome; in the same way, the fairies living on the peak of Moehau obviously could not be molested, for their homes were inside thickets of supplejack. Sometimes as well the plants were spoken of metaphorically, so that a chief boasting of the strength of his warriors and his pa might tell an enemy,

E kore koe e tata mai, i ngā tairo a Tū-te-koropanga!

You won't get near me, because of Tu-te-koropanga's obstructions!

When the warrior chief Te Rauparaha in 1822 led his people southwards to a new home on Kapiti Island, the difficulties encountered during the second part of their long journey were so great that it became known as *te heke tātarāmoa,* 'the bush lawyer migration'.

Birds and People

Birds were an endless source of imagery and ideas. Recognising them as their distant kin, surrounded by them in their everyday lives, with an expert knowledge of their habits, dependent upon them for much of the food they most enjoyed, all the more aware of their presence because of the absence of large animals, wearing their plumes in their hair and treasuring cloaks covered with their feathers, the

Maori thought about birds a great deal. Often they identified themselves with them.

Like other peoples, they associated birds in many contexts with the world of the spirits. With their power of flight, birds have a freedom and unpredictability of movement similar to that possessed by supernatural beings, and in their homes above us they are close to the sky — which is tapu, sacred, being high and unreachable. Their songs seem certainly to mean something, yet their speech is strange, it requires interpretation.

When travellers heard a bird singing as they were passing a tapu place where stood the tombs of chiefs and warriors, they knew it was the spirit of one of these men, and they anxiously speculated as to its message: was it telling of storms and other troubles to come, or was it saying that all would be well? An early trader, J. S. Polack, describes meeting a chief who at first was greatly afflicted by the death of a son but later seemed very cheerful. He explained to Polack that as he had been passing a bush a few days before, his son had whistled to him in the form of a little bird and told him to dry his tears, as he felt perfectly satisfied with the quarters he now occupied. ' "Shall I grieve at his happiness?" the sagacious old man enquiringly demanded.'

Polack also tells us that offerings were made to the spirits of departed chiefs. Persons soliciting their assistance would place a small basket containing kumara, fish or other food on the branch of a tree near the tapu place, then wait patiently; if a small bird were seen picking at the food, they would know that the spirit had accepted the offering and would help them. Sometimes the dead were asked to return as birds and communicate with the living. In an old song a chief is urged,

Kia kōrero koe i te ngutu o te manu,
Kia hoki ana mai tō wairua ki te ao nā ī!

Speak with the bill of a bird,
Let your soul come back to us in this world!

Finely carved waka huia, containers for huia plumes, hung from the rafters of chiefs' houses.

Rods with carved heads were placed before the tuahu as resting-places for atua, or spirits. The spirits were thought to respond to the tohunga's karakia in much the same way that birds did.

When a tohunga seated before his tuahu, shrine, wished to communicate with the spirit of an ancestor, or some other spirit, his first aim was to ensure that it answered his call. Here again, the relationship with birds provided a model, a way of visualising the invisible. To make the spirit come, the tohunga placed an offering of food upon a small framework of sticks which was termed a *tiepa;* and this word was also used of a karakia that was recited to make birds flock to a forest and be easily caught there. Other, similar coincidences of meaning confirm that in the Maori mind there was an association between snaring birds and catching unseen spirits. The method worked with birds, so it must work with spirits as well.

The only way of entering the sky, the realm of the unknown, was by flying a kite — or rather, a bird, for Maori kites were called birds, or sometimes hawks. For a people who do not have aeroplanes there is something almost magical about sending a kite high into the air, and the flying of a large, elaborate kite was a festive occasion for which people came from far and near. Such kites were in the form of birds, with outstretched wings made from toetoe stalks and hung with strings of feathers. Sometimes there would be horns on the head, and a face of paper mulberry cloth with tattoo markings painted upon it. A writer named Hamiora Pio tells us that a large bird would be sent up by two chiefs wearing their best apparel; one waved it into the air while the other held the cord. After it had started to go up 'it swooped down and thrust with its horns at the people flying it, making them dance and leap about. The rope was tightened by the man holding it, the bird climbed upwards and a cry of joy went up from the people. When it had gone up, water was sent to it; a ring was sent to travel up the cord. Then the people gathered to chant a karakia to charm the bird.' The first words of this karakia were:

Piki mai, piki mai
Te mata-tihi o te rangi, te mata-taha o te rangi!
E, ko koe kai whāunumia, e koe,
Ki te kawe tuawhitu, ki te kawe tuawaru.
Tahi te nuku, tahi te rangi!

Climb up, climb up
To the summit of the sky, the sides of the sky!
Oh you, you will be given drink
In the seventh region, the eighth region.
Earth and sky are one!

The bird was to unify the earth and the sky, bringing them together in a mystical harmony. Water from the earth was sent up the cord in a ring, and there it joined the waters of the sky, which were believed to have special, magical properties.

Apart from such associations with the supernatural, birds were envied for their freedom of movement. This idea was often expressed in songs, as

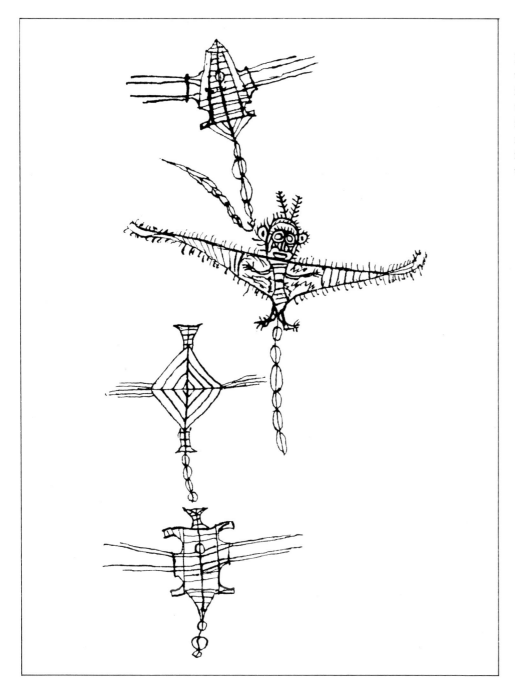

Kites of different shapes and sizes were made from raupo leaves, with frameworks of rods and twigs. Some of the larger, elaborate ones were in the form of hawks. This drawing was made in 1819 by Titore, a young chief from Te Tai Tokerau (Northland) who was visiting England at the time.

when a man lamented the fact that he could not visit his beloved daughter, who lived far away with her husband:

He manu hoki koā, e taea te hokahoka,
E taea te whanawhana te whare i moe ai?

Am I a bird, able to take flight
And fold my wings in the house where she sleeps?

Their singing at dawn was a sign of the triumph of light over darkness, and it was associated with oratory. Departed chiefs might be praised as *taku manu whakaoho i te ata,* 'my bird that woke the dawn'. And in a song addressed to a child who had died, a relative tells him:

Kīkī-ā-manu, aroaroā ō tāngata i a koe
Hei nui mōhou, hei tangi mōhou.

Your kinsmen speak like birds, they voice their thoughts
To praise you, and lament you.

Someone with bad manners could be said to have been hatched by a bird, and a babbler might be accused of making as much noise as a baby bird. Usually, however, comparisons with birds were complimentary. Brave warriors were 'flapping birds' and 'stubborn birds', and the young fighting men who formed the vanguard in battle were *pī-rere,* 'young birds able to fly' — that is, old enough to venture from the nest. People who were abandoning their homes to move to new territory could be spoken of similarly, also those who had lost a parent:

Amio noa ana te kāhui pī nei,
Kāore nei he mātua! Tēnā ka riro
I te herenga kakano, i te huanga miro.

This flock of young birds keeps flying about,
Fatherless! He is gone as the birds are speared
Among the berries, as the miro fruit ripen.

And since nests are snug, safe havens, the word might be used of a pa or a person's birthplace. When a high-ranking woman had a child, she and

The silvereye is a newcomer, having been blown over from Australia in the middle of the last century, and it was accordingly named *tauhou,* 'stranger'. Other names given it include *karu-pātene,* 'button eyes', and *kanohi mōwhiti,* 'spectacle eyes'.

OPPOSITE ABOVE Pigeons feeding on fruit in a painting in Rongopai, a meeting-house decorated in transitional style in 1888.

OPPOSITE BELOW The fat, peaceable pigeons, with their splendid plumage, were the main game birds.

her new baby lived for the first few weeks in a specially constructed building which was termed a nest house.

The Maori also assigned to each kind of bird a particular significance, and often associated its habits with those of human beings. In the forests, in the open country and in the swamps and rivers these other children of Tane went their different ways, each kind with its well-understood characteristics, each with its own relationship with humans, each a source of ideas and metaphor.

Birds of the Forest

Pigeons were the most important game birds, being large, plentiful and very good eating. In the autumn and winter they gorge themselves on the fruits of trees, and their greed was proverbial. Their gorgeous plumage was said to be due to the mischievous hero Maui, who wanted to find where his mother went each day at dawn, so one night delayed her departure by hiding her loincloth and belt. In the

end she fled down to the underworld without them. Maui became a pigeon and flew after her, still carrying her garments, and the bird wears them today. Its white breast and purple-green ruff are the mother's loincloth and belt.

Another story tells of a man named Rupe who is identified with the pigeon, being claimed as its first parent. Rupe had a sister, Hinauri, whose mythic role was that of wife and mother; in this respect she provided a pattern for all women to follow. Rupe's role was that of a woman's brother — for in Maori society a man had a special relationship with his sister, often having a claim upon the children she produced. Asserting this relationship, Rupe turned himself into a pigeon and went seeking his sister, who was living with her husband. He found her on the very day that she had given birth to a son, and after greeting her he swooped down and carried off both sister and nephew; some story-tellers said that he later restored the boy to his father, others that he did not. In real life also a pigeon's behaviour could indicate a special concern with the fate of an infant boy, for an early missionary tells us that if a pigeon should coo 'at the moment when a man-child is born, it is a prognostication that by him some great things are to be brought about'. Probably this pigeon was thought to be Rupe himself.

The aggressive, noisy kaka were often kept as pets, and served as decoys when wild kaka were being taken. Their perches were sheltered by pieces of bark, and contained troughs for food and water. Sometimes the birds were taught to talk, though they were not as good at this as tui.

Next to the pigeon the main game bird was the kaka, a large, gregarious parrot as clamorous and active as the pigeon is quiet and peaceful. The bird's raucous cries were much spoken of in proverbs. A silly, talkative fellow might be called *he kākā waha nui*, 'a big-mouthed kaka'; boastful enemies were chattering kaka who would soon meet their fate; and the pigeon's greed was contrasted with the kaka's habit of politely nibbling its food. Another saying contrasted the pigeon's gentle cooing and the kaka's harsh screams:

He kūkū ki te kāinga, he kākā ki te haere.

He's a pigeon at home, a kaka when he travels.

This was said of a man who remained silent among his own people, being of no consequence, but behaved as if he were important when he went elsewhere. It was also applied to a man who would not call an invitation to travellers approaching his home, but who when himself a traveller would loudly sound his trumpet to make his presence known when nearing

Large flocks of kakariki, or parakeets, fed on seeds and other vegetable foods on the outskirts of the forests. They were taken with snares after being attracted by decoys or bait such as berries.

a village, then afterwards complain noisily about the quality of the food he had received. In Maori such comparisons have a satisfying ring to them, all the more so because of the similarity of the onomatopoetic names of the two birds, *kūkū* and *kākā*.

In the North Island most kaka are predominantly olive-brown in colour, but there is much variation, and the Maori had a number of terms for birds with different kinds of plumage. They were especially interested in the rare birds which are mainly white or red, thinking them the chiefs of the flocks to which they belonged. Red kaka feathers were bound around the heads of taiaha and they were used on feather cloaks, usually in combination with the feathers of other birds. Cloaks entirely covered with red kaka feathers were rare treasures worn only be a few men of very high rank.

All kaka have a few scarlet feathers, hidden under their wings. A well known tale explains that these used to belong to the kakariki, the little parakeet, but they were stolen by the kaka, so that the kakariki now sings reproachfully,

> *E te kākā e rere atu rārā, hōmai aku kura!*
> *Nāku anō aku kura i tiki ki te motu tapu na Tinirau!*

> You kaka flying up there, give me back my treasures!
> It was I who fetched them from Tinirau's tapu island!

The Maori were always concerned to trace things to their source, so it was satisfying that this story explained where the feathers had come from in the first place: the kakariki had got them from a mythical land of origin. Even without them the kakariki is brilliantly coloured, bright green with red, yellow or orange markings on the head; but since the Maori valued red things so much and green ones so little, it seemed to them that this could have been no consolation for the loss of its stolen treasures. The bird's name, *kākāriki*, means literally 'little kaka', and by a process of extension this word came to be used for the colour green, also for a species of green lizard; some said that when the young birds hatched, the fragments of their shells turned into these lizards. Kakariki used to feed on seeds in such large flocks that their great numbers were proverbial. Their chattering provided a simile for noisy talk and continual gossip: *ko te rua porete hai whakarite,* 'just like a nest of kakariki'.

The strange nocturnal parrot known as the kakapo, literally 'kaka of the night', was found mostly in mountainous parts of the South Island and was somewhat uncommon in the north even before the arrival of the Pakehas. Its plumes were highly valued, and there was an ironical proverb that was used when someone complained too much of the cold:

> *Me kauhi rānei koe ki te huruhuru kākāpō, pū mai o te tonga?*

> Shall I cover you with a cloak made of kakapo feathers
> Heaped up here from the south?

The implication was, 'Would nothing else be good enough for you?'

The kakapo is almost flightless, and it was hunted with dogs. The kiwi, a flightless bird of ancient origin, was similarly treated. During the day this remarkable bird lies hidden, then at night it emerges to walk through the forest on its stumpy legs, tapping its long, sensitive bill from side to side and sniffing and probing for grubs and big bush worms. Kiwi lay their enormous eggs in burrows they dig under logs or the roots of trees, and the male must sit upon the eggs for seventy-five days before the chicks hatch. This is such a long time that it seemed even longer; some said the eggs took two years to hatch, and others three years. It was thought that the roots grew over the eggs, and that young birds were sometimes trapped inside.

In the second half of the nineteenth century, feather cloaks became very popular. The chief Pera Te Watutu, photographed at Turanga (Gisborne), probably in the early 1870s.

Though kiwi have very poor sight by day, at night they move around confidently, and they are very fast runners. When they are disturbed they stretch their heads forward and crash wedge-shaped through the undergrowth, pounding along on their big strong feet, or if they cannot escape they defend themselves with powerful backward kicks, first tucking their heads into corners. A kiwi that is running from a dog knows that if its pursuer is gaining it must stop in a suitable place and start kicking. To find out what is happening it will sometimes look back as it runs, so a person giving sidelong glances might be said to be *whakakiwi*, 'acting like a kiwi'. And a man running from enemies, or after them, would try to find breath enough to recite a tapuwae, footsteps spell, that names the kiwi and the weka in the hope of gaining the speed of these two birds:

Tuku atu au kia rere me he matakōkiri ānewa i te rangi,
Te rokohina taku tapuwae nei!
Ko te tapuwae o wai? Ko te tapuwae o Kiwi, o Weka!

Let me fly like a meteor falling through the sky,
Let me achieve my footsteps spell!
Whose are these footsteps? The footsteps of Kiwi and Weka!

The weka is another flightless bird. A member of the same family as the pukeko and banded rail, it is so bold and inquisitive that it is quite easy to snare. But weka are intelligent, and when they did learn about snares they became very wary. A much-quoted proverb remarked that,

Ka motu te weka i te māhanga, e kore a muri e hokia.

When a weka breaks from a snare, it won't be back.

The lively beautiful tui was an important food item, being taken in the early winter when it was fat from feeding on the fruits of trees. Its glorious singing, so rich and varied, was also much appreciated, and it was high praise when a witty and poetical orator was said to speak *me he korokoro tūī,* 'like a tui's throat'. With its extraordinary powers of mimicry it was a popular cage bird, and some were taught recitations containing as many as forty or fifty words. Only young males were chosen for this. First the trainer trimmed off the brush on the tongue which is used in sipping nectar, then he put the bird's cage in a quiet place away from the village, as it would otherwise learn to imitate the cries of children, the barking of dogs and other domestic sounds. Every day he visited it, feeding it berries

The sharp-nosed, bushy-tailed dogs brought by the ancestors of the Maori were used in hunting the flightless birds that they found here.

This small figure of a dog (OPPOSITE) was worn as a pendant; it belongs to the Canterbury region and the Archaic phase of Maori culture. Later, in the Classic phase, the main birds hunted with dogs were the kakapo (OPPOSITE BELOW), the weka (BELOW), and the kiwi.

and roasted kumara and repeating a short phrase; when one was memorised, he would teach another. Often the bird would learn a recital telling of approaching guests:

Whārikitia te whare mo te manuhiri,
Kia pai te whare mo te manuhiri!
Tahia te marae, ē, tahuna he kai ma te manuhiri!

Spread mats in the house for the visitors,
Let the house look good for the visitors!
Sweep the marae, cook food for the visitors!

When a tui chose to utter these words it was thought that people were

Kiwi-feather cloaks are rare and much treasured. This unknown woman was probably photographed in the 1870s.

coming, and an oven would be lit. Sometimes the bird's master would greet his guests with his pet perched upon his shoulder or on the ground beside him, its speech of welcome being received with acclamation.

There were stories about strangely gifted tui which could repeat karakia, even the most tapu ones, and knew genealogies, and history, and recitals of all kinds. In the seventeenth century a chief living in the Wairoa district owned a tui which was so learned that it was entrusted with the performance of all the religious rituals. When another chief stole this wonderful bird a war was fought over it, and the thief and his people had to migrate south to new homes.

The smaller, olive-green bellbird belongs to the same family as the tui, and is another sweet singer. Bellbirds greet the dawn, especially the sunrise, with loud, chiming choruses of song, and this seemed appropriate to the Maori, who disliked the darkness and associated daylight with life and success. A performance by a good singer or a graceful speaker might be praised as being *he rite ki te kōpara e kō nei i te ata,* 'like a bellbird pealing at day-break'. An early missionary, Richard Taylor, says that at Taupo it was the custom, at the ceremony marking the birth of a boy of high rank, to cook a bellbird in a tapu oven 'that the child might have a sweet voice, and become an admired orator'. Taylor adds that 'in imitation of this bird, which only sings in the mornings, the high chiefs give their commands, and scold their slaves, with the first dawn of the day'.

Another of the bellbird's habits was thought less worthy of imitation. They are restless creatures, always on the move, and when they are feeding on the nectar of the fuchsia or kowhai they hang and swing upside down to reach the drooping flowers. A flighty woman sure to get into trouble might be called *he kōpara kairerere,* 'a female bellbird, that keeps flitting about'.

Eloquent orators and sweet singers were said to sound like the tui (TOP) and the bellbird (ABOVE). The tui was valued for its ability to imitate human speech, and the words it uttered were often thought to be meaningful.

Huia were found in the high ranges in the southern part of the North Island. Their skins and tail plumes, carefully prepared and packed between layers of totara bark, were sent to tribes in other parts of the country as items of exchange. The southern tribes gave presents of greenstone in return, and those in the far north gave the teeth of the mako shark.

The stitchbird, also a honeyeater, was of interest to the Maori mainly because the male bird has a band of bright yellow feathers across its breast. These were highly valued, and were used to ornament cloaks. The ubiquitous Maui was responsible for their presence, having one day in a fit of rage thrown the male bird on to a fire, so that its feathers took the colour of the flames. The female, which escaped this treatment, has much duller plumage.

Another bird greatly prized for its feathers was the huia. This was large and black, with orange wattles, a white beak and twelve long, white-tipped tail feathers which it could spread and display. Though it lived only in the rugged ranges to the north of Te Whanga-nui-a-Tara

A painting of a female huia in a small meeting-house which formerly stood at Ohau, north of Wellington.

LEFT An unknown woman, photographed in about the 1880s, wears two huia plumes in the traditional manner.

(Wellington Harbour), its tail feathers were worn by people of rank throughout the country, being passed from one owner to the next. They were the most treasured of plumes, along with those of the white heron, and they were stored in finely carved wooden boxes, long and narrow to accommodate them, which hung from the rafters of chiefs' houses. Men used them, as the missionary William Yate tells us, 'to ornament their hair on grand occasions, or when going out to battle'. Women were permitted to wear them, and it was a high honour when a woman of rank was able to appear at a festival adorned with two huia plumes, one on each side of her head.

A chief whose death was mourned in a lament might be called by the poet *he huia tū rae,* 'a huia plume on my brow', and in love songs a sweetheart was sometimes *te huia kai-manawa,* 'the huia that consumes my heart'. And apparently they were noisy, for a talkative know-all might be said to be a ngutu-huia, a huia-lips or huia-beak. They were trusting creatures, quite easily caught; when a man whistled their cry of alarm, *huia, huia,* they came hopping down to look for the bird they thought was in distress there. When the Pakehas arrived with their guns, collectors of specimens for foreign museums killed great numbers of them. Many more were shot by Maoris, for their tail feathers, which previously had been worn only by people of the highest rank, were now desired by all. Early this century, the last of the huia disappeared from their mountain home.

The grey kokako, a related bird, is said once to have brought Maui a drink of water in its bright blue wattles when he was tired and thirsty; as a reward, Maui pulled out its legs so that it now moves with swift, bounding hops through the trees. But in another story a kokako became envious of the beautiful huia and wished to attract the admiration which that bird received. After much searching he found a dead huia, and borrowing its plumage he strutted about in front of the other birds, hoping for their praise. They only laughed at him, however, and said, 'Just look

A kokako feeding its chick. Fortunately for this bird, its plumes were not in demand, and though it was eaten sometimes, it was not much liked.

at that kokako! He's pretending to be a huia, but he still looks like a kokako!'

Another relative of the huia is the saddleback, a dark bird with a chestnut 'saddle' and orange wattles. To the Maori its role was that of a guardian. Ancient, buried treasures were sometimes guarded by this bird, and when the mythical Mataatua canoe set sail from Hawaiki a pair of saddlebacks accompanied its crew and guided them to this country. These two saddlebacks are named Mumu-hau and Takere-tou. At the entrance to the Hauraki Gulf they were left at Repanga (Cuvier Island), and they are living there still; they are wise birds that foretell the weather by their cries and their manner of flying. In fact the cries of all saddlebacks were taken to be good or bad omens. An early writer says that if a party of travellers heard a saddleback cry on their right, lucky side, they knew that the people they were visiting would welcome them with feasting. If the cry came from their left, unlucky side, it warned of murder.

The ability to foretell the future is appropriate in a bird that is a guardian. As to why it had this role, the main reason must be that in the days when saddlebacks were common, they had the habit of following large flocks of whiteheads through the forest to snap up insects that had been disturbed by the whiteheads but were too big for these little birds to manage. There would be a pair of saddlebacks doing this, or perhaps four or five, and to the Maori they must have looked like the whiteheads' guardians, all the more so because of the sharp, rapid cries they utter when alarmed. The usual Maori name for the saddleback is *tieke*, a word imitative of these loud cries, but sometimes it was known as a *tiaki* — and this similar-sounding word ordinarily means 'guard, keep watch'. So not only did the saddleback guard other birds, it uttered a cry that sounded as if it were speaking of its duties.

A saddleback bathing.

Apart from this, the saddleback is mentioned in a saying used about an object, such as a piece of wood, that was full of holes: it was *me te mea i houhoua e te tieke*, 'as if it had been pecked by a saddleback'. Because the bird often nests in clumps of kiekie growing on trees, a person making a cloak from kiekie leaves might be told, *Ka mahi koe te whare o te tieke*, 'Well done, you're making a saddleback's house'. And because it bathes energetically, sending water in all directions, something that was being done to excess might be said to be *me he wai tā tieke*, 'like the water spread around by a saddleback'.

One of the most conspicuous of the small forest birds is the fantail, with its spread tail and fearless, darting flight. A very small man might be nicknamed *Piwakawaka*, (Fantail) and *he tou tīrairaka*, 'the tail of a fantail', was an expression for a restless person. The trickster Maui once tried to overcome death by entering the sleeping body of Hine-nui-te-po, Great-woman-of-the-night, by the pathway that children follow when they are born, but when he went to do this the fantail and the rail burst out laughing at the ridiculous sight, and the fantail danced for joy. Hine-nui-te-po woke at the sound, she killed Maui, and in this way death came into the world. Probably because of this association with death, it was a bad omen when a single fantail entered a house.

Another flycatcher, the little tomtit, has very sharp eyesight, so that someone able to see small objects was said to have *he kanohi hōmiromiro*, 'a tomtit's eyes'. A man whose wife had left him might wait till the wind was blowing in her direction then recite a spell to make her love him once more, releasing as he did so a tomtit he had previously caught. This tomtit was his messenger. It was thought that it would fly straight to the woman and perch upon her, and that she would at once be overcome with longing for her husband and set out to return to him.

Captive birds were released in other rituals too, sometimes as a means of communicating with spirits. On some parts of the East Coast their ceremonial release occurred in the rituals performed over a new-born child, at the initiation of a visionary tohunga and at the removal of the tapu, sacredness, from a newly built pa. The birds used in such ceremonies were tomtits and whiteheads, and the intention was to acquire for the person or persons concerned — for the child, the tohunga, the people who were to live in the pa — the wellbeing symbolised by the bird's flight to freedom.

Quite a few small species of birds were employed in rituals, or were thought to have the power of foretelling the future. Perhaps this was because it was assumed that all creatures were significant in one way or

The fantail is proverbially restless. When one of these birds enters a house, it is considered a bad omen.

another, and since these little birds were not important as a source of food it was felt that their importance must lie elsewhere. The robin's cry was a good omen when it was heard on someone's right side, and a bad omen on the left. The grey warbler's call could be an ill omen, and the direction in which it built its hanging nest was an indication of the weather to come: if the entrance faced towards the east, westerly winds would prevail and the summer would not be a good one. In spring the grey warbler's song could have a different significance, for then it called upon people to bestir themselves and prepare the ground for their crops. If a man's food-supplies ran short and he had to ask his neighbours for assistance, he was likely to hear the old question:

I whea koe i te tangihanga o te riroriro, ka mahi kai māu?

Where were you when the grey warbler was singing,
That you didn't work to get yourself food?

Some little birds provided a convenient metaphor for enemies whom it was wished to insult. Robins were one species spoken of in this way. A certain Te Tuhi, having been badly treated by some people living at

The grey warbler (BELOW) and the robin (LEFT) are other small birds whose actions were thought to foretell the future.

Whiteheads fly in flocks, feeding in the forest canopy. In the Whanganui region it was said that they were the spirits of the dead.

Paranui, visited another tribe and asked for their assistance by saying, 'Kill me these robins at Paranui!' In a cursing song, a poet first speaks of her enemies as chattering, rashly boastful kaka, then says scornfully that they are only whiteheads and robins:

> *He upoko kākā no Taurua, no Tamarehe,*
> *Kai runga kai te rākau e tarahae ana!*
> *He taki tātāeto, he tīeke rere,*
> *He p̄itoitoi ketuketu para rākau!*

Kaka-heads from Taurua and Tamarehe
Are jabbering up in the trees —
A flock of whiteheads with saddlebacks flying around,
Robins scratching about in dead leaves!

Saddlebacks are mentioned here because of their habit of accompanying the whiteheads as they flew through the forest.

Usually it is the grey warbler that has the task of raising the young of the shining cuckoo; even when the outsized chick bursts the sides of its home it remains nearby, calling insistently, and the little birds hurry to feed it. The long-tailed cuckoo, a larger bird than the shining cuckoo, often chooses whiteheads and yellowheads as foster parents. Both cuckoos occur in sayings about indolent, shiftless folk, and a fatherless baby might be called *he pōtiki na te koekoeā*, 'the youngest child of the long-tailed cuckoo'. In a song, a poet claims to be without the support of kinsmen:

> *Ko te uri au i te whēnakonako, i te koekoeā:*
> *E riro nei ma te tātaihore e whāngai.*

I am the offspring of the shining cuckoo, the long-tailed cuckoo:
It is left for the whitehead to feed me.

Some said that the cuckoos travelled each autumn to the homeland of Hawaiki, some that they spent the winter on the backs of whales, and others that they lost their feathers, retreated into burrows and turned into lizards. In the spring they appeared again as the messengers of Mahuru, Spring, to let people know it was time to prepare for the planting season. In particular, the long-tailed cuckoo was heard calling *kōia, kōia,* 'dig, dig!' In Taranaki, men digging the fields sang this song as they worked:

> *Tangi te kawekaweā, waiho kia tangi ana!*
> *Tangi te wharauroa, waiho kia tangi ana!*
> *E tatari atu ana kia aroaro-mahana,*
> *Ka taka mai te āhuru!*
> *Kōia!*

The shining cuckoo's cry announces the coming of spring, but at first the bird complains of the shortage of food. Later, as the summer approaches, its cry becomes a promise of success and prosperity.

The long-tailed cuckoo sings, let it sing!
The shining cuckoo sings, let it sing!
They are waiting for the summer,
When the warmth will come!
Dig!

When the shining cuckoo first appears in early spring it keeps crying *kūī*, 'no food', but later, when the warm weather comes and it knows that all will be well, it adds the words *whiti, whiti ora,* 'changing, changing to plenty'. This call told the people that the summer would be a good one, and as a promise of prosperity and wellbeing it is quoted by poets.

Hunting in the darkness on noiseless wings and hooting in its melancholy fashion, the morepork, as always with owls, was associated with the night and with spirits. Many family groups, perhaps most of them, were thought to have a special relationship with an ancestral spirit, and most of these spirits took the form of a morepork, one particular bird recognisable by its behaviour. Its presence was usually a warning that someone in the family had died. It would sit boldly in a conspicuous place, or keep knocking on a window or even enter a house.

A morepork's cry was also ominous when it was heard as men were discussing a plan of action, and when it called from a place associated with

A morepork with its chicks. Ancestral guardian spirits were often thought to take the form of an owl. These special birds were usually seen in times of trouble. They made themselves known by their bold behaviour.

the dead, or a crossroads. A poet addressing his beloved, and lamenting their separation, spoke of its cry as an ill omen:

Tangi a te ruru ra kei te hokihoki mai ē,
E whakawherowhero ra i te pūtahitanga.
Nāku nei ra koe i tuku kia haere,
Tē puritia iho, nui rawa te aroha.

The morepork's cry keeps coming to me,
It is hooting out there where the paths meet.
I was the one who allowed you to go,
My great love did not detain you.

Moreporks could be associated with lonely isolation, as when a woman defending herself against gossip sang that *kei te ruru koukou au ki te wāhi mokemoke*, 'I am like a morepork hooting in a lonely place'. And sometimes its round, staring eyes were identified with a state of watchful alertness. A man replying to insults told his enemies that he was well aware of their slander:

Etia anō aku mata me te mata-ā-ruru e tīwai ana,
Me te mata kāhu e paro noa ra kai te tahora!

My eyes are like a morepork's, staring from side to side,
Like the eyes of a hawk that soars over the plain!

A myth explains that a man named Rongo built the first carved house after acquiring a knowledge of this art from a house in the sky. It was necessary to bury a tapu offering under the rear wall, and for this purpose Rongo sacrificed Kou-ruru, the personification of the morepork. That is why carved figures now have large, glaring eyes. They are the eyes of Kou-ruru, or Morepork.

A second species of owl, the laughing owl, is now extinct. It was a larger bird with an unearthly cry which inhabited high rocky bluffs, mostly in the South Island. A person who disapproved of a garden that had been made in a steep or stony place might say, with some exaggeration, that it was *me te pari hakoke*, 'like a laughing owl's cliff'.

Birds of the Open Country

The large round eyes of carved figures, inlaid with rings of paua shell, are known as *mata-ā-ruru*, 'owl eyes'. They are said to be the eyes of Kou-ruru, the personification of the morepork. This figure of a female ancestor is from Whangara, on the East Coast.

There are two species of hawk, and different characters were assigned to them. The New Zealand falcon lives in the forests, especially their outskirts, and also the open country. Its rapid, dashing flight and sustained ferocity make it an impressive sight, especially when it has a nest to defend, and though it preys mostly on small creatures it sometimes attacks even such large, well-armed birds as herons and shags. The harrier hawk on the other hand is essentially a bird of the open spaces, and unlike the falcon it is a scavenger, devouring dead creatures as well as live ones. With a much larger wing-span than the falcon, the hawk soars and glides over fernlands, plains and marshes, scanning the ground below. It is slow, methodical and wary, where the falcon is swift and recklessly courageous.

The power and the predatory instincts of these two birds were often spoken of in proverbs. But, as George Grey tells us, the hawk was 'a symbol

The harrier hawk (RIGHT) was associated with chieftainship and success in battle. The fierce falcon (BELOW), a smaller bird, is an enemy of the harrier hawk. In proverbs it is seen as being cruel and aggressive, and dangerous to established authority. FAR RIGHT Though the kea, an alpine parrot, is a familiar bird in the South Island high country, no folklore concerning it has been recorded.

for a great chief' and the falcon was 'a symbol for a treacherous, cruel man'. This distinction was expressed in the maxim,

Hōmai te kāeaea kia toro-māhangatia,
Ko te kāhu te whakaora: waiho kia rere ana!

The falcon must be snared,
And the hawk must be saved: let it fly on!

Hawks were in fact snared from time to time when their feathers were wanted, and they then formed a meal for the fowler. This saying is not about birds but about people. Great men must be saved, and treacherous ones destroyed.

The hawk's larger size, long wings and effortless flight must have made it seem the more impressive of the two, while the falcon's boldness and rapacity were associated with men whose aggression and upstart ambition made them untrustworthy allies, all the more so because the falcon is in reality an enemy of the hawk, attacking it whenever it gets the chance. Since it could represent a great chief the hawk was associated with victory in battle, and it must have been this bird which an early writer had in mind when he wrote that 'For a hawk to fly over the heads of those who are settling the affairs of war, is a certain assurance of success in whatever they undertake'. From the wide blade of the tewhatewha, a long-handled wooden weapon, there hung a bunch of feathers which was meant to confuse and distract an opponent; because of the hawk's association with warfare, these feathers were usually those of the hawk.

As hawks become older they slowly acquire a greyish, almost white plumage. The Maori valued these birds very much, for they were fond of white feathers and they liked rarities also. High chiefs might be spoken of as white hawks, as in the saying *Me haere i raro i te kāhu kōrako*, 'Travel under the protection of a white hawk': if one moved about the country in the party of a powerful chief, one could be sure of a good reception. And because of its gliding flight the hawk was associated with the idea of a smooth, effortless passage. A poet tells her daughter of the places she could so easily visit if only she had the wings of a hawk; and on the East Coast, workmen hauling a log or some other heavy article would chant this song to make it move easily:

The tewhatewha was employed as a spear at one end and a club at the other. The bunch of hawk feathers attached to the heavy end was symbolic of chiefly prowess.

> *Te kāhu i runga whakaaorangi ana ē rā,*
> *Te pērā koia tōku rite inawa ē!*

> The hawk up above moves like clouds in the sky.
> Let me do the same, *inawa ē!*

Not many birds live all the year round in the open country, though some shore birds visit it to nest and rear their young. The pipit is common in scrub lands, tussock foothills and river beds, but it is seldom referred to in Maori folklore. And no proverbs, myths or songs have been recorded about the kea, the clowning, thievish parrot of the South Island high country, though with such a bird these must surely have existed. Their absence must be due to the fact that the folklore of the South Island was not very well recorded.

A handsome quail used to be abundant in the open country, especially on the grassy plains of the South Island. Like all quails it flew up quickly when startled, and a man coming suddenly upon an enemy might liken his frightened response to that of a quail, taunting him because he could not fly off like one:

Whiti koreke, ka kitea koe!
Haere whakaparirau i a koe, haere whakamanu!

The quail springs up, you're found!
Go and get yourself wings, go and turn into a bird!

By 1870 the Pakehas' guns, dogs, cats, stoats, weasels, rats and forest fires had destroyed the last of the native quails.

Quails were useful game birds in some areas. Like many small birds, they were taken with snares and nets.

The white heron was very rare in the north, and uncommon even in the south. Its feathers were treasured, especially the long tail plumes.

Birds of the Waterways and Wetlands

In the North Island the rarest of the swamp and river birds was the tall, stately white heron, said to be seen once in a lifetime: *He kōtuku rerenga tahi,* 'A white heron of a single flight'. An orator may honour a distinguished visitor by comparing his visit to that of a white heron: such an important man comes as seldom as that bird.

The heron's plumes were treasured by people of rank, being exchanged only for the most valuable property. Each kind of plume had its own name. The longest ones, which were the most highly valued, were regarded as tapu, and women were forbidden to wear them, being warned

An eighteenth-century warrior robed in a fine dogskin cloak, holding a tewhatewha and wearing plumes in his hair.

that if they presumed to do so, all their hair would fall out. This prohibition is not surprising, for in Maori symbolism the white heron could represent the male, just as the huia, that other prized bird, could be associated with the female. When a man dreamt he saw the skulls of his ancestors adorned with plumes, it was a sign that his wife was to have a baby: if the feathers were those of the white heron the child would be a boy, if they belonged to the huia it would be a girl. This identification of white things with the male and dark ones with the female was very much in accord with Maori thinking generally.

In laments for the dead, men are compared to the plumes of the white heron or the birds themselves:

Ngā kōtuku awe-nui o te uru
Ka moe whakaāio ki te mate.

The long-plumed white herons of the west
Sleep peacefully in death.

Because herons stand motionless in the water as they await their prey, a proverb spoke of *he kōtuku kai whakaata,* 'a white heron, that feeds upon its reflection'. The bird has a beautiful reflection to gaze upon, and it was apparently felt that this sight was a compensation for its long wait. William Colenso explains that this proverb was used of a chief who concerned himself with feeding his guests — for the Maori ate after their visitors, not with them — 'also, of one who quietly and courteously awaits the arrival and sitting of others to their repast before he eats his own food'. Such manners were a sign of good birth.

There is little in the folklore about the blue reef heron, perhaps because the white heron was such a glamorous bird that it drew attention away from it. But another member of the heron family, the bittern, had a most distinctive character assigned to it. Bitterns are large, elegant, shy birds which live on eels and other creatures in raupo swamps and sedgy lagoons, and hide in the reeds with necks stretched up, bills pointing skyward; with their dark-brown and tawny markings they are well camouflaged. In the evening during the spring and early summer the male bird calls to its mate, its deep, booming calls, three or four times repeated, carrying far into the surrounding countryside. The Maori thought the bitterns were expressing their loneliness and melancholy, and they spoke of them in metaphor. A woman unhappy in love might liken herself to a bittern, and so might an invalid:

Me he hūroto au kei rō repo,
Me he kāka, e whakarāoa ana!

I am like a bittern in the swamp,
A bittern with its choking cry!

Bitterns were not much liked, and were not regularly eaten. When the male birds called to their mates in the spring, their booming cries were thought to be expressive of loneliness and unhappiness.

LEFT Pukeko were snared in their swamps, all the more so because they raided kumara and taro plantations.

Birds were employed in many rituals. The first one taken at the beginning of the season was ceremonially presented to Tane, who was both the birds' creator and the birds themselves. Some other birds had specialised roles, such as the fernbird (BOTTOM), which was regarded as sacred. Among Te Arawa and some neighbouring tribes, a fernbird was sacrificed at a tangihanga or funeral and at a ceremony that was performed when men returned empty-handed from battle. BELOW A tohunga seated at his tuahu, or shrine. He is communicating with a spirit thought to be temporarily present in the figure before him.

The evening and night were times associated with the expression of sorrow, so it must have seemed appropriate for the bitterns to be lamenting then. If their cries continued far into the night, this was thought to be a warning that floods were coming.

With its long, ungainly legs and striking plumage, the pukeko is common in swamps and marshes and along the banks of streams. These birds eat the soft parts of raupo and other plants, along with everything else they can find, and when there are crops growing nearby they set out early in the morning on raiding expeditions. This annoys people now, and it did so then. Maori gardeners spent much time and energy chasing pukeko away from their cultivations of kumara and taro, sometimes shouting as they did so a song telling them to go back to where they came from, that is, to their original ancestress:

> Hie, hie! Haere ki te hūhi, haere ki te repo,
> Haere ki a Hine-wairua-kokako! Hie, hie!

> Away, away! Go off to the swamp, go off to the bog,
> Go off to Hine-wairua-kokako! Away, away!

Though the birds could usually be kept out by building fences around the gardens, they were determined and cunning adversaries. A stubborn person might be said to have taringa pākura, 'the ears of a pukeko', someone who had gained much experience of life might be said to have become like a pukeko (kua pūkekotia), and one name for the bird itself was tangata tawhito, 'old man'.

Liking red things as much as they did, the Maori must have thought it remarkable that this objectionable bird should have such a large red bill and shield. One explanation was that while Maui was obtaining fire for mankind he caused a blaze that singed the pukeko's head. Another story dealt ingeniously with the incongruity by saying that the pukeko was the offspring of Punga, who was also the father of sharks, lizards and other enemies of mankind. This Punga was the uncle of Tawhaki, who was the archetypal figure of a handsome high chief and was associated with the colour red. When the pukeko was born, Tawhaki claimed him from Punga as an adopted son (being a close relative, he could do this); and since he had just cut his hand while adzing some wood, he marked the bird's forehead with his blood as a sign of their relationship. So the pukeko behaves badly, like all the sons of Punga, but he bears upon his brow the mark of the noble Tawhaki.

A smaller, secretive relative of the pukeko is the banded rail, also a swamp-dweller. Proverbially, this bird disappears with great speed when discovered (he pōpōtai numanga kino). In mythology its main claim to fame was that along with the fantail it was responsible for the death of Maui, when that hero went to conquer death in the person of Hine-nui-te-po, Great-woman-of-the-night. The birds' laughter woke the woman, and Maui's death set the pattern for mankind.

In swamps and some scrub lands, another bird that is usually well hidden is the small, speckled fernbird. This runs along the ground through reeds and manuka searching for insects and spiders, every now and then briefly darting up above its home then disappearing down again. Fernbirds were sacrificed in some ceremonies, and they were thought to be able to foretell the future. Their ordinary call of *te, te* was of no significance, but if a person heard one crying *kore tī, kore tī* he knew it was useless to continue with the task he was engaged in, for he would not succeed. When on the other hand the cry was *toro kī, toro kī,* he could be sure that all would be well.

The kingfisher, perched on its lookout, was seen as boldly and persistently waiting for its meal, and people could be likened to it:

He peo koe, he pītoto koe,
He pīnono koe, he piri noa —
He kōtare koe!

You come quickly, you sit begging,
You keep asking for it, you won't go away —
You're a kingfisher!

The kingfisher is proverbially patient as it awaits its moment.

Platforms projecting over the palisades of pa looked like the kingfisher's perch, so were sometimes called by the bird's name, *kōtare*. And there was a song that was sung by children when they had grown tired of the rain:

> *E rere, e te kōtare, ki runga ki te pūwharawhara,*
> *Ruru ai ō parirau! Ka mate koe i te ua!*
> *Tihore mai i uta, tihore mai i tai,*
> *He rangi ka maomao! Mao, mao, mao te ua!*

Kingfisher, fly up to the shore astelia
And there close your wings! You're unhappy in the rain!
Clear up over the land, clear up over the sea,
Let the sky stop raining, let it stop, stop, stop!

One would expect the kingfisher to mind the rain less than most land birds, and no doubt that is the point of the song. If rain is heavy enough to bother a kingfisher, it really is something to complain about.

With so many swamps, ducks were extremely numerous in many places, the commonest and most widely distributed species being the grey duck. Multitudes of men might be compared to flocks of grey ducks, a greedy eater was *he pārera apu paru*, 'a grey duck that gobbles up mud', a

Crested grebes (BELOW) are excellent swimmers and spend nearly all their time on the water. Both sexes have a tuft of feathers at the top of the head which they erect and display when they meet in mutual courtship. The Maori, whose high-ranking men bound their hair into topknots on important occasions, termed these crests *tikitiki*, 'topknots'.
BOTTOM Grey ducks were numerous in shallow water in nearly all parts of the country.

person who could not swim was *he pārera māunu,* 'a grey duck that's moulting', and when flintlock muskets made their appearance they became known because of their shape as *ngutu pārera,* 'duckbills'. Other kinds of ducks are seldom mentioned in the folklore, but in a pretty simile referring to ducks in general, the rapid quivering of women's hands in the dance was said to be *me te paihau turuki,* 'like the wings of fledgling ducks'.

In some inland lakes there were crested grebes, handsome, uncommon birds rather larger than ducks which spend nearly all their lives on the water and are very good divers, able to stay down for a long time. Though the Maori knew their habits well, including the fact that they nest on vegetation floating on the water, in the Taupo district they believed that grebes with special powers, with not one but two crests or 'topknots' upon their heads, lived in beautiful Roto Pounamu, or Greenstone Lake, upon the north-west slopes of Mount Pihanga. These wonderful birds used to dive right down to the lake bed, and there lay their eggs and rear their young.

The rapid quivering of dancers' hands was likened to the fluttering wings of young ducks. A ceremonial dance at a festival at Hokianga in 1834.

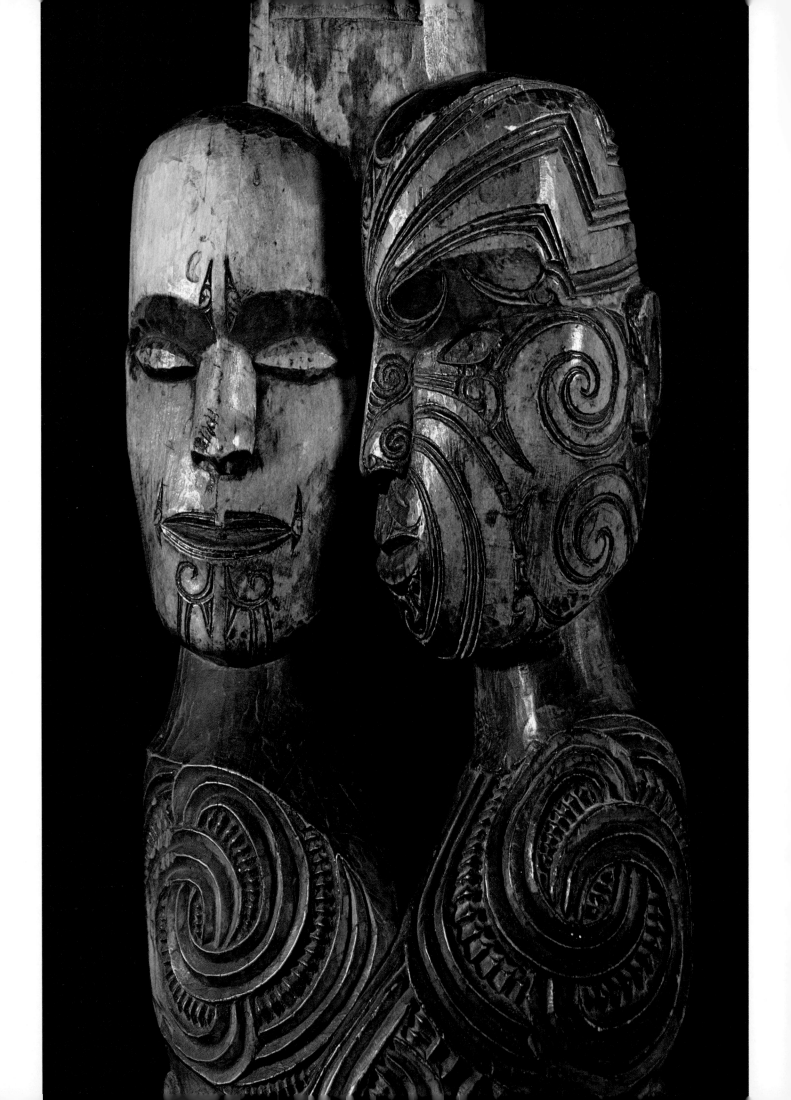

Epilogue

In modern, western society we speak of nature and the natural world and we contrast this, at least by implication, with culture, by which we mean human activities and thought. In traditional times the Maori did not think in these terms, for they did not see their existence as something separate and opposed to the world around them. Birds, fish, insects and plants, also natural phenomena such as the moon, mist, wind and rocks, were felt to possess a life essentially similar to that of human beings. And all forms of life were related, for all were descended from Rangi, the sky, and Papa, the earth. Men's relationship to other living things, and to the world itself, was expressed and explained in the form of a whakapapa, a genealogy.

The early history of the world, which is recounted in the myths, established the natural and proper behaviour, the *tikanga*, of all these beings: the pattern was set in the beginning, and they behave now as their ancestors did then. This word *tikanga* is used in speaking of the characteristic behaviour of natural phenomena, plants and animals, and it is also a term for human nature and human custom. All *tikanga* have a common origin in history, in the first ancestors and the relations between them.

Since these ancestors and their descendants are bound by the indissoluble ties of kinship, there is an underlying harmony in the world. Inevitably, though, there is conflict as well, and the myths explain the reasons for this. The wind and the rain batter the earth because in the beginning the wind, Tawhirimatea, was angry with his brothers for having agreed to the separation of Rangi and Papa; he attacked them from the sky, and he does so still. Men going out fishing on the ocean are siding with their creator, Tane, in his ancient quarrel with Tangaroa, which began when the reptiles and the fish disagreed as to the best place to hide from Tawhirimatea. And when human beings kill birds or fish, dig up plants or cut down trees, they are enacting the role of another mythical brother, Tu. This brother represents mankind, and is a warrior.

In the great fight with Tawhirimatea, Tu is the only one who stands firm. Then afterwards he turns and attacks his brothers upon the earth: he snares birds and cuts down trees, destroying Tane; he catches fish, which are Tangaroa; and he digs up fernroot, which is Haumia, and kumara, which are Rongo. Tu finds a justification for this slaughter in his brothers' having failed to help him in his struggle with Tawhirimatea, and he also tells himself, in the oldest of excuses, that his brothers' progeny are becoming too numerous, and that they might attack him if he does not act first. But really he kills his elder brothers because his circumstances give him no choice. The name Tu means literally Upright, or Standing. As men must do, he asserts himself strongly, winning a place for himself in the world. And because Tu set the pattern in the beginning by subduing the birds, fish and plants, destroying their tapu, human beings can now do likewise. When the proper rituals are performed, people can safely take the lives of these elder relatives, acquiring from them the food and materials they need for their survival.

Tu fights with the natural world. But three of these earliest ancestors have a dual aspect: they are part of nature, and at the same time they provide patterns of behaviour to be followed by their human descendants. Rangi, or Sky, is the model for all men in that he possesses the high status and tapu associated with human males, as opposed to females. Papa, or Foundation, is the model for human females, for she is noa, or profane, of lower status, yet a dearly loved mother who nurtures and sustains her children. And Tane, the ancestor who makes the world by separating these parents and who then fathers the birds, plants and humans, is a second figure with whom men are identified, for his name means Male and his life-giving potency is a power that was thought to belong exclusively to males. So in the myths the main characteristics of human beings are established and represented by the sky, the earth, and the fertility of the living things upon the earth.

The ancestors who follow are men and women, people such as Maui, Hinauri and Tawhaki who have adventures which determine the human condition and provide models for human behaviour in more specialised ways. Most of their archetypal exploits take place in Hawaiki, the mythical land of origin. They in their turn are followed by ancestors who make the voyage from Hawaiki to Aotearoa, preparing the way for human beings and founding tribes. Gradually the names in the whakapapa become legendary rather than mythical, and finally we are in the realms of ascertainable history. But to the owners of the whakapapa, all was history. The nature of existence had been determined in the remote past, by the earliest ancestors. Tribal and personal identity had been established by the more recent ancestors, many of whom, as atua, or spirits, now watched over their descendants, assisting and sometimes punishing them.

Maori thought and mythology were centrally concerned with the human situation and human experience, as all systems of thought have necessarily been, but in their thought, as in their way of life, a balance was maintained between human beings and the environment. Their closeness to nature and the immediacy of their dependence upon it, their intimate and profound knowledge of plants, animals and landscape, led to a view of the world which recognised the tapu, the sacredness, of other life forms and the landscape itself. By seeing themselves in the natural world and thus personifying all aspects of the environment, they acquired a fellow-feeling for the life forms and other entities that surrounded them, and they saw a kinship between all things. Their thinking was ingenious and subtle, and quite often it followed a logic that is familiar to us; for example, certain life forms which appeared to be related, such as the flax and the kiekie plants, were said to have once lived together but then to have chosen different homes, so that the flax now lives in swamps and the kiekie grows in trees. But because they had no modern scientific knowledge, the Maori were free to project human presences and values on to the world. Thought and feeling were one. Their poets drew confidently upon a rich store of shared imagery and ideas; and while there was a term for 'ritual', *karakia*, no words were needed to distinguish 'science' from 'religion'.

Though Maori thought and imagery were shaped by ideas brought here from tropical Polynesia and also very much by the conditions existing in this country, they were generally similar to those of other traditional peoples. Even in countries with monotheistic religions, even in Europe, ancient patterns of thought gave way fairly slowly and in piecemeal fashion until the late seventeenth century, when the pace of change quickened with the evolution of modern science and technology. It is more difficult for us now, despite all the information that we have, to understand that everything is related, and that if we fail to show respect for our mother the earth, we do so at our peril. It is more difficult to feel at home in the world, and to feel in the landscape the continuity of human experience. In post-colonial countries this is especially a problem for people of European descent, for they have suffered a most abrupt break with the traditions of the past. But everywhere a realisation of the interconnectedness and the sacredness of things is more important for our survival than it has ever been. While we cannot go back, we can learn from those who were here before us.

Notes

There is a vast literature on traditional Maori poetry, mythology, religion and history. The references given below are in many cases far from comprehensive.

Subjects are listed below alongside the numbers of the pages on which they are discussed; quotations are identified by their first words. In each case there is a reference to the source of information. For example, for the origins of the Maori (discussed on page 5), the source is 'Bellwood 1978:45-65'. This refers to pages 45-65 of a book by Peter Bellwood which was published in 1978. Information about this book is in the list of references, arranged alphabetically under the names of authors, which starts on page 223.

CHAPTER ONE   LAND AND PEOPLE

5   The origins of the Maori: Bellwood 1978:45-65.
5   Iro, in Mangaia: Gill 1894:130-42.

ENVIRONMENTAL CHALLENGE

7   The first centuries: Bellwood 1978:130-45; Davidson 1981; Prickett 1982.
11   Horticulture: Green 1974; Davidson 1981; Bellwood 1978:48-59; Prickett 1982; Lenski and Lenski 1974:185-97.
13   Motuopuhi: Angas 1847a: plate VIII.
14   War party near Kororareka: Earle 1838.

CHAPTER TWO   WAYS AND MEANS

HUNTING AND FISHING

21   Birds: Best 1909; Best 1942:137-416.
21   *Kāhore he tārainga:* Grey 1857:35.
24   Taking kaka: Ranapiri 1895: 135-7, 146-7.
26   Kiore: Best 1942:416-56.
28   *Tāne rou kākahi:* Grey 1857:82.
28   Fish and eels: Best 1929.
29   School sharks: Matthews 1910; Keene 1963:32.

FOOD PLANTS

33   Yam: Best 1925:120-2.
33   Taro: Best 1925:123-8; Colenso 1880:14-5.
34   Gourd: Best 1925:129-34; Colenso 1880:15-6.
35   *Ko te wā tonu ia:* Ngata and Te Hurinui 1961:240.
37   Kumara: Best 1925:47-119; Colenso 1880:7-14.
38   Fernroot: Best 1942:85-105; Best 1902:49-53; Colenso 1880:20-5; Taylor 1870:495; Williams 1971: pitopito; Shawcross 1967.
39   Kumarahou: Brooker, Cambie and Cooper 1981: 84.
40   Other food plants: Best 1942; Best 1902; Colenso 1880; Te Rangi Hiroa 1950:85
40   *He toa piki rākau:* Best 1952:195.
41   Cabbage tree: Best 1925a:135-44.
43   *Ka katokato [au]:* Grey 1857:36. Compare Colenso 1880:27.

CLOTHES AND ORNAMENTS

44   Paper mulberry: Colenso 1880:18; Best 1899:626.
44   Garments of flax: Colenso 1879; Best 1899; Best 1908:231-4; Best 1924:II, 503-31; Mead 1969. The account of the evolution of weaving techniques is derived from Te Rangi Hiroa 1950:144-78. Some other techniques were used in some areas, especially in the far south.
47   Kiekie and other materials: Best 1907:213, 227, 231.
48   Maurea: Best 1899:648.
48   Tying of cloaks: Thomson 1859:I, 205; Best 1924:II, 508; Makereti 1938:71.
49   Women's dress: Reed and Reed 1969:143.
49   *Kia hei taku ate:* Orbell 1978:20.
49   Girdles in Marlborough Sounds: Mead 1969:64. Like Mead, I assume these kaka feathers were red ones.
50   Personal adornment: Best 1924:I, 532-57; Best 1899:654-5; Angas 1847:I, 244, 321-8.

WOODWORKING

52 Greenstone: Brailsford 1984; Chapman 1891.
54 Houses: Best 1924:II, 558-91; Davidson 1981:9.
60 *He whare maihi:* Williams 1971: maihi.
61 Like a seagull: Proverbial expression used of canoes —
me te remu karoro, 'like the tail of a black-backed gull'.
Best 1924:II, 591.

CHAPTER THREE   THE WORLD OF LIGHT

65 Rangi and Papa: Grey 1956:1-11; Taylor 1870:118-24.

THE SACRED SKY

67 *E te hihi o te rā:* McGregor 1898:21.
67 Hawaiki: Orbell 1975.
68 Tane and Hine-titama: Best 1924:I, 114-20.
68 *Tātai whetū:* Cowan 1930:112.
69 Mackerel sky: Elder 1934:138; Williams 1971: māra.
69 Meteor: Elder 1934:77; Polack 1840:I, 273.
69 Stars: Best 1955; Best 1924:II, 206-16; Best 1899a:105-12.
69 Left eye a star: Elder 1934:77; Polack 1838:II, 71.
69 *Kua whetūrangitia koe:* personal communication from Mr Te Waaka Melbourne.
71 *Tirohia atu nei:* Orbell 1978:78.
71 *Me i penei te mate:* Orbell 1978:54-5. Compare Grey 1857:20 and Taylor 1870:54.
72 Moon is husband: Best 1924:I, 134.
72 Rona: Orbell 1968:18-9.
72 Tawhaki: White 1887-90:I, 55-67; Grey 1956:46-61; McLean and Orbell 1975:28.

THE EARTH AND ITS WEATHER

72 *He wahine, he whenua:* Best 1902a:127.
74 *Ka puta koe:* Orbell 1978:64-5.
74 The earth's seasons: Grey 1857:71, 69, 26; Williams 1971: kōrehu.
75 *Tēnei ka noho:* McLean and Orbell 1975:143.
75 If a man's wife: Best 1924:I, 467.
76 *Ka tōkia tō kiri:* Orbell 1978:46-7.
76 Brightly glowing sunset: White 1885:179.
77 Waterspout, rainbow: Polack 1840:I, 273.
77 Rainbow: Grey 1857:25, 52.

THE UNDERWORLD

78 An early missionary: Simmons 1973:47-8.
78 *Takoto rawa iho:* Ngata 1959:226.
78 Te Reinga: Best 1905:232-6; Best 1924:II, 30; Simmons 1973:48-9; Oppenheim 1973:93-100; Taylor 1855:97-106; White 1885:117-9.

80 *Ka eke ki runga ra:* Ngata and Te Hurinui 1970:120; Paerau is another name for Te Reinga.
81 *E hopu tō ringa:* Orbell 1978:36-7. This is a song from the Lake Rotoehu district.
81 *Whakaū:* Polack 1838:I, 245; Taylor 1855:104; Williams 1971: ū. This term apparently has the same meaning as *uruuru-whenua.*
82 *E tae ki Te Rerenga:* Orbell 1978:36-7.
83 *Tirohia iho ra:* Ngata and Te Hurinui 1961:230.

THE HIGH PLACES

84 Mount Tarawera: Taylor 1855:248.
85 Putauaki: Mair 1923:78; Cowan 1926:I, 195.
85 Two battles in Taranaki: Smith 1910:138.
86 Maungaroa: Pomare and Cowan 1930-4:I, 226-7.
86 *Terā te uira:* Ngata 1959:14.
87 Tu-whakairi-ora: Turei 1911:29.
87 Mount Taupiri: Hamlin 1842:259.
87 Mount Hikurangi: Johansen 1958:31-2; Polack 1840:I, 234-5; Cowan 1910:57.
89 Moa: Best 1942:225-35.
89 *Kia tū tonu au:* McGregor 1893:20. This song apparently belongs to Ngati Ira, a branch of Ngati Porou in whose speech *n* substitutes for *ng.* Information from Arapeta Awatere, 1974.
89 Dieffenbach on Taranaki: Dieffenbach 1843:I, 155-6.
89 Tongariro: Taylor 1870:451-2; Cowan 1927:25-7, 106-9; Te Hata 1917:180.
90 *E hōmai ana koe:* Grey 1853:201.
91 Kuha-tarewa and Tuhi-o-Kahu: Best 1899a:117.
92 Te Heuheu's meeting: Smith 1920:60-1.
92 Patupaiarehe: Orbell 1982.
95 Pa seen by Banks: Beaglehole 1963:I, 432.
95 *Taku taumata tonu:* Ngata and Te Hurinui 1961:136-7.

CHAPTER FOUR   SHAPING THE LAND

99 Maui: Grey 1956:12-44; Taylor 1855:23-31. For South Island traditions, Pomare and Cowan 1930-4:I, 41.
101 Kupe: Orbell 1977; for Kupe at Waikaremoana, Best 1897: 93-4.

THE ANCESTRAL CANOES

101 Toi: For Toi as Maui's descendant, Gudgeon 1893. For his uncultivated plant foods and lack of fire, see Best 1942:91; Tarakawa 1893:250; St John 1892.
103 *E tama mā e!:* Orbell 1978:18-9.
104 Tumutumu-whenua, or sometimes Tuputupu-whenua: White 1880:15, 16.
104 Hawaiki: Orbell 1975.
104 Rainbow: Beattie 1940:47.
104 Back of albatross: White 1885:113.

104 Tarawhata: Tarakawa 1911a.
104 Manawa-tere: Graham 1921.
104 Wairakewa: Tarakawa 1894:61, 67.
104 Paikea: Fowler 1974:15-7.
104 Ancestors who came on calabashes: Fowler 1974:22-3;
    Taylor 1870:254-5.
105 Te Arawa: Grey 1956:109-27; Tarakawa 1893.
105 *Eke, eke:* Grey 1928:63 (though in this version, they are
    not quite the last words). The exact meaning of the last
    line is uncertain; the translation given follows Te Rangi
    Hiroa (1950:47), and conveys its general significance.
    The use made of the chant in oratory was explained to
    the writer in 1973 by Arapeta Awatere.
106 *Nguaha te kakau:* Part of a karakia in Cowan 1910:54-5.
    See also Tautahi 1900:205. I take it that *nguaha* is
    another form of *nguha*. But another version (Houston
    1965:200) has *uaha*, which may perhaps be another form
    of *uakaha*, 'be vigorous, strenuous'.
106 Hauling the Tainui: White 1880:5-6; Orbell 1975:346.
107 Canoes turned to stone: For Aotea, see Hammond
    1924:143; for Takitimu, Beattie 1915:109; for Mamari,
    Andersen 1946:51 and White 1885:107-8.
109 Araiteuru: Andersen 1942:128-41; Beattie 1957:25-7;
    Beattie 1941:37-9.
109 Te Punga o Tainui: Cowan 1930: 180-1; Te Rangi
    Hiroa 1950: 52.

THINGS BROUGHT FROM HAWAIKI

112 Whetstone: Best 1912:107.
112 Greenstone: Grey 1956:106-8; Best 1912:195-219.
    Fishing for greenstone: Best 1912:215; Reed and Reed
    1969:238; Polack 1838:I, 345. Greenstone travelling
    along waterways: Te Hurinui 1960:16.
113 Kakau-matua: Fletcher 1913.
115 Te Awhio-rangi: Best 1912:240-5.
115 Mangarara canoe: Turei 1876; White 1887-90:II,
    189-93. Some writers have misread this account, taking
    Wheketoro to be an octopus. In fact he is said to be a
    man and an ancestor.
115 Whakaotirangi: Mair 1923:53; Te Rangi Hiroa
    1950:61-2.
116 Pourangahua: Best 1925:I, 918-24.
116 Horouta canoe: Johansen 1958:112-24. The existence of
    this ritual is established in Johansen's masterly analysis
    of this myth and other evidence.
118 Ngatoro-i-rangi: Te Hata 1916; Kerry-Nicholls
    1884:181-3; Cowan 1927:25-7. For Tama-o-hoi, see
    Cowan 1930:146-8. Sometimes Ngatoro-i-rangi's sisters
    start from Whakaari (White Island), rather than
    Hawaiki; sometimes they send two burrowing taniwha
    with the fire; and sometimes it is his wife who comes.

THE EXPLORERS

122 Rakataura: Pomare and Cowan 1930-4:I, 43-7.
122 Paoa: Kapiti 1912:160; Large 1923; Fowler 1974:24;
    Ngata 1959:102-3; Gudgeon 1892.
123 Taramainuku: White 1940:193-4; Pomare and Cowan
    1930-4:I, 119; Best 1925:I, 383, 839. Other information
    given by Arapeta Awatere in 1974.
123 Tamatea: Diamond and Hayward 1979:32; Cowan and
    Hongi 1908:105; Beattie 1915:109-10; Beattie 1940:77,
    113; Best 1917:147; McLean and Orbell 1975:264-5.
125 Rakaihaitu: Beattie 1915:104-7; Beattie 1918:79-85.

THE BURROWING TANIWHA

126 Te Whanga-nui-a-Tara: Best 1917:147.
126 Hokianga: White 1874:1-3.
126 Waikaremoana: Best 1925:I, 190-1, 978-80.
127 Kaiwhare: Frost 1947:56-9. For a version where he is
    killed by a man named Hakawau, see Diamond and
    Hayward 1979:22-3.

MOUNTAINS THAT MOVED ABOUT

129 Mountains in the centre: Best 1925:I, 982-5; Best
    1899a:118-9; Cowan 1927:106-8, 112-3.
130 Kakepuku: Cowan 1910:207-8.
130 Manaia: Cowan 1910:208-9; Smith 1897:62-3; White
    1885:138.; Keene 1963: 159-68.
131 Rangitoto: Diamond and Hayward 1979:37.

CHAPTER FIVE THE REALM OF TANGAROA

135 Symbolism in love poetry: Orbell 1983.
135 *Ka ngaro hoki ra:* Orbell 1978:44.
137 Rua-te-pupuke: Best 1928.
137 Hinauri (sometimes known as Hine-te-iwaiwa): Grey
    1956:62-8; Best 1929:86-7.
137 *Haere mai ki uta:* McGregor 1893:103.
137 *Kua riro te whenua:* Ngata and Sutherland 1940:346.
137 *I nāianei kua hā:* Houston 1965:206.
137 Te Parata: White 1885:119.
138 *Haere ra, e tama e!* Best 1902:131.
138 *Kāti te tangi:* Best 1905:226.
138 *Ka pū te ruha:* Williams 1971: ruha.

CREATURES OF THE SEA

141 Ngahue: Grey 1956:106-8.
142 *He maroro kokoti:* Williams 1971: maroro.
142 *Tē ai he mahara:* Ngata 1959:48.
142 *Kia mate ururoa:* McGregor 1898:62.
142 *A, me he kawenga pioke te pīkau ana i te ākau ki Ōhope:*
    Ngata and Te Hurinui 1970:102.
142 Ropata Wahawaha: Best 1902:130.

143 *Anā tā te uaua:* Grey 1857:1.
143 *He rei ngā niho:* Grey 1857:26.
143 *I muri o te tira:* Grey 1857:104.
144 Mauri at Te Mahia: Fowler 1974:14-5.
145 White whale: Personal communication from Ms Moyra Johnston, 1960.
146 *Ka whano nei au:* McGregor 1893:36.
146 *He honu manawa-rahi:* Grey 1853: xcix.
146 *Ngā tama korowhiti:* Williams 1971: korowhiti.
146 *He aua:* Williams 1971: aua.
147 The eel has slipped: *Kua kaheko te tuna i roto i aku ringaringa.* Grey 1857.63.
147 *He ika paewai:* Williams 1971: paewai.
147 *Whano ake:* Orbell 1978:24.
147 *Etia me te wheke:* Grey 1857:7
147 *Me te waha kahawai:* Grey 1857:72.
147 *Me te ihe:* Grey 1857:70.
147 *He rarī-kai-pō:* Williams 1971:rarī.
147 Mackerel: Williams 1971:tawatawa.
147 Cockle shell: Grey 1857:71, 69.
147 Trevally: Grey 1857:69.
147 Paua: Grey 1853:289.
147 Crayfish: Grey 1857:18, 86.
148 *E hoki te pātiki:* Grey 1857:4.
148 *Me he kōrinorino:* Grey 1857:68.

BIRDS OF THE SEA AND SHORE

148 Hurumanu: Best 1982:263-4.
148 Battle of the birds: Best 1982:561-2
149 Shag guardians: Phillipps 1963.
149 *E kore te kawau:* Williams 1971: kawau.
149 *Me he kawau ka tuku:* Best 1923a:20.
149 *Ka mārō te kakī:* Williams 1971:mārō.
149 *He kawau mārō:* Williams 1971:kawau.
149 Houmea: Orbell 1968:xiv-xvii, 64-71.
150 *He karoro inu tai:* Williams 1971:karoro.
150 Gull a bad omen: Best 1902:61.
150 *Tangi amio ana:* McGregor 1898:30. Compare McGregor 1898:77.
150 Kai karoro: For example, Elvy 1949:49.
150 Mokoia Island: Pomare and Cowan 1930-4:I, 241-6.
152 *Ko wai rawa:* McGregor 1898:47.
153 Who can tell of the nest: Taylor 1907:93 (Maori text not given).
153 *Rārangi noa ra:* Davis 1855:178.
154 *He tītī hua tahi:* Grey 1857:91.
154 *He tītī kainga tahi:* Grey 1857:91.
154 *He manawa tītī:* Williams 1971:tītī.
154 *He pōkai tara:* Williams 1971: pōkai.
154 *He tāhuna-ā-tara:* Williams 1971: tāhuna.
154 *Taku pōhoi toroa:* Ngata and Te Hurinui 1961:226.

155 *Waiho kia whana atu:* Davis 1855:198.
155 *Me he toroa ngungunu:* Grey 1857:69.
155 *Ka pā te muri:* Williams 1971: toroa.
157 *Taku hau amokura:* McGregor 1898:55.

REPTILES

157 Lizards and tuatara: Best 1923; Best 1908:235-8; Downes 1937; Tarakawa 1911.
159 Ngarara Nui: Phillipps 1958:27.
159 Lizard chest in museum: Cheeseman 1906.
159 Te Rehu o Tainui: Best 1897.
161 Tuatara and gurnard: Taylor 1870:303.
162 Ngaiterangi and gurnard: Puata 1919:14
163 The woman and the ngarara: Orbell 1968:38-45.

CHAPTER SIX   THE CHILDREN OF TANE

167 Tane: Best 1907:189-9, 247-9; White 1887-90:I, 158-9.
169 Rata: Best 1907:197, 250; White 1887-90:I, 68-80.

PLANTS AND PEOPLE

169 Hinau: Tregear 1926:40.
169 Pohutukawa: Pomare and Cowan 1930-4:I, 89.
169 *Ka ū ki Mata-nuku:* Best 1907:192-4; Taylor 1870:170-1.
170 Plants worn in mourning: White 1874:207-8; Davis 1876:124; Keene 1963: 176-9
170 *Rākau rangatira:* Best 1907:218; Best 1942:130.
170 *He tangata māmore:* Williams 1971: māmore.
170 *He kōkōmuka:* Williams 1971: kōkōmuka.
171 *Kei whea ko te tau:* Ngata 1959:240.
172 *Ehara i te tangata:* McLean and Orbell 1975:158.
173 *He iti hoki te mokoroa:* Grey 1857:18.
173 Pourangahua: Best 1925:I, 919-31.
174 Kauri: Taylor 1870:303.
174 Rata: Best 1907:222; Grey 1857:49, 74; Colenso 1879:124.
174 Pohutukawa: Best 1907:222; White 1880:11.
175 Maire: Colenso 1879:140; McLean and Orbell 1975:300.
175 Kanuka: Taylor 1870:298.
175 Pukatea and kohekohe: Kohere 1951:40; Grey 1857:89; Colenso 1879:138.
175 *Nāu i eke atu:* Ngata and Te Hurinui 1970:414-5.
175 Pikirangi, or pikiraki: Beattie 1920:72
176 Spiders: Taylor 1870:294, 641.
176 Stick insect and praying mantis: Miller 1970:53.
176 *Wētā Punga* (perhaps *wētā [a] Punga*): Williams 1971: wētā.
176 *Ka whati te tī:* Best 1942:106. Compare Grey 1857:3.
176 *E hine kaitu:* Davis 1855:177-8.
177 *I whea koe:* Grey 1857:34-5; Colenso 1879:117; Taylor 1870:297.
177 Rewarewa: Orbell 1968:46-51.

177 Whau and paper mulberry: Taylor 1870:305.
178 Rangiora and kawakawa: Grey 1857:70; Cowan 1922-3:I, 382.
179 *He aha te tohu:* Andersen 1946:14, 65-6.
179 Mamaku: McLean and Orbell 1975:264. Compare Ngata and Te Hurinui 1961:250.
179 *Ko te rite i aku kamo:* Cowan 1930:94.
179 Obstructing plants: Orbell 1977:129; Beattie 1940:62-3; Wohlers 1876:110-3.
180 *E kore koe e tata mai:* Grey 1857:5.
180 *Te heke tātarāmoa:* Smith 1910:129.

BIRDS AND PEOPLE

181 Birds as spirits: Polack 1838:I, 147-8; II, 262; Polack 1840:I, 235-6; McLean and Orbell 1975:74 (for tūāhu).
181 *Kia kōrero koe:* Ngata and Te Hurinui 1970:358.
182 Kite: Pio 1910.
183 *He manu hoki koā:* Ngata and Te Hurinui 1961:272.
183 *Taku manu whakaoho:* Grey 1853:407.
184 *Kīkī-ā-manu:* Orbell 1978:66-7.
184 *Amio noa ana:* Chapman MS (no page number). The writer is indebted to the Librarian of the Hocken Library, Dunedin, for permission to publish this passage.
184 Silvereye: Williams 1971: kanohi.

BIRDS OF THE FOREST

185 Pigeon: White 1887-90:II, 96; Grey 1857:59, 68; Yate 1970:91.
187 *He kākā waha nui:* Grey 1857:14-5; Best 1942:238-41.
187 *He kūkū ki te kāinga:* Grey 1857:19; Colenso 1879:129.
188 Kakariki: Best 1942:373-7.
188 Kakapo: Grey 1857:70.
189 Kiwi: Best 1942:205-7; Williams 1971: kiwi.
190 *Tuku atu au:* Best 1903:155.
191 Weka: Best 1942:216.
191 Tui: Grey 1857:68; Best 1942:338-73.
193 Bellbird: Best 1942:377-8; Taylor 1870: 185.
194 Stitchbird: White 1887-90:II, 120.
194 Huia: Best 1942:221-5; Yate 1970:61; Phillipps 1963a; Taylor 1855:401.
196 *He huia tū rae:* Ngata and Te Hurinui 1961:254.
196 *Te huia kai-manawa:* Williams 1971: huia.
196 Ngutu-huia: Williams 1971: ngutu.
196 Kokako: White 1887-90:II, 120; Best 1942:379. The South Island kokako had orange wattles. It is now extinct.
197 Saddleback: White 1885:133.
197 Two birds brought by Mataatua (some say they came on Te Arawa): Best 1908:282; Tarakawa 1893:235.
197 *Me te mea i houhoua:* Grey 1857:71.
197 *Ka mahi koe te whare o te tieke:* Grey 1857:37.
197 *Me he wai tā tieke:* Kohere 1951: preface, 37.
197 Fantail: Polack 1838:II, 82; Best 1942:389; White 1887-90:II, 107.

198 Tomtit: Williams 1971: hōmiromiro; Grey 1857:66, 81; Best 1942:386-7; Best 1924:I, 280.
199 Grey warbler: Best 1942:388-9.
199 Robin: Best 1942:382; Gudgeon 1905:66.
200 *He upoko kākā:* Best 1902:147-8.
200 Cuckoos: Grey 1857:44, 80; Best 1942:396-9.
200 *He pōtiki na te koekoeā:* Grey 1857:25.
200 *Ko te uri au:* Williams 1971: whēnakonako.
200 *Tangi te kawekawea:* Orbell 1978:76-7.
201 Owls: Best 1908:281; Schwimmer 1963; Phillipps 1963; Yate 1970:90.
202 *Tangi e te ruru:* Ngata 1959:298-9.
203 *Kei te ruru koukou:* McGregor 1893:37.
203 *Etia anō aku mata:* McGregor 1898:73.
203 Kou-ruru: Best 1942:391.
203 *Mata-ā-ruru:* Williams 1971: mata.
203 *Me te pari hakoke:* Best 1942:393.

BIRDS OF THE OPEN COUNTRY

203 Falcon and hawk: Grey 1857:32; Yate 1970:91; Best 942:393-6; McLean and Orbell 1975:172.   1
205 *Te kāhu i runga:* Ruatapu and Potae MS 1876:II, 59. The writer is indebted to the Librarian of the Alexander Turnbull Library, Wellington, for permission to publish this song.
206 *Whiti koreke:* Grey 1857:96.

BIRDS OF THE WATERWAYS AND WETLANDS

208 White heron: Best 1942:402-3; Cowan 1930a:156.
208 When a man dreamt: Tregear 1926:40.
208 *Ngā kōtuku awe-nui:* McGregor 1898:78.
209 *He kōtuku kai whakaata:* Grey 1857:19; Colenso 1879:129.
209 *Me he hūroto au:* Ngata 1959:72.
210 *Hie, hie!:* Best 1942:234-5. The Mataatua people, whose song this is, believed that both the pukeko and the kokako were descended from Hine-wairua-kokako.
210 *Taringa pākura:* Williams 1971: pākura.
210 *Kua pūkekotia:* Williams 1971: pūkeko.
210 *Tangata tawhito:* Williams 1971: tawhito.
210 Origin of the pukeko: Best 1942:235.
210 *He pōpōtai:* Grey 1857:25.
211 Fernbird: Best 1942:176, 387.
211 *He peo koe:* Grey 1857:24.
212 *E rere, e te kōtare:* Grey 1853:29.
212 *He pārera apu paru:* Grey 1857:24.
213 *He pārera māunu:* Williams 1971: māunu.
213 *Me te paihau turuki:* Grey 1857:71.
213 Crested grebe: Best 1942:404; Williams 1971: manapou.

EPILOGUE

215 The word *tikanga:* Johansen 1954:172-6.
217 Flax and kiekie: Best 1907:213.

References

These books and articles are referred to in the Notes. Works which provide a substantial amount of further information about subjects discussed in this book are marked with asterisks. The following abbreviations are used:

JPS Journal of the Polynesian Society
TPNZI Transactions and Proceedings of the New Zealand Institute

Andersen, Johannes C. 1942. *Maori place-names* Wellington.

_____ 1946. *Polynesian literature: Maori poetry* New Plymouth.

Angas, G.F. 1847. *Savage life and scenes in Australia and New Zealand* 2 vols. London.

_____ 1847a. *The New Zealanders Illustrated* London.

Beaglehole, J.C. 1963. *The Endeavour journal of Joseph Banks, 1768-1771* 2nd ed. Sydney.

Beattie, J. Herries. 1915. 'Traditions and legends collected from the natives of Murihiku (Southland, New Zealand)' Part 1. *JPS* 24:98-112.

_____ 1918. 'Traditions and legends collected from the natives of Murihiku . . .' Part 8. *JPS* 27:137-61.

*_____ 1920. 'Nature-lore of the southern Maori' *TPNZI* 52:53-77.

_____ 1940. *Tikao talks* Dunedin.

_____ 1941. *Moriori; the Morioris of the South Island . . .* Dunedin.

_____ (ed.) 1957. *Folklore and fairy tales of the Canterbury Maoris: told by Taare Te Maiharoa . . .* Dunedin.

* Bellwood, Peter. 1978. *The Polynesians: prehistory of an island people* London.

Best, Elsdon. 1897. *Waikare-moana . . .* Wellington.

*_____ 1897a. 'Te Rehu o Tainui' *JPS* 6:41-66.

*_____ 1899. 'The art of the whare pora: notes on the clothing of the ancient Maori . . .' *TPNZI* 31:625-58.

_____ 1899a. 'Notes on Maori mythology' *JPS* 8:93-121.

*_____ 1902. 'Food-products of Tuhoeland . . .' *TPNZI* 35:45-111.

_____ 1902a. 'Notes on the art of war . . .' Parts 1-4. *JPS* 11:11-41, 47-75, 127-62, 219-46.

_____ 1903. 'Notes on the art of war . . .' Parts 5-8. *JPS* 12:32-50, 65-84, 145-65, 193-217.

_____ 1905. 'Maori eschatology . . .' *TPNZI* 38:148-239.

*_____ 1907. 'Maori forest lore . . . of the Tuhoe or Urewera district' Part I. *TPNZI* 40:185-254.

*_____ 1908. 'Maori forest lore . . .' Part II. *TPNZI* 41:231-85.

*_____ 1909. 'Maori forest lore . . .' Part III. *TPNZI* 42:433-81.

_____ 1912. *The stone implements of the Maori* Wellington.

_____ 1917. 'The land of Tara . . .' Part 1. *JPS* 26:143-69.

*_____ 1923. 'Notes on the occurrence of the lizard in Maori carvings' *Journal of science and technology* 5:321-35.

_____ 1923a. 'The origin of the Maori' *JPS* 32:10-20.

*_____ 1924. *The Maori* 2 vols. Wellington.

_____ 1925. *Tuhoe: the children of the mist* 2 vols. New Plymouth.

*_____ 1925a. *Maori agriculture* Wellington.

_____ 1928. 'The story of Rua and Tangaroa' *JPS* 37:257-60.

*_____ 1929. *Fishing methods and devices of the Maori* Wellington.

*_____ 1942. *Forest lore of the Maori* Wellington.

_____ 1952. *The Maori as he was* Wellington. (First pub. 1924)

*_____ 1955. *The astronomical knowledge of the Maori* Wellington. (First pub. 1922)

_____ 1982. *Maori religion and mythology . . .* Part 2. Wellington.

*Brailsford, Barry. 1984. *Greenstone trails: the Maori search for pounamu* Wellington.

*Brooker, S.G., R.C. Cambie and R.C. Cooper. 1981. *New Zealand medicinal plants* Auckland.

Chapman, F.R. MS. Song texts written down in 1890s at Waikouaiti. MS1 416A. In Hocken Library, Dunedin.

*_____ 1891. 'On the working of greenstone . . .' *TPNZI* 24:479-539.

Cheeseman, T.F. 1906. 'Notes on certain Maori carved burial-chests in the Auckland Museum' *TPNZI* 39:451-56.

Colenso, William. 1879. 'Contributions towards a better knowledge of the Maori race' Part II. *TPNZI* 12:108-47.

*_____ 1880. 'On the vegetable food of the ancient New Zealanders before Cook's visit' *TPNZI* 13:3-38.

*Cowan, James. 1910. *The Maoris of New Zealand* Christchurch.

_____ 1922-3. *The New Zealand wars . . .* 2 vols. Wellington.

_____ 1926. *Travel in New Zealand* 2 vols. Christchurch.

_____ 1927. *The Tongariro National Park* Wellington.

*_____ 1930. *The Maori yesterday and today* Auckland.

_____ 1930a. *Fairy folk tales of the Maori* 2nd ed. Christchurch.

_____ and Hare Hongi. 1908. 'The story of the "Takitimu" canoe' Part 2. *JPS* 17:93-107.

*Davidson, Janet M. 1981. 'The Polynesian foundation' in Oliver, W.H. and Williams, B.R. (eds.), *The Oxford history of New Zealand* Oxford and Wellington. pp. 3-27.

Davis, C.O.B. 1855. *Maori mementos* Auckland.

_____ 1876. *The life and times of Patuone* . . . Auckland.

Diamond, John T. and Bruce W. Hayward. 1979. *The Maori history and legends of the Waitakere Ranges* Auckland.

Dieffenbach, Ernst. 1843. *Travels in New Zealand* . . . 2 vols. London.

*Downes, T.W. 1937. 'Maori mentality regarding the lizard and taniwha in the Whanganui River area' *JPS* 46: 206-24.

Earle, Augustus. 1838. *Sketches illustrative of the native inhabitants of New Zealand* London.

Elder, J.R. (ed.) 1934. *Marsden's lieutenants* Dunedin.

Elvy, W.J. 1949. *Kaikoura coast* Christchurch.

Fletcher, H.J. 1913. *Ngahue's ear-drop JPS* 22:228-9.

Fowler, Leo. 1974. *Te Mana o Turanga* Auckland.

Frost, E.T. 1947. *Maori trails and Pakeha tracks* Wellington.

Gill, William Wyatt. 1894. *From darkness to light in Polynesia* . . . London.

Graham, George. 1921. ' "Te Tuhi-a-Manawatere" and other legends of Marae-tai, Auckland' *JPS* 30:252-3.

*Green, R.C. 1974. 'Adaptation and change in Maori culture' in Kuschel, G. (ed.), *Ecology and biogeography in New Zealand* The Hague. pp. 1-44.

Grey, George. 1853. *Ko nga moteatea* . . . Wellington.

*_____ 1857. *Ko nga whakapepeha me nga whakaahuareka* . . . Cape Town.

*_____ 1928. *Nga mahi a nga tupuna*. Wellington. (3rd edn. ed. by H.W. Williams, with additional matter).

*_____ 1956. *Polynesian mythology* 3rd edn. Christchurch.

Gudgeon, W.E. 1892. 'Paoa' *JPS* 1:76-9.

_____ 1893. 'Maori tradition as to the kumara . . .' *JPS* 2:99-102.

_____ 1905. 'Mana tangata' *JPS* 14:49-66.

Hamlin, James. 1842. 'On the mythology of the New Zealanders' *Tasmanian journal of natural science* 1:234-64, 342-58.

Hammond, T.G. 1924. *The story of Aotea* Christchurch.

Houston, John. 1965. *Maori life in old Taranaki* Wellington.

*Johansen, J. Prytz. 1954. *The Maori and his religion* Copenhagen.

*_____ 1958. *Studies in Maori rites and myths* Copenhagen.

Kapiti, Pita. 1912. 'The history of "Horouta" Canoe' *JPS* 21:152-63

Keene, Florence. 1963. *O Te Raki: Maori legends of the North* Auckland and Hamilton.

Kerry-Nichols, J.H. 1884. *The King Country* . . . London.

Kohere, Reweti T. 1951. *He konae aronui* Wellington.

Large, J.T. 1923. 'Tawhiti' *JPS* 32:49.

Mair, Gilbert. 1923. *Reminiscences and Maori stories* Auckland.

Makereti. 1938. *The old-time Maori* London.

*Matthews, R.H. 1910. 'Reminiscences of Maori life fifty years ago' *TPNZI* 43:598-605.

McGregor, John. 1893. *Popular Maori songs* Auckland.

_____ 1898. *Popular Maori songs* Supplement No. 1. Auckland.

*Lenski, Gerhard and Jean Lenski. 1974. *Human societies* New York.

_____ 1905. *Popular Maori songs* Supplement No. 3. Auckland.

McLean, Mervyn and Margaret Orbell. 1975. *Traditional songs of the Maori* Wellington.

*Mead, S.M. 1969. *Traditional Maori clothing* Wellington.

*Miller, David. 1970. 'The insect people of the Maori' *JPS* 61:1-61.

Ngata, Apirana T. 1959. *Nga moteatea* Part I. Wellington.

_____ and I.L.G. Sutherland. 1940. 'Religious influences' in Sutherland, I.L.G. (ed.), *The Maori people today* Wellington. pp.336-73.

_____ and Pei Te Hurinui. 1961. *Nga moteatea* Part II. Wellington.

_____ and Pei Te Hurinui. 1970. *Nga moteatea* Part III. Wellington.

*Oppenheim, R.S. 1973. *Maori death customs* Wellington.

Orbell, Margaret. 1968. *Maori folktales* . . . Auckland.

*_____ 1975. 'The religious significance of Maori migration traditions' *JPS* 84:341-7.

*_____ 1977. 'The Maori traditions of Kupe: a religious interpretation' *The artefact* 2:123-31.

_____ 1978. *Maori poetry: an introductory anthology* Auckland.

*_____ 1982. 'The other people: Maori beliefs about fairies' in Simms, Norman (ed.), *Oral and traditional literatures* (Vol. 7:2 of *Pacific Quarterly Moana.*) pp. 83-92.

_____ 1983. 'The paddler and the canoe: a sexual image in Polynesian poetry' *Journal of New Zealand literature* 1:55-66.

Phillipps, W.J. 1958. *Maori carving illustrated* Wellington.

*_____ 1963. 'Notes on the owl and shag as guardians or familiar spirits' *JPS* 72:411-4.

*_____ 1963a. *The book of the huia* Wellington.

Pio, Hamiora. 1910. 'Te manu aute' *JPS* 19:191-93.

*Poata, Tamati R. 1919. *The Maori as a fisherman and his methods* Opotiki.

Polack, J.S. 1838. *New Zealand* . . . 2 vols. London.

_____ 1840. *Manners and customs of the New Zealanders* 2 vols. London.

Pomare, Maui and James Cowan. 1930-4. *Legends of the Maori* 2 vols. Wellington.

*Prickett, Nigel (ed.) 1982. *The first thousand years: regional perspectives in New Zealand archaeology* Palmerston North.

*Ranapiri, Tamati. 1895. 'Nga ritenga hopu manu a te Maori, o mua.' *JPS* 4: 132-52.

Reed, A.H. and A.W. Reed (eds.) 1969. *Captain Cook in New Zealand* 2nd edn. Wellington.

Ruatapu, Mohi and Henare Potae. 1876. MS among the Elsdon Best papers in the Alexander Turnbull Library, Wellington: 'Maori material by Henare Potae and Mohi Ruatapu' 2 vols.

Savage, John. 1807. *Some account of New Zealand* . . . London.

*Schwimmer, Erik G. 1963. 'Guardian animals of the Maori' *JPS* 72:397-410.

*Shawcross, Kathleen. 1967. 'Fern-root, and the total scheme of 18th-century Maori food production in agricultural areas' *JPS* 76:330-52.

Simmons, D.R. (ed.) 1973. *Customs and habits of the New Zealanders, 1838-42* by C. Servant. Wellington.

Smith, S. Percy. 1897. 'The peopling of the north' (Part 2). *JPS* 6:23-108 (Supplement).

_____ 1910. *History and traditions of the Taranaki coast* New Plymouth.

_____ 1920. 'Clairvoyance among the Maoris' *JPS* 29:149-61.

St John, Lieut.-Col. 1892. 'The tradition respecting the aboriginal inhabitants of Whakatane' *TPNZI* 24.470.

*Tarakawa, Takaanui. 1893. 'Ko te hoenga mai o Te Arawa, raua ko Tainui i Hawaiki' *JPS* 2:220-52.

*_____ 1894. 'Ko te rerenga mai o Mata-atua, me Kurahaupo me era atu waka, i Hawaiki' *JPS* 3:59-71.

_____ 1911. 'Ko Tuatara raua ko Kumukumu' *JPS* 20:39-41.

_____ 1911a. 'He korero mo Tara-whata' *JPS* 20:185-8.

*Tautahi, Hetaraka. 1900. 'Ko "Aotea" waka: te haerenga mai a Turi ki Aotea-roa nei' *JPS* 9:200-33.

Taylor, Richard. 1855. *Te Ika a Maui* ... 1st edn. London.

*_____ 1870. *Te Ika a Maui* ... 2nd edn. London and Wanganui.

Te Hata, Hoeta. 1916. 'The Ngati Tuwharetoa occupation of Taupo-nui-a-Tia' (Part 1). *JPS* 25:104-16.

_____ 1917. 'The Ngati Tuwharetoa occupation of Taupo-nui-a-Tia' (Part 2). *JPS* 26:180-7.

Te Hurinui, Pei. 1960. *King Potatau* ... Wellington.

*Te Rangi Hiroa (Peter Buck). 1950. *The coming of the Maori* Christchurch.

Thomson, Arthur S. 1859. *The story of New Zealand* ... 2 vols. London.

Turei, Mohi. 1876. 'He korero kauwhau Maori' *Te Waka Maori o Niu Tirani* 12:201-3.

_____ 1911. 'Tu-whakairi-ora' *JPS* 20:17-34.

White, John. 1874. *Te Rou, or the Maori at home* London.

_____ 1880. 'Legendary history of the Maoris' *Appendices to the House of Representatives* G-8.

*_____ 1885. *Maori customs and superstitions* Bound together with *The history and doings of the Maoris* by T.W. Gudgeon. Auckland. (First pub. 1861.)

*_____ 1887-91. *The ancient history of the Maori* 7 vols. Wellington.

_____ 1940. *Revenge: a love tale of the Mount Eden tribe* Wellington.

White, Taylor. 1907. 'On the use of birds in navigation' *JPS* 16:92-3.

*Williams, Herbert W. 1971. *A dictionary of the Maori language* 7th edn. Wellington.

Wohlers, J.F.H. 1876. 'The mythology and traditions of the Maori in New Zealand' *TPNZI* 8:108-23.

Yate, William. 1970. *An account of New Zealand* ... Wellington. (First pub. 1835.)

Some Books on the Natural History of Aotearoa

There are many books on the natural history of New Zealand. These are representative works of interest to the general reader.

General

AA book of New Zealand wildlife: a guide to the native and introduced animals of New Zealand C. O'Brien (Lansdowne Press Auckland 1981).

Native animals of New Zealand A.W.B. Powell (Auckland Institute and Museum, Auckland, 2nd ed., 1951).

New Zealand's nature heritage R. Knox (ed.) Published in serial form. (Hamlyn, Hong Kong 1974-6).

The ancient islands: New Zealand's natural environments Brian Enting and Les Molloy (Port Nicholson Press, Wellington 1982).

Plants

A field guide to the native edible plants of New Zealand, including those plants eaten by the Maori Andrew Crowe (Collins, Auckland 1981).

New Zealand flowers and plants in colour J.T. Salmon (Reed, Wellington, 1963).

The native trees of New Zealand J.T. Salmon (Reed, Wellington 1980).

The Oxford book of New Zealand plants L.B. Moore and J.B. Irwin (Oxford, Wellington, 1978).

Birds

New Zealand's birds Geoff Moon and Ronald Lockley (Heinemann, Auckland 1982).

The birds around us: New Zealand birds, their habits and habitats Geoff Moon (Heinemann, Auckland 1979).

The new guide to the birds of New Zealand and outlying islands R.A. Falla, R.B. Sibson and E.G. Turbott (Collins, Auckland 1979).

Insects

New Zealand insects and their story Richard Sharell (Collins, Auckland, 2nd ed., 1982).

Fish and shellfish

A treasury of New Zealand fishes David H. Graham (Reeds, Wellington, 2nd ed., 1956).

The New Zealand sea-shore J.E. Morton and M.C. Miller (Collins, Auckland 1968).

New Zealand Freshwater Fishes: a guide and natural history: R.M. McDowall (Heinemann, Auckland 1978).

Index

Numerals in *italic type* refer to illustration
captions

Adzes, 19, 52, 53, 55, 58, 112, 115, 167
albatross, *31*, 50, 116, 154ff., *155, 156*
Altair, 69
amokura, 157
Angas, G.F., *46*, 50
Antares, 69, 85
Aonui, 109
Aoraki (Aorangi), 111, *111*
Aotea canoe, 106, 109, 115
— Harbour, 109
Arahura, 112, 141
Araiteuru canoe, 109, *109*, 111, 112, 124
— (taniwha), 126
Arapawa Island, 101
Arawa canoe, 105, 106, *106*, 107, 112, 118,
    123, 144, 175
— tribes, 150ff., *161*
Archaic phase, 13, 191
Arowhana, Mount, 123
Ashburton, 109
Atea, 65
Atiamuri, *129*
Auckland, *12*, 106
— Museum, *58*, 107, 159
Austral Islands, 5
Awakino, *109*
Awatere valley, 109
Awhitu, 107, 129

Banana, 5, 19
Banks, Joseph, 95
Banks Peninsula, 33, 124
bat, 19, *22*
Bay of Islands, 38
Bay of Plenty, 13, 23, 80, 85, 118, 121,
    129, 130, *142, 144*
beech, *28, 175*
bellbird, 21, 193, *193*
bindweed, *36*, 43, 116
bird-kites, 44, *183*
'bird-men', *8*

birds, 7, *8*, 19, 21ff., 50, 51, 83, 89, 104,
    112, 122, 125, 148ff., 159, 167, 180ff.,
    210
— preservation for food, 25, 35, *35*
bittern, 23, 209, *209*, 210
blackfish, 143
bracken, *7*, 11, *37*, 38, *38*, 57
breadfruit, 5, 19
bulrush, *42*
bur cucumber, 116
bush lawyer, 101, 179, 180
butterfish, 147

Cabbage tree, 29, 39, 41, *41, 44*, 47, 54,
    176
calabash, 25, *27*, 35, *35*, 109, *109*
canoes, *60*, 61, *61, 78*, 83, 101ff., 121ff.,
    138, 177
Canterbury Plains, 38
Cape Reinga, 78, *79*
Cape Runaway, *140*
caterpillars, 37
cats, 206
celery, wild, *42*
centipede, 115
Chalky Sound, 124
charcoal, 54
— drawings, *8*
Chatham Islands, 7, *7*
chisels, 19, 51, *52*, 53, 58
Christchurch, 109
Classic phase, 13, *191*
clematis, 170, *171*
Clutha River, 109
coconut, 5, 19, *40*
Colenso, William, 43, 177, 209
Coleridge, Lake, 125
convolvulus, New Zealand, *36*, 43
Cook, James, 49, 57, 112
Cook, Mount, 111, *111*
Cook Islands, 5
Cook Strait, 53
cooking, 55
Coromandel Peninsula, 52, 95, 145
crayfish, 28, 29, *30, 31*, 129, 147, 179
cricket, 115

crocodile, 157
cuckoo, long-tailed, 50, 163, *163*, 200, 201
— shining, 163, 200, 201, *201*
curlew, bristle-thighed, 7
Cuvier Island, 197

Dieffenbach, Ernst, 89
dog, 19, 21, *22*, 26, 83, 99, 101, 104, 109,
    123, 189, *191*, 206
dogskin cape (cloak), 45, *46, 47*, 48, 49,
    209
dolphin, 7
dotterel, 152
Doubtless Bay, 123
duck, 23, 212ff., *212, 213*
Dunedin, 109, *109*
D'Urville Island, 52

Ear fungus, 43
earthworms, 83
East Cape, *86*, 115
East Coast, 13, 34, 43, 87, 99, 101, 103,
    105, 115, 116, 122, 137, *140*, 144, 148,
    149, 173, 177, 198, *203*, 205
East Island, 115
Edgecumbe, Mount, 85, 129, *129, 142*
eel pots, 29, 44, *45*, 109, *109*, 147
eels, 7, 28, 29, *30*, 32, 112, 147, 148, 149,
    209
Egmont, Mount, 85, *87, 128*, 129
Ellesmere, Lake, 125
exploration, 5, 7, 121ff.

Fairies, 84, 85, 92ff., *93*, 104, 149, 180
falcon, 203ff., *204*
fantail, 197, *198*, 210
feather cloaks, *189, 192*
fern, *22*, 42, 43, 167, 169, *170*, 179
fernbird, *210*, 211
fernroot, 7, *7*, 11, *12*, 13, 38ff., *38*, 103, 215
Fiji, 5
Fiordland, 21, 52
fish, 7, *8, 9*, 13, 19, 28, 32, 44, 104, *118*,
    135, *140*, 141ff., 153, 181

fishhooks, *31, 32,* 51, *51*
fishing, 5, 12, 14, 15, 26ff., 129, 135ff., 140, *141, 177*
flax, 19, *27,* 29, 31, 39, 44ff., *44, 48,* 55, *59,* 92, 109, *110,* 118, 179, 180, 217
flounder, *29,* 127, 147
Forsyth, Lake, 125
Foveaux Strait, 123, 125
fowl, 5, 89
Frenchman's Gully, *8*
fuchsia, 176, 193
fungus, 43, 115

Galaxias, 28, 118, *147,* 148
gannet, 50, 154, *155*
Gannet Island, 130
garfish, 147
gecko, *115,* 157ff., *158, 159*
Giant's Causeway, 124
Gisborne, 89, *143, 169,* 173, *189*
godwit, 152, *153*
gourds, 25, 33ff., *35,* 72, 104, 115, 116
grayling, 28, 148
grebe, *212,* 213
Green Island, 123
greenstone, 8, 49, 50, *51,* 52, *52,* 53, 58, 112, 113, *113,* 129, 141, 157, *194*
Greenstone Lake, 213
Grey, George, 203
Grey, Mount, 109
grey warbler, 199, *199,* 200
groper, *140*
gull, *26*
— black-backed, *36,* 37, 149ff.
— black-billed, 150, *150,* 151
— red-billed, 150, *150,* 151
gurnard, 161, 162, *162*

Haere-awaawa, 167
Hamiora Pio, 182
hangi, *27*
Hanmer, 124
Hape-ki-tuarangi, 121
hapu, 14, 95
hapuku, 33, *140*
harpoons, 51
Hauhungatahi, 90
Haumapuhia, 126, *126*
Haumia, 215
Hauraki Gulf, *80,* 81, 123, 129, 131, 197
Hauraki Plains, 95
Hawaiki, 37, 67, 68, 77, 78, 80, 87, 93, 99, 101, 103, *103,* 104, *104, 105, 106,* 112ff., *113, 115, 116, 121,* 122, 131, *140,* 141, 145, 173, 175, 180, 197, 200, 216
Hawea, 125

hawk, 50, 182, 203ff., *204, 205*
Hawke Bay, 99
Hawke's Bay, 91, *92,* 106
Heretaunga, 91, *92,* 106
heron, 7, *9,* 49, 50, 195, 203, 207ff., *207*
Heron, Lake, 125
herring, 146
Hicks Bay, 87, 123
Hikurangi, Mount, 87, 89, *89*
hinau, *24, 40,* 41, *48,* 169
Hinauri, 137, 186, 216
Hinemihi, *122*
Hine-nui-te-po, 68, 197, 210
Hinetapora, *104*
Hine-titama, 68
Hine-tua-hoanga, 112
Hipo, 109
Hokakura, 125
Hokianga, 101, *103,* 109, 126, 153, 159, *159, 213*
hongi, *75*
Horokau, 111
Horouta canoe, 116, 122
Horowhenua, Lake, *10*
Horse Range, 109
horticulture, 11, 12, 19, 33ff.
Hotunui, *58*
Hoturoa, 115
Houmea, 149
houses, *45,* 54ff., *55, 56, 57,* 67, 83, 137, 172, 185, 195, 203
huhu grub, 173, *173*
huia, 50, *53, 181,* 194ff., *194, 195,* 208
hunting, 12, 21ff.
Hurumanu, 148

Inanga, 118
insects, 115, 167, 211
Invercargill, 111
Iro, 5

Kahawai, *32,* 147
kahikatea, *24,* 31, *39,* 40, 51, 170, 172ff., *173*
Kaikoura Ranges, 99, 109
Kaipara Harbour, *95*
Kaitangata, 111
Kaitotehe Pa, *89*
Kaiwhare, 127, *127*
kaka, 21, *24,* 49, 122, *186,* 187ff., 200
kakapo, 21, *22,* 50, 188ff., *191*
kakariki, 21, 115, *116, 187,* 188
Kakau-matua, 112, *113*
Kakepuku, 130
Kakiroa, *110,* 111
kanuka, 175
Kapiti Island, 101, 180

Ka puna-wai karikari a Rakaihaitu, 125
karaka, 7, *7,* 40, *40,* 107, 115
karamu, 169
Karekare, 131
karengo, 43
Karewa, 130
kauri, 37, 51, 60, 72, 170, 172, *172*
Kautu-ki-te-rangi, 106
Kawa, 130
kawakawa, 37, 169, 170, 178, *178,* 179
Ka whata tu a Te Rakihouia, 126
Kawhia, *47,* 109, 130, 169
kea, *204,* 205
kiekie, 43, *47,* 197, 217
kina, *33*
King Country, 122
kingfish, 146
kingfisher, 211ff., *211*
kiore, 26, *28,* 104, 115
kite-flying, 44, 182
kites, 44, *183*
kiwi, 7, 21, *89,* 189ff., *191, 192*
kohekohe, 175
kokako, 23, 196, *196*
kokopu, 118, *147,* 148
koromiko, 169, *170*
Kororareka, *14*
korowai, *48*
kotare, 211ff.
Kou-ruru, 203, *203*
kowhai, *24,* 193
Kuha-tarewa, 91
kumara, 11, 12, *12,* 13, 14, *27,* 33, 36ff., *36,* 39, 40, *58,* 69, *71,* 77, 83, 103, 109, *109,* 112, *112,* 115, 116, *116, 142,* 144, 181, 192, 210, 215
kumarahou, *39*
Kupe, 101, *103,* 180

Lamprey, 28, 127, 148
lily, New Zealand, 43, *43*
lizards, *8,* 89, 115, 135, 157ff., *161, 163,* 180, 188, 200, 210

Mackerel, 147
— sky, *71*
Mahia Peninsula, 99, 144
Mahu, 127
Mahunui, 99
Mahuru, 200
Maia, 104
maire, *24,* 170, 175
Makaro, 101
Maketu, 109
mamaku, *40,* 41, 103, 179
Mamari canoe, *107,* 109

Manaia, 130, *130,* 131, *131*
Mana Island, 101
Manapouri, Lake, 125
Manawa-tere, 104
Mangaia, 5
Mangarara canoe, 115
mangemange, *147*
manuka, 34, 54, *55,* 104, 175, 211
Manukau Harbour, 122, 123, 127
Manutuke, *143*
mapou, 145, 169
marakihau, *126*
Marama, 116
Marlborough, 23
— Sounds, 49
Maroheia, 123
Mataatua canoe, 197
matagouri, 101, *103,* 179, 180
matai, 40
Matakaea, 109
Matariki, 69, 71
Matata, *142*
Matau, 109
Mataura River, 109
Matiu, 101
Maui, 68, 87, 99, 101, *101,* 104, 141, 185,
    194, 197, 210, 216
Maukatere, 109
Maunga-haumi, 122
Maunga-kakaramea, 130
Maungakiekie, *12*
Maunganui Bluff, *107,* 109
Maungapohatu, 130
Maungaraho, 131
Maungaroa, 86
mawhai, 116
Mayor Island, 52
meeting-house, *21,* 57, *58, 104, 105,* 107,
    122, 143, 156, 161, 169, 184, 195
Melanesia, 157
Mercury Bay, 95
Milford Sound, 113
Milky Way, 123
miro, 21, *23, 24,* 26, 184
mistletoe, *175*
moa, 7, 19, 21, 51, 89, *89, 143*
Moehau Range, 80, 95, 180
Moeraki, 109, *109*
Mokau Heads, *109*
Mokau River, *30*
moki, 33, *140*
moko, *50,* 51
Mokohiku-aru, 115
Mokoia Island, 150
mollymawk, 154
morepork, 201ff., *202, 203*
Moriori, *7*
moss, *25,* 170
moths, *36,* 37, 83

Motu River, 123
Motuhora Island, 129
Motuopuhi, *13*
mountain daisy, *50*
Moutohora, 129
mullet, 31, 146
Mumu-hau, 197
Mumuwhango, 167
Mungakahu, *46*
Murirangawhenua, 99
Muriwhenua, 78
mussels, 28, 32, 147
muttonbird, 23, 25, *26,* 149, 153, 154

Napier, 49
needles, 51, 179
Nelson, 33, 52
nettle, stinging tree, 101, *103,* 179, 180
Ngahue, 112, 141
Ngaiterangi, *162*
Ngapuhi, 150ff.
ngarara, 163
Ngarara Nui, 159, *161*
Ngati Awa, *58, 85, 129*
Ngati Kahungunu, 91
Ngati Mahanga, *27*
Ngati Mahuta, *46*
Ngati Maniapoto, *109,* 122
Ngati Maru, *46, 171*
Ngati Porou, 87, 101, 115
Ngati Raukawa, *24*
Ngati Ruanui, *87*
Ngati Toa, *46, 155*
Ngati Tuhourangi, *85*
Ngati Tuwharetoa, *46, 48,* 83, 89, 90, *91,*
    92, 99
Ngati Whatua, *46*
Nga Toenga, *171*
Ngatoro-i-rangi, 89, 93, 105, 106, 118, *118,*
    121, *121, 122,* 124
Ngauruhoe, 89, *91,* 118, *121*
Ngongotaha, 95
nikau palm, *23, 40,* 41, 54, 55
Northland, 13, 29, *84,* 99, 101, 104, *107,*
    130, 146, 153, 157
Nukutawhiti, 109

Oamaru, 124
obsidian, 52, 58
octopus, 129, 147
Ohaki, 118
Ohau, Lake, 125, *125*
Ohinemutu, 121
Ohiwa, 122
Ohope, 142
Ohou, 125, *195*
Old Man Range, 109

One Tree Hill, *12*
ongaonga, *103*
Opoe, 123
Orakei Korako, *121*
orchid, *43*
Otago, 52
Oturoto, 125
owl, 7, 78, 201, *202, 203*
oyster, 32
oystercatcher, 115, *116,* 152, *152*

Pa, *12,* 13, *13,* 14, 53, *55,* 59, *59,* 61, *75,*
    83, 95, *95,* 180, 184, 198, 212
paewai, 147
Paikea, 104, *105,* 145
Pakihiwi-tahi, 111
Palmerston, 109, *110*
Paoa, 123
Papa, *38,* 65, 67, 215, 216
paper mulberry tree, 19, 44, 115, 116, 177,
    177, 182
Papua New Guinea, 5
parakeet, 21, *187*
Paratene Maioha, *46*
parawai, *46*
Para-uri, 167
Parengarenga, *29*
Parkinson, Sydney, *31*
patu, *10*
Patutahi, *169*
paua, 32, *32,* 49, 147, *203*
pendants, 50, *51,* 53, 112, *113, 143, 191*
Pera Te Watutu, *189*
petrel, 149, 153, 154
pig, 5, 19, *59*
pigeon, 7, 21, *23, 24,* 50, 122, *184,* 185ff.
Piha, 127, *127*
Pihanga, Mount, 90, 213
pikirangi, *175*
pingao, 47
Piopio-tahi, 113
pipi, 31, 32, *32*
Pipiriki, *78*
pipit, 115, *116,* 205
Pipitea Pa, *46*
Pirongia, Mount, 93, *93,* 130
piwakawaka, 197
Pleiades, 69
Pohaturoa, *129*
pohutukawa, 78, *79,* 82, 169, 174, *174*
poi, *47*
Polack, J.S., 112, 181
Polynesia, 5, *9,* 13, 15, 19, 34, 44, 65, 89,
    177, 217
Porirua, *45*
Potatau Te Wherowhero, 91
potato, *11,* 34, *37, 142*
— sweet, 11, 36

Potoru, 106
Pourangahua, 116, 173
Poutini, 112
Poututerangi, 69
Poverty Bay, 123
praying mantis, *115, 176*
Pu, *46*
puha, 42
Pukaki, 125
pukatea, 175
Pukeamaru, 87
pukeko, 50, 115, *116,* 191, *209,* 210
puriri, 170
puriri moth, *82*
Puketapu, 109, *110*
Punaweko, 148
Punga, 161, 167, *176,* 210
Putauaki, 85, 129, *129, 142*

Quail, 205, *206*
Queen Charlotte Sound, *31, 55*

Raggedy Range, *109*
Raglan, *27*
rahui, 26
rail, 191, 197, 210
Rainbow Mountain, 130
Rakaihaitu, *124,* 125, *125*
Rakataura, 122
Rangi, 65, 67, 215, 216
rangiora, 109, 169, 178, *178*
Rangipopo, 87
Rangiriri, 104
Rangitoto, 81, *81,* 95, 131, *141*
rat, 19, 26, *28,* 206
Rata, 137, 169
rata, *25,* 167, 170, 172, *173,* 174, *174*
Ruakawa, 53
raupo, *42,* 43, 54, *54,* 209, 210
Rehua, 69, 85
rengarenga, 43, *43*
Repanga, 197
rewarewa, 177, *177*
rimu, 40, 170, 172
Riripo, 109
robin, 199, *199,* 200
Roko-i-tua, 77
Rona, 72
Rongo, 203, 215
Rongokako, 123
Rongopai, *169, 184*
Ropata Wahawaha, 142
Rua-te-pupuke, 137
Rotoaira, Lake, *13*
Rotoehu, Lake, 49, 80
Rotoiti, Lake, 125
Rotokawa, 118

Rotomahana, *118*
Roto Pounamu, 213
Rotoroa, Lake, 125
Rotorua, 83, 84, *85,* 105, 112, 159
— Lake, 28, 95, 150, *150*
Roto-ua, 125
Rough Range, 109
Ruapahu, 90, *128*
Ruapehu, Mount, 89, 90, *90, 128*
Ruatahuna, *21*
Ruatoria, *104*
Rupe, 186

Saddleback, 197, *197,* 200
Samoa, 5
sandflies, 49
sandhopper, 147
Savage, John , 67
sculpture, 12, 53, 58, 143
sea-egg, *33*
seahorses, 50
seals, 7, 8, *9,* 19
seaweed, 43, *82,* 83, 138
sedge, 48, 209
Sefton, Mount, *110,* 111
shag, 148ff., *148, 149,* 203
Shag Point, 109
shark, 29, *31,* 32, 33, 50, 142, *142,* 161, 163, *194,* 210
shearwater, *26,* 153
shellfish, 7, *9,* 19, 32, *32,* 127, 152
shells, 50, 51, *137, 146*
silvereye, *184*
snakes, 157
snapper, 33
Society Islands, 5
Somers, Mount, 109
Southland, 109, 123
sow thistle, 42
speargrass, 47, *50*
Sperm Whale Bay, 144
spiders, *82,* 83, 159, *176,* 211
squid, 153
Stewart Island, 99
stick insect, 115, *115, 176*
stilt, 152, *152*
sting-ray, 147
stitchbird, 194
stoats, 206
storehouses, 59, *59, 67,* 83, 116, 144, *144*
Sumner, Lake, 125
supplejack, *25,* 179, *179,* 180

Tahiti, 15, *41*
tainui, *39*
Tainui canoe, 106, 107, 109, *109,* 115, 122, 144

Takapo, *124,* 125
Takere-tou, 197
Takitimu canoe, 106, 109, 115, 123, 144
Takitimu Mountains, 109
Takuira, 75
Tama, 113, 180, *180*
Tamaki, *12,* 106, 123
Tama-o-hoi, 121, *122*
Tamatea, 115, 123, 124
Tamatekapua, 105, *106,* 123
Tamati Ranapiri, *24*
Tamure, 129
Tane, 65, 67, 68, 83, 115, 116, 135, 148, 167, 169, 173, *175, 176, 210,* 215, 216
tanekaha, *48*
Tangaroa, 65, 105, 135, 137, 146, *177,* 215
tangihanga, 69, *86, 210*
taniko, 45ff., *47*
taniwha, 105, 126ff., *126, 127,* 137, 163
tapa cloth, 19, 44
Tapuaeharuru, 118
Tapuaenuku, Mount, 109
Taramainuku, 123
Taranaki, 13, *61, 75,* 85, *87,* 89, 99, 106, *112,* 115, *128,* 129, 144, 175, 200
Taranga, *84*
Tarawera, Mount, 84, *85,* 121, *122*
Tarawhata, 104
taro, 5, 33, 34, *34,* 38, 83, 115, 210
Tasman, Mount, 111
tattoo, 51, 147, 161, 179, 182
'Tauaki, 95
Tauhara, Mount, 118
Taupiri, Mount, 87, *89,* 130
Taupo, 43, 83, 89, 105, 121, 124, 172, 193, 213
— Lake, 28, *48, 57, 90,* 92, 99, *101,* 118, *118, 137*
Tauranga, *162*
Tauwhaki, *48*
Tauwhare, 86
tawa, 21, *22,* 26, 41
tawari, *24*
Tawera, 109
Tawhaki, 72, 104, 137, 174, *174,* 210, 216
Tawhirimatea, 65, 215, 216
Tawhiti, 95
Taylor, Richard, 193
Te Ahi a Tamatea, 124
Te Anau, 125
Te Aotaki, 87
Te Aroha, 95
Te Awamutu, 130
Te Arawa, 123, *210*
Te Atiawa, *61, 87*
Te Awhio-rangi, 115
Te Haruru o te Rangi, 89
Te Heuheu, 92, 112, *113*
Te Kaha, *144*

Tekapo, Lake, *124*, 125
Te Karehu o te Ahi a Tamatea, 124
Te Kauati a Tamatea, 123
Te Kawau, *46*
Te Kiekie, 109
Te Kupenga a Taramainuku, 123
Te Kuri a Paoa, 123
Te Mahia, 144
Te Mana o Turanga, *143*
Te Matapihi o Rehua, 85
Tene Waitere, *161*
Te Onionga, *48*
Te Pakaru, *47*
Te Parata, 105, 106, 137
Te Poho o Tamatea, 124
Te Punga o Tainui, *109*
Te Puta o Paretauhinau, *95*
Te Rakihouia, 125
Te Rangihaeata, *155*
Te Rapa, *137*
Te Rarawa, 29
Te Rauparaha, 180
Te Rehu o Tainui, 159
Te Reinga, 78, *79*, 83
tern, 154, *154*
Te Tai Tokerau, *107, 183*
Te Tara ki 'Tauaki, 85
Te Tarata, 75
Te Tatau o te Rangi, 85
Te Tawhiti Nui a Paoa, 123
Te Wairoa, *122*
Te Whai a Te Motu, *21*
Te Wetere, *109*
Te Whanga-nui-a-Tara, 99, 101, 126, 194
Te Whanga-nui-o-Hei, *95*
Te Wharerangi, 172
tewhatewha, *205, 208*
Tia, 121
tikanga, 215
Tikitere, 121
tikumu, *50*
Timaru, *8*
timber, 19, 55, 60, 172, 175
Tinirau, *143*
Tirau, 83
titi, 23, *26*
titoki, 50
Titore, *183*
toetoe, 55, *58*, 109, *110*, 182
toheroa, 32
Tohi, *46*
tohunga, 26, *39*, 44, 67, 84, 93, 105, 153, 158, 183, 198, *210*
Toi, 101, 103
Tokaanu, 118
Tokatoka, *95*, 131
Tokomairiro, 111
Tokomaru Bay, 123
Tokomaru canoe, 144

Tolaga Bay, 57
tomtit, 198
Tonga, 5
Tongariro, Mount, *13*, 89, 90, *91*, 92, 118, 124, 129
— River, *90*
tools, *11*, 51ff.
Torlesse, Mount, 109
totara, 40, 54, 58, *58*, 60, 118, 167, 170, 172, *172*, 194
tree fern, *24*, *40*, 41, 55, *58*
tree nettle, 101, *103*, 179, 180
tropic bird, 50, 157
Tu, 65, 215, 216
tuatara, 115, 135, 157, 161ff., *162*
tuatua, 32
Tuhi-o-Kahu, 91
Tuhoe, 91, 99
tui, 21, *25*, 122, 167, 191ff., *193*
Tumutumu-whenua, 104
Turanga, 123, *169*, 173, *189*
Turi, 106, 115
turtle, 146
tussock, 180, *180*
tutaekoau, *42*
Tutangata-kino, 115
Tu-te-koropanga, 180
tutu, *24*, 39, 41
Tutunui, *143*
Tu-whakairi-ora, 87

Uawa, 57
Uhia, 159
Ureweras, 47, 91, *92*, 99, *126*, 130, 159, 167, 169
Uruao canoe, 125

Wading birds, 152, *152*
Waiapu River, 123
Waihemo, 109, *110*, 111
Waihora, 125
Waikaremoana, Lake, 28, 91, *92*, 101, 126, *126*
Waikato, 13, 23, 86, 87, *89*, 93, 122, 123, 159
— River, *90*
— War, 86
Waima River, 109
Waimamaku, *159*
Waimangu, *118*
Waimahana, 121
Waioeka River, 123
Waiotapu, 118
Waipa valley, *56*, 130
Waipaoa River, 123
Wairakewa, 104
Wairarapa, Lake, 99

Wairewa, 125
Wairoa, 89, 193
— River, *95*, 131
Waitahanui, 80
Waitakere Ranges, *127,* 131
Waitotara, 115
waka huia, *53, 181*
Wakatipu, Lake, 125
Wanaka, 125
warfare, 12, 14, 84, 90, 141, 142, 149, 169, 175, 179, 193
weasels, 206
weaving, 44ff., *45*
weka, 7, 21, *22*, 167, 190, 191, *191*
Wellington, 99, 101, 126, 195, *195*
West Coast, 52, 53, 112
weta, *176*
Whaingaroa, 27
Whakaari, 118, *121, 128,* 129
Whakamatau, 125
Whakaotirangi, 115, 116, *116*
whakapapa, 215, 216
Whakarewarewa, 121
Whakatane, 104, 122, 142
Whakatau, 104, 137
Whakatipu-wai-maori, 125
whales, 50, 59, *105*, 143ff., *143, 144, 145,* 163, 174, 200
Whanganui, 106, *200*
— River, *7, 8*, 90, 124, 129
Whanga-o-keno, 115, *115*
Whangaparaoa, *140*, 144
Whangara, *105, 203*
Whangarei Heads, *130*, 131, *131*
Whangaroa, 49
Wharekahika, 87, 123
whau, 29, 116, 177, *177*, 178
Wheketoro, 115, *115*
whitebait, 28, 32, 142, 148
whitehead, 197, 198, 200, *200*
White Island, 118, *121, 128,* 129
Whitireia, *105*

Yams, 5, 33, 38
Yate, William, 195
yellowhead, 200
Young Nick's Head, 123